T0365916

That I May Know Him

THRESHOLD TOPICAL BIBLE COMMENTARY

DANIEL E. ARMOUR

WESTBOW
P R E S S®
A DIVISION OF THOMAS NELSON
& ZONDERVAN

WestBow Press books may be ordered through booksellers or by contacting:

WestBow Press
A Division of Thomas Nelson & Zondervan
1663 Liberty Drive
Bloomington, IN 47403
www.westbowpress.com
1 (866) 928-1240

Because of the dynamic nature of the Internet, any web addresses or links contained in this book may have changed since publication and may no longer be valid. The views expressed in this work are solely those of the author and do not necessarily reflect the views of the publisher, and the publisher hereby disclaims any responsibility for them.

Any people depicted in stock imagery provided by Thinkstock are models, and such images are being used for illustrative purposes only. Certain stock imagery © Thinkstock.

ISBN: 978-1-4908-8131-7 (sc)
ISBN: 978-1-4908-8132-4 (hc)
ISBN: 978-1-4908-8130-0 (e)

Library of Congress Control Number: 2015908066

Print information available on the last page.

WestBow Press rev. date: 06/30/2017

THIS BOOK IS DEDICATED
TO EVERY CHRISTIAN SEEKING TO WALK IN
GROWING SANCTIFICATION AND A DEEPER KNOWLEDGE OF
OUR LORD AND SAVIOUR JESUS CHRIST

TABLE OF CONTENTS

ACKNOWLEDGEMENTS

I am forever grateful and marvel at the unwavering love and support of my wife, Nancy. Throughout our twenty-eight years of marriage, she has shown me her kindness and grace in the face of so many insurmountable trials. She has been a living example to our girls as to what true love is and what it can do within a marriage between two people who love each and never give up on God, no matter what they are facing.

Through trying times, her dignity and hope in Christ allowed God to bring stability, peace, and joy to my family. In times of despair, in particular a time when she faced the end of everything she knew and God seemed to be hidden from her eyes, her Faith in Him never failed. As she waited for the Lord to rebuild her strength, I watched her learn from God that He alone was her only source. Throughout the years, and many of my failures, God has shown me what it truly means to love her. Today, it is an honor to have Nancy as my wife.

Contributors

I would like to thank Nicole Armour for the many, many hours of proofreading and editing, as well as exemplifying the true meaning of Faith, hope, and love. It has been remarkable to see her heart of mercy in action toward the broken-hearted, and her unyielding determination in Christ, regardless of the circumstances. As her dad, it is an honor to walk with her as she walks in Christ.

I would like to thank Holly Armour for proofreading, and her tireless humor that has brought so much laughter and support in the years it took to write this book. I have watched her heart quietly treasure the things of God, yet stand so strongly in His Principles, regardless of what else is being said and done. As her dad, it is an honor to stand with her as she stands in Christ.

INTRODUCTION

As a young boy, my life was filled with adventures of exploring, building tree houses, and trying to fly. However, as life would have it, things began to happen. One significant event of many was the sexual abuse by an older man that would consume my life from the age of six until eleven. It was not until this that I began to realize the impact of not having a dad and somehow, the innocence of life began to fade. This was probably when my view changed from a life of extraordinary adventures to protecting others; if I saw someone getting beat up, I stepped in to stop it. It was not something I thought about; it was just the way it was.

The town we lived in was somewhat small, and over time my exploits attracted those looking to involve themselves with confrontation. By the time high school rolled around, these types of people became narrowed down to just a few whose parents owned the local martial arts clubs. Eventually, helping others and looking over my shoulder would end in an event that would forever alter my life.

One night I heard screaming in an alley and, as I looked in, I could see a man backed up against a pole with a street gang in front and on either side of him. One of the gang members, with a wine bottle in his hand, broke the bottom off by hitting it against the pole, and then thrust it into the man's face. In his cries for help, I ran over without thinking and grabbed the man's jacket. I began to drag him a long way, or so it seemed, but I was later told it was only a few feet. Nonetheless, in these moments, the gang converged on me, spread me out against the wall behind the pole, and began stabbing me. This would have ended my life if it had not been for a courageous man that stepped in front of me to keep them from stabbing me more. As the man shielded me, two officers rushed over to help. One of the officers picked me up and the other, not knowing any other way, placed his hands into the holes in an effort to stop the bleeding. The events that occurred when the ambulance came are another story, but eventually I would get to the hospital and, after some time, I was able to go home.

The reason I am telling this story is because, regardless of the physical experiences of the sexual abuse and stabbings, the pain in my mind grew much worse than the physical pain these events caused. The biggest problem became me locking it all away, unaware that it was consuming me.

I did not go back to school after the stabbing. Instead, I followed my dream of becoming a carpenter; I began to excel in this field throughout the years. It was on one particular job that I had the opportunity to work with a gentleman by the name of Bobby, who also happened to be a pastor. Late one afternoon he led me to the Lord, and I vividly remember it today. After receiving Jesus Christ as my Lord and Saviour, I felt clean for the first time in my life. It was the single most amazing thing I had ever experienced. About four days later, Bobby came to my apartment to pray with me to receive the baptism of the Holy Spirit. Though I did not speak in tongues that day, the most wonderful language came out as I was praying. From then on, I poured myself into the things of God.

A year passed by; the day before Christmas, one of my close friends invited me to his parents' house for their annual Christmas party. I had been out of school for years and was reluctant to go. Nonetheless, I went and was introduced to a lot of people I did not know. As the evening came, so did a girl I had never seen before, and as I gazed upon her, I fell in love. It was a storybook love at first sight thing, and it was happening to me. We married three years later, continued to fall deeply in love, and began a family of three beautiful girls.

However, as time went by, all that I locked away began to rage out of control within my heart and mind. I would pray, read my Bible religiously for hours every day, and because of the stabbing that caused severe limitations on the amount of food I could eat, I dedicated myself to a life of fasting. Still, in all this, my mind was filled with chaos and pain and I could not shut it down. In addition, I began to experience insomnia. One night, sleep never came. The first couple of days, I plowed through it with all my strength, but after a week I would just sit through the night and weep until the sun came up. This event lasted ten days, and it was the first of many that would so badly distort the anger and lust that suicide seemed to be the only option. The condemnation became too much. I thought I was holding onto God, but as I look back, I can now see He was the One holding me. I was trying to do as much as a man could do, until one day my pain turned into my sin, and my actions tore my family apart and forever changed the world as we knew it. In time, the Lord met me where I was, to keep me from taking my life, so that He could bring me to discover the answer to my question: why did I do the things I hated?

Exhausting every effort to overcome without any lasting results, I became desperate for the answer. My desperation turned into determination, and a nine-year journey would pass before I found what I was looking for. In finding it I was made free, yet it did not stop with me; this answer brought healing in my family beyond what we ever thought possible. Though I was desperate and determined, it was this sovereign act of God revealing His Truth, without which my family and I would have been left in despair. Today, I thank God through Jesus Christ for His faithful loving and tender kindness toward an undeserving man, and a family in need.

If you have never experienced the pain of hurting someone you love so deeply, then it is not possible to understand the desperate brokenness of those crying out because they have. More often than not, it will be those who love the Lord with all their heart, those who are using all of their strength to defeat the evil they see and feel within their heart and mind. Without knowing the way God has established their victory, the sin they are trying to overcome continues to destroy them. It will be those who so desperately desire to be free from the sin they see hindering them, those who love the Truth, but do not understand why they are doing the things they hate. They feel no matter how hard they try, they are not doing enough. In this, they are compelled to do more and more until the sin they are trying to overcome consumes them.

There is not one person on the face of the earth exempt from experiencing the effects of sin and the nature of it. When an individual receives Jesus Christ as Lord and Saviour, all things have become new, and he or she is now alive in Christ. The new Christian longs to know more of the Lord because of the newness knowing the Truth. However, the inevitable struggle with the sin nature will be an unavoidable journey he or she will have to face. Those facing it now are looking for the answer to shutting it down; some in such despair have given up on life and are planning suicide. Will they follow through with it?

This year, approximately 5,000 teens between the ages of 13 and 19 will commit suicide; 80% of them will talk about it before taking action. There is only one way to victory, but trying to overcome in your own strength can destroy your life. There are many Christians coming home from church each week okay for a while, then once again they find sin consuming their heart and mind and they think it is only them. It is not. There is an answer, but only one. *That I May Know Him* unveils this magnificent answer in a way the Christian has not known.

SALVATION

This book is for every Christian man, woman, boy, and girl. It has been written to bring hope and the only answer for their victory and rest. If Jesus Christ has not been received as Lord and Saviour of your life, start your new life in Christ now. If, as a Christian, hope has faded away because of failure and condemnation, understand that nothing has separated you from His Love. He does not confuse who you are with what you have done, and His Love for you has never changed. All that is required from you is that you turn to Him and believe, and He will do the rest.

Receiving Eternal Life is remarkably easy. It is simply by believing – that is all we can bring to God. If the desire to receive Salvation has come, it is God Who is drawing you, so He can be trusted to bring you all the way. The theme of the Bible is easy: it is God revealing the Creation of Man, the Fall of Man, and His Redemption of Man. It is all about His Love toward Man.

These are just five Scriptures to help bring understanding to the Biblical Truth in your need for Salvation, the way for Salvation, and the simplicity of receiving Salvation from God:

"Jesus answered and said unto him, Verily, verily, I say unto you, Except a man be born again, he cannot see the kingdom of God" (John 3:3).

"For God so loved the world, that He Gave His Only Begotten Son, that whosoever believes in Him should not perish, but have Everlasting Life" (John 3:16).

"Jesus said, "I am the Door: by Me if any man enter in, he shall be Saved, and shall go in and out, and find pasture" (John 10:9).

"That if you shall confess with your mouth the Lord Jesus, and shall believe in your heart that God has raised Him from the dead, you shall be Saved. For with the heart man believes unto Righteousness; and with the mouth confession is made unto Salvation" (Romans 10:9-10).

My Brother and Sister, from a sincere and believing heart, Prayer for Salvation can be made like this: Dear Father, I know that I am a sinner and understand that my sin has separated me from You. I am sorry for the way I have lived and ask You to forgive me. I believe in my heart that You gave Your Son, the Lord Jesus Christ, to die on the Cross for me, and through His Shed Blood, I can receive forgiveness for my sins. Father, I believe that You raised Him from the dead, and I am asking You to forgive me of all my sins. Lord Jesus, right now, I accept all that You have done on the Cross for me, and I ask You into my heart to be the Lord and Saviour of my life. Accomplish Your Will in me, in Your Name Jesus I pray. Amen.

Congratulations in your new life in Christ!

Upon Salvation, the Bible declares that your name has been written in the *Lamb's Book of Life*, and now God is preparing for you a home in Heaven; His Love is so incredible! Now, keep your Faith forever anchored in Jesus Christ, and what He has done at the Cross. In this, the Holy Spirit will help you grow in triumph and holiness in every way.

ABOUT THIS BOOK

S in promises but never delivers; as it has been from the beginning, it is today. Our fight is to resist the lie that there is something more to learn about life in darkness. However, as it has always been, when darkness is engaged, emptiness and horrific loss are all that is found.

There are two places for our Christian walk: one is that of triumph, the other is that of defeat. Our walk is either after the Spirit or, by default, it will be after the flesh. If we say we are walking after the Spirit, but our experience is condemnation because of continual failure, we fool ourselves, robbing ourselves of what it truly means to know Him. This is the plight before discovering the guidelines that God has set in place through His Son, and what His Son has done on the Cross through His Death.

These guidelines are spiritual Laws, and they have been established for us through the Cross so that we can walk with God in a deeper, more intimate relationship; relationship filled with victory and peace resulting from true rest, and abundant life blossoming from His love.

The word "Law" might be thought of as a set of rigid rules; however, this is not the case in regard to spiritual Laws. Spiritual

Laws are like the Law of Gravity; though you cannot see gravitational forces, the forces of gravity work within a set parameter, an established guideline. For the sake of this preface, we will touch on just two Laws: "the Law of the Spirit" and "the Law of Sin." The most powerful Law is the Law of the Spirit, which God established through the Cross for our freedom, as we walk with Him. If the Law of the Spirit is not understood, by default, the Law of Sin will rule our life *(Rom. 7:23)*.

Due to the importance of knowing just these two Laws, we would think the fundamentals of them would be a preaching and teaching priority. However, this is not the case. Coming from the governmental, social, and religious pulpits are answers that bear little, if any, understanding of these two unseen powers. The governmental pulpit says, "Together we can fix the world." The social pulpit says, "We can fix ourselves." Today, much of the Church is saying both. As Christians, we must be careful to see if what is being said, taught, and preached is scriptural and not error *(Acts 17:11; Col. 2:8, 20)*.

Much of what we see and hear is not as it seems. Satan desires chaos and complexity; he is the author of it, and he delivers it through this world system and his erroneous gospels *(II Cor. 11:3-4; Gal. 1:6-9; I Tim. 4:1)*. On the other hand, regardless of how many complex obstacles we face or how significant any obstacle may appear, God is the Author of Peace. If we wade through the smoke and mirrors of Satan's complexities, we have just two core problems: one within us (that is, in our flesh), and one outside of us. Still, God the Father has one answer that takes care of them both.

The first core problem within all of us as human beings is the nature of sin that needs to be dealt with due to Adam's decision to eat from the Tree of the Knowledge of Good and Evil, and there is no getting around this fact, regardless of what we desire to believe *(Gen. 2:16-17; Chptr 3; Psalms 51:5; Rom. 5:12; 7:9, 23)*. Furthermore, even though we may be born again and the body of sin incapacitated upon Salvation *(Rom. 6:6)*, it remains within our physical body and can revive if we do not understand the principles that revive it *(Rom. 7:8-11, 15, & 23)*.

Another aspect of this first core problem is a fallen condition due to the Fall of Adam, in which all thinking and behaviors are fully dependent upon living by the Law through the flesh. This is what is referred to as carnal thinking *(Rom. 7:9, 14; II Cor. 10:4)*. In general, the problem with the carnal mind is that it is not subject to the ways of God *(Rom. 8:7)*.

The Apostle Paul writes, *"Knowing this, that our old man is Crucified with Him, that the body of sin might be destroyed, that henceforth we should not serve sin" (Rom. 6:6)*. However, though our old man is Crucified upon receiving Salvation, the significant dilemma we will have is that the ways of our old man are remembered *(Rom. 7:9)*. Now Saved, all carnal thinking regarding spiritual matters needs to be put away *(Gal. 5:7; Eph. 4:22; Col. 3:9)*.

Though we are Redeemed and are a new creation, there is an innate residue of carnal thinking because of our mortal condition that has a desire to live by the Law *(Rom. 7:14)* or any law aside from the way that God has established for walking with Him. The dilemma is, if our old man's ways are engaged, the nature of sin is given occasion to revive *(Rom. 7:8; I Cor. 15:56; II Cor. 3:6)*. With unsaved Man, they are constantly under the influence and rule of this nature because they have no alternative way to live other than the scope of their fallen condition and its carnal mind *(Rom. 2:14-15)*. Not so with us who are Saved; we have a new way to live. We have been given the opportunity to live by Faith apart from living by the Law through our flesh.

The second core problem is Satan; he is the problem outside of those who are Saved on the mere fact that, for a season, he is allowed to be the god of this world, and therefore continues to blind, tempt, and deceive Mankind *(II Cor. 4:4)*. He desires the Christian to use his or her willpower through the ways of the old man so he can bring bondage, condemnation, and death *(Rom. 7:9)*.

Satan has always had answers that look and sound good *(Gen. 3:1-5; II Cor. 11:14)*, but from the beginning, his ways have never brought freedom, they have only brought death, and it has not changed *(John 10:10)*. Examples are seen in the manifold disciplines of psychology. The Apostle Paul writes, *"Beware lest any man spoil you through philosophy and vain deceit, after the tradition of men, after the rudiments of the world, and not after Christ" (Col. 2:8)*. Though a form of freedom may be found for a while, defeat and slavery are all that is there; thus the lie of trying to find life in darkness.

As Believers, we know why those who are unsaved suffer this, yet it is terribly real and widespread throughout much of today's Christianity. For example, there are many Christians today who love the Lord with all of their heart; however, because they are not being taught the truth, they are left thinking and feeling as if they have not done enough. Although this is a lie, the result is looming condemnation at best. In this place, efforts will be made to find freedom, but if the truth for freedom is not found, continued failures will produce tormenting guilt, all of which becomes an isolated and inescapable prison of darkness.

This book was written for two purposes: first, to provide the answer to those who are desperately searching for it and second, to teach the amazing principles going on within and around us. To the one desperately seeking the truth, my prayer is that you find what I have found. To one endeavoring to learn more about the Word of God, my prayer is that God Himself would unveil to your heart and mind the magnificent Revelation of His Wisdom, Love, and Power, wrapped in the finished work of the Cross.

LANGUAGE

The Scriptures I chose to use in the development of this book are from the King James Version, unless otherwise noted. In the case of the Elizabethan language, such as "ye," "hast," "seeketh," etc., I have made use of today's language, such as "you," "has," "seek," etc.

METHOD OF BIBLICAL APPLICATION

In developing all of the Scripture expositions within this book, biblical hermeneutics became the most effective form of application. The application of biblical hermeneutics is simply a discipline of a broader field of hermeneutics which involves interpretational principles for understanding biblical text. The main goal for this method of study is to provide an accurate biblical exegesis, sometimes referred to as a biblical exposition.

The biblical exegesis used in the draft of this book deals with the examination of a Scripture and the words within it. Properly applied, the Scripture context must be maintained in this examination in order to carry out a true biblical exegesis. The role of biblical hermeneutics is to keep us from improperly interpreting Scripture, and thereby ensuring accuracy. This application is critical in defining spiritual principles to better understand and draft what is happening within the Scripture, and the context of the Scripture.

Though these applications may seem rigid, and seem as though they might limit the role of the Holy Spirit revealing the Word of God in its true meaning, this is not the case. The Scripture itself is the inspired Word of God *(Heb. 4:12).* The value of biblical hermeneutics is that it ensures the accurate explanation as the

Holy Spirit reveals and teaches the Word of God *(I John 2:27)*. This research application results in a true biblical exegesis or exposition that can be summarized in *II Timothy 2:15 – "Study to show yourself approved unto God, a workman that need not to be ashamed, rightly dividing the word of Truth."*

PART I

Opening Commentaries

CHAPTER 1

The Design, Creation, and
Making of Adam

As youngsters, our imagination filled in the details as we were taught that God created Adam from the dust of the ground. This view comes from just one of two accounts unveiled in the Book of Genesis. When both accounts are investigated as a literal chronology, we can see the grand theme of not only two accounts, but also God's magnificent, kind, and loving Hands in the creating of Adam and the making of Adam that we might not have known before. Let us begin by looking into these two biblical accounts.

Account One: *Genesis 1:26-27 – "²⁶And God said, Let Us make man in Our Image, after Our Likeness: and let them have dominion over the fish of the sea, and over the fowl of the air, and over the cattle, and over all the Earth, and over every creeping thing that creeps upon the Earth. ²⁷So God created man in His Own Image, in the Image of God created He him; male and female created He them."*

Account Two: *Genesis 2:7 – "And the Lord God formed man of the dust of the ground, and breathed into his nostrils the breath of life; and man became a living soul."*

3

These two biblical accounts are a Divine chronology. *Genesis 1:26-27* is a literal account of God first creating Adam in spirit, and *Genesis 2:7* is the literal account of God bringing Adam into the tangible world with a soul. Let us start this chronological investigation with *Genesis 1:26-27*.

THE GENESIS 1:26-27 ACCOUNT

Genesis 1:26 begins by providing the pronouns *"Us" and "Our,"* which speak of the Three Persons of the Divine Trinity: God the Father, God the Son, God the Holy Spirit – One God *(Mark 12:29; Gal. 3:20)*. This Divine discussion, in and of itself, is most remarkable, yet it reveals God's intention: the design of Adam and what man would be like – *"And God said, Let Us make man in Our Image, after Our Likeness...."* Verse 26 clearly reveals the intention of God and the overall design of Adam; Adam will be made in the image, after the likeness of God. As we move into *Genesis 1:27*, we clearly see that God performed His intention – *"So God created man in His Own Image, in the Image of God created He him...."* This is qualified by the past tense *"created."* Also, knowing that God is a Spirit *(John 4:24)*, we can take *Genesis 1:27* literal in that God performed His intended desire and *"created"* Adam in His image, after His likeness. Therefore, He began by first creating Adam, in spirit: intangible as God Is *(Gen. 1:26-27; Exod. 3:14)*. Thus, with certainty, God *"created"* Adam first in spirit on the sixth day; God does not *"make"* the man, Adam, until He forms his physical body as seen in the *Genesis 2:7* account. This will become easier to see by looking into the theological significance of the verbs *"make"* and *"create (-ed)."*

The biblical Hebrew word for *"make"* is *'asah* (עָשָׂה, OT: 6213, aw-saw'). This verb *'asah* is found in the Old Testament over 2500 times; however, it is used as a synonym for *"create (-ed)"* only about 50 times. Because *'asah* can describe the most common of human and Divine activities, it is not properly suited to communicate theological meaning except where it is used with *bara'* or other terms whose technical meanings are clearly established. It is only when *'asah* is used as a parallel synonym to *bara'* that we can be sure it implies creation from nonexistent materials. Conversely, outside of this parallel occurrence, *'asah* describes creating from existing materials.

For this reason, let us look into the word *bara'* (בָּרָא, OT: 1254, baw-raw'). The English equivalent for this biblical Hebrew word is "create," and since only God can "create" from nonexistent materials into absolutes, this is the sense implied by *bara'*. This verb expresses creation out of nothing, clearly seen in passages having to do with creation such as *Genesis 1:1*. Therefore, only God is its subject.

We can view the introduction of the verb *bara'* in the creation account – *"In the beginning God created (bara') the heaven and the Earth" (Gen. 1:1)*. Therefore, because God created the heaven and Earth from nonexistent materials, we can see the technical importance of this verb and its contextual setting implications in association with the verb *'asah*. As we move on in the early accounts of creation, we can see occurrences of *'asah*, such as in *Genesis 1:7* – *"And God made ('asah) the firmament...."* However, because *bara'* is not in this passage, *'asah* is not used as a parallel synonym of *bara'*; therefore, it cannot be determined whether or not the firmament was made of non-existing or existing materials.

Remarkably, in *Genesis 1:26-27*, the unusual juxtaposition of *bara'* and *'asah* brings total certainty that God had *"made"* after He *"created"* from non-existent materials. Though the unusual juxtaposition of *bara'* and *'asah* in *Genesis 1:26-27* qualifies the certainty of God creating Adam in spirit from non-existent materials, it does not qualify a simultaneous event, and as a result we have the *Genesis 2:7* account.

Daniel E. Armour

THE GENESIS 2:7 ACCOUNT

By taking *Genesis 1:26-27* literal, in that God created Adam in His image, after His likeness, and thus, God first created Adam in spirit, the *Genesis 2:7* account is not only an extraordinary look into the relationship between God and Adam, but also an extraordinary view into the intimate care and hands-on approach that God took in the final making of Adam. Before we begin, let us look once again into *Genesis 2:7* – *"And the Lord God formed man of the dust of the ground, and breathed into his nostrils the breath of life; and man became a living soul."*

Let us deal with the word *"formed"* within *Genesis 2:7.* In biblical Hebrew, it is defined within the word *yatsar* (יָצַר, OT: 3335, yaw-tsar'); to form, especially as a potter, squeeze into shape; compared to *yatsa'* (יָצָע, OT: 3331, yaw-tsah'), to determine, form a resolution; to strew as a surface: – make [one's] bed, spread.

Accurately defining the word *"formed"* becomes crucial to the full Passage context surrounding it, otherwise the reader would miss the significant insights of *Genesis 2:5-6* that would have given him or her a greater view of God's intimate hands-on approach in the finale of the making of the man, Adam, in the *Genesis 2:7* account.

When taking *Genesis 1:26-27* literal, in that God first *"created"* Adam, in spirit, the deduction of *"formed"* reveals that God, in the *Genesis 2:7* account, determined a resolution, and spread the dust of the ground upon Adam's spirit with His own Hands. Perhaps spreading and pressing smooth, as one makes a bed.

Moving on in *Genesis 2:7,* let us look at the phrase *"the dust of the ground."* The word *"dust"* in this context follows the definite article *"the,"* thus setting this dust apart from all others. This is most likely due to *Genesis 2:5-6* – *"...⁵for the Lord God had not caused it to rain upon the Earth, and there was not a man to till the ground.*

6

⁶But there went up a mist from the Earth, and watered the whole face of the ground."

The significance of these *verses* is that this *"mist" (Gen. 2:6)*, prior to any rain, watered, and thereby moistened the face of the ground. This atmosphere availed the opportunity to produce a fine moistened dust (clay) unlike any material known today. Therefore, the biblical Hebrew word for *"the dust"* is defined within the word *'aphar* (עָפָר, OT: 6083, aw-fawr); from *'aphar* (עָפַר, OT: 6080, aw-far'), dust, clay, earth, ground.

In conclusion, due to the *mist*, the biblical Hebrew definition for *"the dust"* is defined as "fine clay," and this becomes significantly insightful in regards to the *Genesis 2:7* account – *"And the Lord God formed man of the dust of the ground...."* We will see this insight of "fine clay" when we bring *Genesis 1:26-27* and *Genesis 2:7* together. Until then, let us look into the ending portion of *Genesis 2:5* – *"... and there was not a man to till the ground."* The significance of this is Adam could not till the ground because it was tangible and Adam was not. Adam was first *"created"* in spirit, intangible, existing in the image God, after the likeness of God *(Gen. 1:27)*.

THE CORRELATION
OF
GENESIS 1:26-27 AND GENESIS 2:7

As we bring the account of *Genesis 1:26-27* and *Genesis 2:7* together, let us recap *Genesis 1:26-27*. *Genesis 1:26* reveals God's intention, the design of Adam, and what man would be like – *"And God said, Let Us make man in Our Image, after Our Likeness...."* *Genesis 1:27* reveals the literal account of God performing His loving intention by first creating Adam in spirit – *"So God created man in His Own Image, in the Image of God created He him...."* Therefore,

Adam was not yet made, but *"created"* in spirit, intangible, existing in the image God, after the likeness of God. This account took place on the sixth day *(Gen. 1:31; 2-5)*. The seventh day however, Scriptures reveals – *"And on the seventh day God ended His work which He had made; and He rested on the seventh day from all His work which he had made" (Gen. 2:2)*. Although there is much that can be said about *Genesis 1:31* through *Genesis 2:5* (the ending events of the sixth and seventh day) very simply, they are dealt with through the application of the words *"make"* and *"create (-ed)."*

Nonetheless, we are pausing on the seventh day to deal with *Genesis 2:2* – *"And on the seventh day God ended His work...."* The significance within *Genesis 2:2* is found in *"God ended His work,"* which may be the reasoning for separating the *Genesis 1:26-27* account from the *Genesis 2:7* account. It is highly possible that the separation of the two accounts was so that the forming (i.e., the tangible making) of the man, Adam, would not be included in the scope of God's work. God did not want Man to be thought of as a work of God; He desired Man to know that he was much different.

God set the two accounts apart to reveal the crowning expression of His love, and His desire to have a loving and unique relationship with Man.

Therefore, sometime after the seventh day – *"...⁵for the Lord God had not caused it to rain upon the Earth, and there was not a man to till the ground. ⁶But there went up a mist from the Earth, and watered the whole face of the ground" (Gen. 2:5-6)*. The atmosphere described within *Genesis 2:5-6* must have been remarkable; a mist, prior to any rain moistening the face of the ground. It is quite possible that God had not caused it to rain for this purpose, which in and of itself is unique to ponder. Nonetheless, God within this atmospheric condition, God produced the fine clay unlike any material known today.

As we move into the extraordinary finale, let us view the first part of *Genesis 2:7 -"And the Lord God formed man of the dust of the ground...."* Though we do not know whether or not God explained to Adam what He was going to do before forming him, or if God explained to Adam as He began to spread the fine moist clay over him; nonetheless, we do know that it was done in God's Kindness, Gentleness, and Love. The intent for tangibility may have been two fold at minimum. First, God desired Adam to fully enjoy all of creation. Second, in God's incomprehensible love, Adam entered into a probationary journey.

There is a lot to ponder in the wonderful event of God forming the man, Adam, and we might have had the idea that God formed Adam in the ground, and then God breathed into his nostrils, whereupon Adam then stood to his feet. However, it is more likely that God and Adam were standing in this event in gentle, loving anticipation as God finished the last details of Adam's body. God, in His Power and Love, looking into Adam's eyes, and Adam, peering into God's eyes as he waited in the wonderment of what was about to take place. In this extraordinary moment we can now glimpse into the balance of account two -*"And the Lord God ... breathed into his nostrils the breath of life; and man became a living soul" (Gen. 2:7).*

THE ATTRIBUTE–COMPONENTS OF MAN

Man is a spirit with a soul, and both the spirit and soul live in the human body. Man was created a triune being. Still, the Bible bears out six attribute–components of the human being: the spirit, soul, heart, mind, body, and the ghost *(Gen. 25:8; Matt. 22:37; Acts 12:21-23)*. Although the wonders of God forming the man, Adam, are remarkable, we will not know the whole story in all the splendor of details until we are in Eternity with God. Until then, we do know Adam became separated from his Creator because he chose to partake of the Tree of the Knowledge of Good and Evil. Due to Adam's decision and action, every human, with the exception of Jesus, has been born into the consequences of Adam's Sin. This is an unavoidable fact for all who have been born, will be born today, and those born in the future *(Psalms 51:5; Rom. 5:12)*. Due to this fact, of the six attribute–components that make up the human being, five are significantly affected upon conception and childbirth, and five are significantly affected upon Salvation into Christ. The function of the ghost is unaffected. Coming to understand how each component has been remarkably affected upon our Salvation into Christ can give us a greater degree of awe and thankfulness into Whom God Is and all that He has Done.

OUR SPIRIT

Our spirit is defined within the biblical Hebrew word *ruwach* (רוּחַ, OT: 7307, roo'-akh). In biblical Greek, it is defined within the word *pneuma* (πνεῦμα, NT: 4151, pnyoo'-mah). Our spirit is incorporeal. It is uncarnate – that is, without a body, or without material existence but existing, lacking a physical or material nature, but relating to or affecting by mediating between our body and soul *(Psalms 69:10; 86:4; 143:8)*. Our spirit knows the things of God because we who are Saved are born of the Spirit of God. Thus, God's Spirit dwells within us *(John 3:6; I Cor. 2:11)*. In addition, because we have the Mind of Christ, our spirit can rule our heart and soul. Our spirit has Faith *(II Cor. 4:13; Gal. 2:16, 20)*; one might ask: if our spirit knows God and the ways of God, why do we need Faith? The answer: our spirit resides in our physical body, yet until it is changed by putting on immortality *(I Cor. 15:35-58)* our spirit cannot see intangible things, as originally designed. For this reason, *"Now Faith is the substance of things hoped for, the evidence of things not seen" (Heb. 11:1).*

Before we received Salvation, our spirit was ruled by our heart and our mind, captivated by its deceits *(Rom. 3:10)*. We were ruled by the sin nature because our spirit was separated from God; as a result, our spirit did not know God, nor the things of God, and was dead to the truths of God *(I Cor. 2:14)*. In this condition, our spirit needed to be born again, yet it was impossible to come to God the Father unless He drew us *(John 6:44)*.

Upon our Salvation, our spirit became born again *(John 3:3, 6, 16)*. In this magnificent event, it has become restored to God and, because God is a Spirit *(John 4:24)*, we can now truly come to know what it is like to be created in His image, after His likeness *(Gen. 1:26-27)*. It is here that we can come to know the truths and treasures of God within His Word *(Col. 1:10-29)*. Now growing in the knowledge of God, our spirit can inspire and support our soul to trust the Lord in godly humility *(Psalms 35:13; 57:1; 86:4; 143:8)*.

OUR SOUL

Our soul is defined within the biblical Hebrew word *nephesh* (נֶפֶשׁ , OT: 5314, neh'-fesh). In biblical Greek, it is defined within the word *psuche* (ψυχή, NT: 5590, psoo-khay'). Our soul is intangible; for this reason, God clothed it with a tangible body so that we could experience not only the intangible, but also the tangible wonders of His creation *(Gen. 2:5-7)*. Though our soul is intangible, it experiences the tangible, unlike our spirit. Our spirit resides within our body; we are a living soul – *"And the Lord God formed man of the dust of the ground, and breathed into his nostrils the breath of life; and man became a living soul" (Gen. 2:7).*

11

Our soul can touch *(Lev. 5:2)*, and eat *(Lev. 7:27)*, yet it is intangible. Thus, it can feel emotions *(Psalms 6:3; 23:3; 31:7)*. Our soul can choose *(Job 7:15)* and refuse *(Job 6:7)*; our soul can wait *(Psalms 33:20)* and follow *(Psalms 63:8)*. However, our spirit inspires and has influence over our soul *(Psalms 69:10; 86:4; 143:8)*. Through this, our soul can trust God *(Psalms 57:1)*.

In addition to emotions and feelings, our soul has many types of loves. Still, as with many Hebrew and Greek words, it most often takes two or more English words to define them. For example, the love for a family member, the love for a friend, physical attraction, and sexual love are defined as *Phileo* (φιλέω, NT: 5368, fil-eh'-o). The Greek definition of love for a family member is *Storge*, and the definition for the physical attraction and sexual love is defined as *Eros*. However, *Storge* and *Eros* are not found in the Bible. Therefore, defining *Phileo* love should be expounded upon within the specific passage or Scripture context setting. Nonetheless, the Bible details human love in many ways. The following are biblical Greek words defining love.

The love we have for a dear friend is *phileo* love (φιλέω, NT: 5368, fil-eh'-o). The way we are to love our neighbor is with tenderness, otherwise known as *Agapao* love (ἀγαπάω, NT: 25, ag-ap-ah'-o). The fraternal affection we feel for our Brothers and Sisters in Christ is *Philadelphia* love (φιλαδελφία, NT: 5360, fil-ad-el-fee'-ah). The fondness we may have for Brothers and Sisters in Christ is *Philadelphos* love (φιλάδελφος, NT: 5361, fil-ad'-el-fos). The affection a wife has for her husband is *Philandros* love (φίλανδρος NT: 5362, fil'-an-dros). A general kindness and benevolence toward mankind is *Philanthropia* love (φιλανθρωπία, NT: 5363, fil-an-thro-pee'-ah). General humane acts of courteousness are *philanthropos* (φιλανθρώπως, NT: 5364, fil-an-thro'-poce). There is as well, due to the Fall of Adam, a dark side of human love: the love of money is *philarguria* love (φιλαργυρία, NT: 5365, fil-ar-goo-ree'-ah); covetous love is *philarguros* love (φιλάργυρος, NT: 5366, fil-ar'-goo-ros), and selfishness is *philautos* (φίλαυτος, NT: 5367 (fil'-ow-tos).

These definitions in no way exhaust the array of human love, and it would be impossible to go through life ever trying to discern the variety of these emotions. In conclusion, without *Agape* love (ά γάπη, NT:26, ag-ah'-pay – the Love of God), the true vitality of life cannot be properly experienced. Moreover, without *Agape* love, all of human love remains unstable, fading in and out, remiss of true love.

All of us as human beings have become a living soul with a tangible body *(Gen. 2:7)*. Our soul experiences what our heart imagines, and feels with emotions apart from consciousness. Because our soul connects the intangible to the material, it experiences what our heart imagines as the tangible world is engaged. Moreover, our soul has the opportunity to express emotions and the imaginations of our heart. Before we received Salvation, our soul was not only grossly subject to the deceitfulness of our heart, but was also ruled by the sin nature. As a result, our body manifested this deceitfulness and ruling *(Rom. 2:14-15)*. For this reason, our soul could not experience the likeness of how we were created and made, and our soul could not function properly with our spirit because our spirit was not born again. Thus, our soul was destined into eternity without God *(Matt. 10:28; Rev., Chptr 20)*. In this condition, our entire function was what we were; we were in a fallen state, an unregenerate condition.

Upon Salvation, our spirit became born again *(John 3:3, 6, 16)*; thus, the Spirit of God now dwells in us, and our soul was given the gift of eternal life. In this remarkable event of Salvation, our soul was awakened to the love of God and can now prosper and function with greater clarity in the tangible, and intangible realm *(Rom. 8:1-17; I Cor. 2:16)*. Why? Because the body of the sin nature became incapacitated *(Rom. 6:6)*, and all other components of our makeup

13

have become the new man *(Eph. 4:24)*. Our soul, with true feelings and emotions, through a glass, darkly *(I Cor. 13:12)*, can experience in likeness what God feels, what God sees, and what God knows *(Gen. 1:26-27; Col. 3:10)*. *Agape* love, now dwelling in us, ensures that all other love within our intangible and tangible makeup of feeling and emotions does not fade. It is with *Agape* love we begin to realize and embrace His forgiveness for us, wherein our soul becomes satisfied, and we learn to love in the likeness as He loves *(Eph., Chptr 3)*.

OUR SKIN

Though our body is one of the six components we are dealing with in this chapter, we have delved into the division of our body because many Scriptures refer to the "flesh" or the "body." Very simply, we have skin over our flesh, and both make up our body. Our outer sheath (skin) is defined within the word *'owr* (עוֹר, OT: 5785, ore); from OT: 5783; skin (as naked), by implication, hide, or leather. In biblical Greek our skin is defined within the biblical Greek word *dermatinos* (δερμάτινος, NT: 1193, der-mat'-ee-nos); from NT: 1192; leather, of a skin. Therefore, once again, the skin *(dermatinos)* is the covering of our flesh.

OUR FLESH

Our flesh is defined within the biblical Greek word *sarx* (σάρξ, NT: 4561, sarx); stripped of the skin, or (by extension) the body as opposed to the soul or spirit. In conclusion, the flesh is the interior: that which is stripped of skin. Yet our flesh is our human nature as well with its weaknesses and strengths, both intellectual and physical *(Rom. 7:18)*.

OUR BODY

Our body is defined within the biblical Greek word *soma* (σῶμα, NT: 4983, so'-mah); from, *sozo* (σώζω, NT: 4982, sode'-zo); the body (as a sound whole), used in a very wide application, literally or figuratively – heal, preserve, save (self), do well, be (make) whole. Therefore, the body is the whole of the skin and the flesh.

THE GHOST

The ghost is defined in biblical Hebrew within the word *gava'* (גָּוַע, OT: 1478, gaw-vah'). In biblical Greek, it is defined within the word *ekpsucho* (ἐκψύχω, NT: 1634, ek-psoo;-kho). The ghost is not a ghost as the world might understand; it is "the ghost" unveiled in Scripture, and it is never disassociated with the definite article "the." "The ghost" is a unique entity. In the nineteen times "the ghost" is found in Scripture (eleven in the Old Testament and eight in the New Testament), "the ghost" is directly associated with the death of the mortal human body; for example *"...gave up the ghost, and died" (Gen. 25:8)*. Of these nineteen times "the ghost" is brought out in Scripture, five are in reference to the physical body of Jesus *(Matt. 27:50; Mk 15:37; Mark 15:39; Luke 23:46; John 19:30)*, and fourteen are in reference the physical body of all other men *(Gen. 25:8, 17; 35:29; 49:33; Job 3:11; 10:18; 11:20; 13:19; 14:10; Jer. 15:9; Lam. 1:19; Acts 5:5, 10; 12: 23)*.

Within the Word of God, we find one *verse* that appears, at first glance, to reference the spirit keeping the physical body alive – *"For as the body without the spirit is dead, so Faith without works is dead also" (Jam. 2:26)*. However, this is not the case. *James 2:26* speaks in reference to the spirit of man as it regards being dead to the things of God unless it is born again. For example, without Salvation, the spirit of Man cannot produce works acceptable unto God *(born again – John 3:3-8; unregenerate – Rom. 3:10)*.

The Epistle of James has long been the platform of complex arguments in perspective views of Faith and works. Therefore, further into this book I have addressed this perplexity. Until then, let us continue in the explanation of *James 2:26* in order to understand that it is the ghost keeping the mortal body alive.

James 2:16 is an analogy that is dealing with Faith and works – *"so Faith without works is dead also..."* – and James has likened Faith without works to *"the body without the spirit is dead...."* For this reason, it is important to understand that James is speaking to us who are born again. For us who are born again, the Apostle Paul reveals that our physical body is now dead because of the sin nature – *"And if Christ be in you, the body is dead because of sin; but the Spirit is life because of righteousness" (Rom. 8:10)*. Though *Romans 8:10* and *James 2:16* seem to be in conflict with one another, they are not. They support one another perfectly.

Romans 8:10 reveals that, upon Salvation, our physical body becomes dead; not physically dead, but rendered useless due to the body of the sin nature becoming incapacitated *(Rom. 6:6)*. Now, the Spirit is life within us because of Righteousness *(John 3:6; 8:11-17)*. For this reason, we are to learn how to walk after the Spirit so that all we do is of God. Therefore, in regards to *Romans 8:10*, the Apostle Paul is simply saying that we are not to use our physical body to deal with spiritual matters *(Rom. 7:18)*. Otherwise, the sin nature is given occasion to revive *(Rom. 7:8-11)*. We will be dealing with the sin nature as we get into Part II, Chapter 4, *Our Old Man*. As it regards our physical body and spiritual matters, all manner of walking in Christ comes first by Faith, through which Faith, properly placed, ensures our physical body is quickened by the Spirit of God, and then all good works are acceptable unto God *(Rom. 6:3-5; 7:25; 8:2, 14)*.

Without being born again, this supernatural walk is impossible to achieve just as Faith without works is dead. This is the analogy in *James 2:16*. Prior to our Salvation, we were alive in that our physical body was alive and under the direct reign, influence, and power of the sin nature working in and through our physical body *(Eph. 2:1-5)*. Consequently, the result was that our body was dead to the things of God without our spirit being born again, and we could not produce works acceptable unto God. *James 2:16* states – *"For as the body without the spirit is dead...,"* that is, the body without the spirit being born again is dead as *"Faith without works is dead also."* Therefore, in the nineteen times "the ghost" is referenced, this entity is, without fail, directly related to either "giving up" or "yielding up" the ghost of the mortal human body.

When a human being gives up the ghost, that is, the *ekpsucho* (ἐκψύχω, NT: 1634, ek-psoo;-kho), or expires, which is rendered in the *King James Version* as to "give (yield) up the ghost," it literally means that the human is giving up the last breath of physical life, whereupon his or her tangible mortal body dies *(Gen. 25:8; Matt. 27:50; John 19:30)*. Upon Salvation, there is no indication that the ghost affects the mortal body. Once again, the ghost is that which keeps the physical body alive and, with certainty, it is the breath of life that originated from God in the forming and materializing of the man, Adam *(Gen. 2:7)*.

OUR HEART

Our heart is defined in biblical Hebrew within the word *leb* (לֵב, OT: 3820, labe). In biblical Greek, it is defined within the word *kardia* (καρδία, NT: 2588, kar-dee'-ah). Prior to our Salvation, our heart was covered, hardened, and blind to the truths and ways of God. Thus, it was alienated from God *(Eph. 4:18)*, and we were unable to obey from our heart *(Rom. 2:14-15)*. Our heart was deceitfully wicked and, because we were unsaved, we did not even know the depth of this wickedness *(Jer. 17:9)*. Still, our heart could believe *(Rom. 10:9-10)*. However, God would not violate our will in regards to seeking Him and His ways *(Gen. 3:6-7)*. The sovereignty to believe in God and choose the ways righteousness or unrighteousness was left to us. Even after our Salvation, the sovereignty to believe in God and choose the ways righteousness or unrighteousness is left to us. This sovereignty has always been in the hands of Man, both Saved and unsaved. This is evidenced prior to Adam's Fall *(seeking righteousness – Gen. 2:19-20; seeking unrighteousness – Gen. 3:3-13)*, after the Fall *(seeking righteousness – Gen. 4:1-4; seeking unrighteousness – Gen. 4:1-16)*, and after the events of the Cross *(seeking righteousness – Rom. 10:9-10; seeking unrighteousness – II Cor. 11:4)*, even after an individual's Salvation *(seeking righteousness – Matt. 22:37; seeking unrighteousness – Mark 8:36; Phil. 3:18)*.

Upon our Salvation, our heart became circumcised – the hardness, blindness, and ignorance removed *(the need to become born again – Rom. 2:28-29; now accomplished – Col. 2:11; 3:3)*. Now born again, we can obey from our heart *(Rom. 6:17-18)*. In addition, upon the circumcision of our heart, which is made by God alone, the Author of Hebrews writes – *"This is the Covenant that I will make with them after those days, says the Lord, I will put My Laws into their hearts, and in their minds will I write them…" (Heb. 10:16)*. This sovereign work was done by God in His desire to walk intimately with us who have received Salvation *(Heb. 8:10)*, and now in our own volition we can not only come to know Him, but also come to understand His ways. For example, His ways are found within the Law of Faith *(Rom. 3:27)*, the Law of God *(Rom. 7:25)*, the Law of the Spirit *(Rom. 8:2)*, the Law of Righteousness *(Rom. 9:31)*, the Law to Christ *(I Cor. 9:21)*, and the Law of Liberty *(Jam. 2:12)*. As we seek to know God and His ways from a pure heart, we will come to see that the Laws revealing His ways are not a set of rules to be lived by through our flesh. They are the ways of Righteousness through Faith apart from any works of the Law.

OUR MIND

Our mind is defined in biblical Hebrew within the word *yetser* (יֵצֶר, OT: 3336, yay'-tser). In biblical Greek, it is defined within the word *nous* (νοῦς, NT: 3563, nooce). Prior to our Salvation, our mind had no other resources than that of our fallen carnal nature holding within it the knowledge of good and evil due to Adam's decision to eat from the Tree of the Knowledge of Good and Evil *(Gen. 3:6-7, 22; Rom. 5:12)*. As a result, our mind was not subject to the true ways of God; our mind was hostile against God, and we could only rely on carnal thinking *(Rom. 8:7)*. Through this, our mind could not function properly due to the condition of our spirit, soul, body, and heart. The ghost was unaffected.

Upon our Salvation, we were brought through the carnal veil *(Heb. 10:20)*. We were given the Mind of Christ *(I Cor. 2:16)* and now have the ability to discern *(Heb. 5:14)*, and the opportunity to live a new way through Faith *(Gal. 2:16-20; Phil. 2:5; Heb. 12:2)*. In addition, now that the entirety of our makeup is functioning properly, though for now we see through a glass, darkly *(I Cor. 13:12)*, our mind can direct our thoughts, desire, Faith, and will according to the Word of God *(Matt. 22:37; Rom. 7:25; I Tim. 6:12)*. Now the sky is the limit as to all we will do through His Spirit as our mind is set on no other thing than Jesus Christ, and Him Crucified *(I Cor. 2:2)*.

CHAPTER 2

What on Earth is Going On?

THE HUMAN WILL

After receiving Salvation, due to the current environment we live in *(Gal. 1:4)*, it may be difficult to hang onto the remarkable fact that we are the crowning expression of God's love *(Gen. 1:26-27; 2:2, 7)*. Therefore, I would like to make some applications into our human experience. Why? Although we may glimpse into the wonderful way in which God made man, due to the Fall of Adam, at best, our full ability to experience why and how we were made can still be distorted.

Yes, upon our Salvation all things have become new, yet we can still find ourselves doing some really reckless things. This leaves us to ask: "What on earth is going on?" This is a question asked by a vast majority of Christians. Therefore, within this chapter I am going to lay an altogether different platform for some specifics about humans. Specifically, I want to discuss our will and our body. I am doing this for three reasons: to help us understand what on earth is going on, to lay the groundwork for this book and the terms used, and finally because our walk in Christ is not meant to be happenstance or one of reactions whereby we become participators whether we like it or not.

Our walk is meant to be a joyful experience that comes from proper decisions that can be made when we come to understand what on earth is going on before we participate. Therefore, as we unveil the impact of our decisions, this chapter will begin quite comprehensively. Not to worry, it is okay not to get your mind wrapped around everything at first. It will become clear once we get through the first few paragraphs. Okay, here we go.

THE HUMAN WILL – DEFINED

Our human will is defined within the biblical Greek word *thelo* (θέλω, NT: 2309, thel'-o) and is strengthened by determination as an active option from subjective impulse (i.e., that which takes in our mind). Through the assessment of thoughts (i.e., subjective impulse), a decision must be made in order to determine. Thus, the decision is the active option wherein our determination dictates the direction of our will, whereby will is then strengthened and follows determination.

We must come to understand that the results we experience in our lives are due to the decisions we make. Yet, because we are born again, it becomes paramount that our very first decision must be to place our Faith properly. If the decision is made to place Faith properly, the result is the power of God at work within our lives *(Rom. 8:13; Gal. 6:14; Rev. 12:11)* and not our will working through our flesh. As this becomes the experience, we resonate determination in order to back up our ongoing decision to maintain properly placed Faith. However, if we make a decision whereby our Faith is improperly placed, our will follows our decision and determination trails behind in dysfunctional confusion in order to back up our decision. All the while, our will becomes manifested as willpower working in our body. In conclusion, if the improper decision is made for placing Faith, failure and bondage become the result *(Rom. 7:9, 15, 23)*. This will be qualified in the balance of this chapter and become much clearer as we move our way through the material. The following are four scenarios for our human will.

THE HUMAN WILL – LIFE APPLICATION

Not Making a Decision

If we do not make a decision to place Faith, and place Faith properly, by floundering in a happenstance frame of mind, reflexively our human will is brought back to ourselves by default. Thus, in passive acquiescence (i.e., agreement without protest), our will becomes manifested through our physical body as willpower, and we end up doing things we do not want to do *(Rom. 7:15, 19, 23)*.

Another way this can be viewed: If we do not make a decision when subjective impulses are seen in our mind, by default we passively react wherein our will becomes applied to our body, resulting in willpower. Therein, we are in a constant cycle of doing things we do not want to do whether we like it or not.

In conclusion, properly walking with God cannot be avoided; otherwise we will be operating through our own power. This is due to the fact that we are dealing with ongoing spiritual dynamics that require decisions. By not making decisions, we simply, without choice, get caught up in the movement of the material world and are overcome by the lust of our eyes, the lust of the flesh, the pride of life, the world, and the Devil.

Making the Improper Decision

If we make a decision that improperly places Faith, by default, our human will is brought back to ourselves in the decision to use objective performances in external conditions (i.e., perform in the body). In this case, all power is our human willpower, and reveals our will and not the Will of the Father. For this reason, the Apostle Paul wrote – *"For I know that in me (that is, in my flesh,) dwells no good thing: for to will is present with me; but how to perform that which is good I find not"* *(Rom. 7:18).*

Though the Apostle Paul was not passive, he was without the knowledge of where his Faith was to be placed when he first engaged the struggle with the sin nature. Therefore, Paul found himself in this position before he came to understand the proper decision and resting place for his Faith.

Romans 7:18 was experienced, and thus written by the Apostle Paul due to his love for God and his desire to live for Him. However, although Paul loved God and had Faith, when his will took first place, it was brought back to himself in the decision to use objective performances. All power was his human willpower. Because of this, it revealed his will, and not the Will of the Father. Therein, Paul wrote – *"⁸But sin, taking occasion by the Commandment, wrought in me all manner of concupiscence. For without the Law sin was dead. ⁹For I was alive without the Law once: but when the Commandment came, sin revived, and I died"* *(Rom. 7:8-9).*

Likewise for us, when we make the wrong decision by improperly placing Faith, although we believe in God, upon a proper biblical examination, we would see that our Faith was in our own power and that of our objective performances. Therein, not only did this result in motions of sins in the flesh, which were by the Law *(Rom. 7:5),* the sin nature was given occasion to revive *(Rom. 7:9; I Cor. 15:56).* This cycle continues until the answer as to where Faith is to be anchored is known and embraced. This is the stereotypical condition of most all who love the Lord, and is not a condemning indictment. The Apostle Paul walked through this as well. It is simply the condition when the proper decision is unknown, or is known yet not followed through with.

Let us understand the effects of our decisions. A decision is obviously the subjective (i.e., that which takes place in our mind) and the associated effect of a decision can resonate determination. Still, determination remains in the subjective (i.e., intangible state). However, unlike a decision that can resonate into determination and still remain in the subjective state, human will is not like this. Human will, though beginning in the subjective position, can end up in the objective position by empowering our body to perform, which is based upon a decision to accomplish our will. This results in willpower. The reason for this is that willpower naturally desires to default into the objective position, and to do so, it uses the body. On the other hand, determination stays in the subjective state. Therefore, determination is meant for Faith and willpower is for the body.

The problem is that our willpower and our physical body are not to be joined together in our Sanctification. Therefore, if the two are joined together in the Sanctification process, the result is an illegal combination *(Rom. 7:18; 8:10)*. For this reason, determination must always precede will, yet this biblical sequence can only take place with a proper biblical decision to set Faith in its designed resting place *(Rom. 7:25; Gal. 2:19-20; Heb. 12:2)*.

Making a Decision and Not Following Through
If we make a decision and yet do not follow through with the decision, determination never resonates, and by default our human will is brought back to ourselves in passive acquiescence. In this case, all power is human willpower. We do have an imagination and we are free to ponder the wonders of life and all that God has made. We make decisions throughout each day. In regards to spiritual matters, we cannot flounder, or we will put ourselves in a position of passive acquiescence.

Making the Proper Decision

When we make the definitive decision of properly placing Faith from subjective impulse, determination resonates from the solid and assessed decision wherein our will, now in a subservient position, is strengthened as a constituent, although still, under the authority of the proper decision. This resonates determination and maintains properly placed Faith, and our physical body is energized by the Spirit of God instead of our willpower, revealing the Will of the Father instead of our will. The scope of this happens in an instant, yet is the direct result of the decision to place Faith properly. For this reason, determination is meant for Faith *(I Cor. 2:2)*; this is the good fight of Faith apart from any works of the flesh *(I Tim. 6:12; II Tim. 4:7)*. Let us now look into properly placed Faith.

We are a remarkable creation of God; Scripture says that we are fearfully and wonderfully made. However, due to the Fall, we have three natures. All of us have a divine nature, not in the sense of Divine as God is, but in the sense that we are created in the image, after the likeness of God *(Gen. 1:26-27)*. We are a spirit and we have a soul *(Gen. 2:7)*. The other two natures are simply a human nature *(Gen. 1:28; 2:15)* and a fallen nature *(Rom. 5:12)*. We have three natures: we are a spirit, we have a soul, and we live in a body, but the human nature and the sin nature are melded within our physical body due to the Fall of Adam *(Rom. 6:6; 7:23)*.

For reasons concerning our human nature and the sin nature, our body became dead when we received Salvation *(Rom. 8:10)*. It was not made physically dead, but rendered ineffective so that we do not use our human nature with its natural attributes: our intellect, carnal mind, and even our natural strengths. These can revive the sin nature when engaged improperly, as it regards spiritual matters.

We have subjective impulses all of the time and we need to make decisions with them. We do not have to do this with all of them because we have an imagination. This has much to do with our heart, and we can ponder wonderful things every day – this is part of being human. Yet because of our being born again, we have entered into a spiritual war for the time being. The subjective impulses need to be dealt with so that we are not in just a happenstance frame of mind wherein passive acquiescence in objective performances becomes the result. That is, we cannot use our physical body to live for God because, if we try, the sin nature is given occasion to revive *(Rom. 7:9)*. In conclusion, the proper decision for Faith is the Cross. This is the exclusive and proper object for our Faith *(I Cor. 2:2)*. With this exclusive decision, determination resonates, and our will follows.

Though we may understand the Cross for our Salvation, we must come to understand that God has established through Jesus Christ, and Him Crucified, a life of living yet remaining dead for the benefits of living in the likeness of Jesus' Resurrection *(Rom. 6:3-5, 7)*. This ongoing death is experienced only through Faith placed exclusively in Jesus Christ, and Him Crucified *(Rom. 7:25; I Cor. 1:17-18)*. For this reason the Apostle Paul writes – *"For I determined not to know any thing among you, save Jesus Christ, and Him Crucified"* *(I Cor. 2:2)*. Regarding the ongoing experience of Paul's properly placed Faith he writes – *"I am Crucified with Christ: nevertheless I live; yet not I, but Christ lives in me: and the life which I now live in the flesh I live by the Faith of the Son of God, Who loved me, and gave Himself for me"* *(Gal. 2:20)*. The result of Paul's determination was triumph, wherein he writes – *"But God forbid that I should glory, save in the Cross of our Lord Jesus Christ, by whom the world is Crucified unto me, and I unto the world"* *(Gal. 6:14)*. As Christians we know there is more – we cry out for it, yet the true journey begins with an assessed decision to place Faith properly.

CHAPTER 3

Amazing Love

M ost of mankind is looking for the answer to the origin of creation and their purpose for existence. Yet, we who are Saved may also have an unsettled heart as to our purpose, even though we know Whom our Creator Is. When we come to know our purpose, the void within us becomes filled, and our relationship with the Father grows intimately deeper *(Rom. 8:15-17)*. God has made all of us in His image, after His likeness, to know Him, to experience His love, and to walk with Him in the wonder of all that He has created.

In God's infinite love, He formed man of the dust of the ground, and breathed into his nostrils the breath of life; and man became a living soul *(Gen. 2:7)*. All the while, in His infinite knowledge, He understood the potential for Adam to fall at the devices of Lucifer – the one who attempted to usurp His Throne in Eternity past. Knowing all things, He also knew and, therefore, resolved that it would take the Sacrifice of Himself to Redeem mankind in the event that Adam did fall. Still, in His incomprehensible love, He created and made Adam, then placed him in the Garden of Eden, wherein He intimately walked with him.

Over time, as Lucifer plotted to the extent of his wisdom, he composed himself through the caverns of his darkened mind and caused Adam and Eve to doubt God. By introducing the idea that God was withholding knowledge and wisdom from them *(Gen. 3:4-5)*, they pondered Lucifer's Lie. Though Eve became deceived, believing that there was more, Adam hearkened unto her voice. They took, ate, and gained the knowledge of good and evil *(Gen. 3:6)*.

In this self-reliant act, Adam and Eve became separated from God; their eyes were opened to a conscience of self. The knowledge of good compelled them to overcome the knowledge of evil *(Gen. 3:7, 10, 12)*. This left them and all mankind through Adam's seed, in a fallen state of turmoil. A cyclic turmoil of trying to do good in order to overcome evil resulted, and continues to result, in ongoing failure and condemnation *(Rom. 2:14-15)*. The results are seen in a general evaluation of the world around us.

Due to the catastrophic results of Adam's decision, all of us as human beings, with the exception of Jesus *(Matt. 1:20; Heb. 4:15)*, are and have been born with a void in our heart and mind because of our separation from God. The magnitude of this void is directly tied to our need to feel understood, valued, loved, and everything else associated with what only God can provide. Moreover, regardless of the inexpressible joy we can feel on our very best day, it is not humanly possible to bring another into how we truly feel. Because of this, there can be a peculiar sense of something missing. Likewise, when we are going through a trying time, what we desire most is that someone could feel what we feel so we would not feel alone. In either case, it is not possible to experience fully what another person is feeling.

These voids were not to be within human life *(Gen. 2:17)*, and it is because of these voids that each of us as Christians are driven to search for our purpose. However, regardless of how significant the purpose we pursue, if we engage a semblance of it, the void will not become filled. It is a dilemma for us as Christians because we love God with all our heart and, in this, we desire to serve Him in any way we can. Still, these voids can only be filled through a true relationship with God because He has made man in His image, after His likeness, to walk with Him in the wonder of being created by Him and experience an intimate likeness of what He feels, what He sees, and what He knows.

Man is a created being; he is not God, nor can he ever be, and man cannot be like God in the sense of power, absolute creation, authority or any other thing that touches the Divine attributes of our Thrice Holy God. The notion of attaining such comes from the Devil, and has nothing to do with how and why man became created. Once again, God has made man in His image, after His likeness, to fellowship with Him in a loving and close relationship. It is within this relationship that we learn dependence on Him. It was this way for Adam within in his probationary period, and it is this way for all who call upon His Name.

There are many, many ways in which an individual will try to know God. However, due to the Fall, God in His amazing love has designed one way, the Cross. Upon the Cross, He Redeemed Man through the Vicarious Shedding of His Blood *(John 3:16)*, and destroyed him who had the power of death, through death, that is, the Devil *(Heb. 2:14-15)*. He did all of this in His love so that He could have an intimate and loving relationship with us. It was not God's intention that the Fall took place – it is because of the Fall that He came *(I John 3:8)*.

Now, each of us who call upon His Name, are given the opportunity to experience the benefits of the Cross, by which we can become Crucified to this world and quickened in the likeness of His Resurrection that we might live for Him *(Rom. 8:11-14; Gal. 6:14)*. In this, we come to know Him as He desires.

The Apostle Paul writes – *"⁷But what things were gain to me, those I counted loss for Christ. ⁸Yea doubtless, and I count all things but loss for the excellency of the knowledge of Christ Jesus my Lord: for Whom I have suffered the loss of all things, and do count them but dung, that I may win Christ, ⁹And be found in Him, not having my own righteousness, which is of the Law, but that which is through the Faith of Christ, the Righteousness which is of God by Faith: ¹⁰That I may know Him, and the power of His Resurrection, and the fellowship of His sufferings, being made conformable unto His death; ¹¹If by any means I might attain unto the Resurrection of the dead" (Phil. 3:7-11).*

Though we will be involved within *verses* 7 through 10 of *Philippians Chapter 3* further into the book, as we look into *verse 11* for now, we see that the Apostle Paul wrote – *"If by any means I might attain unto the Resurrection of the dead."* Paul is not speaking of physical death; otherwise, we who believe would have no hope of abundant life while alive in this present world. How then did Paul become dead, still live, yet raised in the likeness of Jesus' Resurrection? Although Paul had Faith, desire, and willpower, he was unable to attain this death *(Rom. 7:15, 23)* until he was taught to place his Faith in Jesus Christ, and Him Crucified *(Rom. 7:25; I Cor. 2:2; Gal. 1:11-12).*

In his walk in Christ, when the Apostle Paul came to embrace the truth of the Cross, he was made in the likeness of Jesus' death, wherein, Crucified with Christ, he was then raised in the likeness of His Resurrection *(Rom. 8:2; Gal. 2:19-20).* For this reason, the Apostle Paul gives us this wonderful disclosure, and in this remarkable place alone, apart from any works, the pursuit of purpose faded in the wonder of truly knowing Him. For this reason, Paul continues by writing – *"¹²Not as though I had already attained, either were already perfect: but I follow after, if that I may apprehend that for which also I am apprehended of Christ Jesus. ¹³Brethren, I count not myself to have* apprehended: but this one thing I do, forgetting those things which are behind, and reaching forth unto those things which are before, *¹⁴I press toward the mark for the prize of the high calling of God in Christ Jesus" (Phil. 3:12-14).*

Within *Philippians 3:12-14*, we find the Apostle Paul following after that which he has been apprehended for. However, as I have stated, there was a time when the Apostle did not understand what he had been apprehended for. This was during a time when he did not know how to walk with God victoriously, but he did not give up *(Rom. 7:24)*. As he sought God, God Revealed a life-changing Truth not known by anyone before him. This Revelation, in due time, became the Gospel that he Preached *(I Cor. 1:17-18, 23)*. For this reason, he writes – *"¹¹But I certify you, Brethren, that the Gospel which was Preached of me is not after man. ¹²For I neither received it of man, neither was I taught it, but by the Revelation of Jesus Christ" (Gal. 1:11-12).*

The Gospel Preached of the Apostle Paul is the Message of the Cross, a Message of Life through death, and though the Apostle Paul had a purpose, once he came to know what it meant to walk with God in victory and freedom, his entire determination was to know Him, at which point he faithfully lived his purpose. For this reason, the Apostle writes – *"For I determined not to know any thing among you, save Jesus Christ, and Him Crucified" (I Cor. 2:2).*

This book is about this determination and the remarkable Resurrection life that comes through Faith in Jesus Christ, and Him Crucified. It is my prayer and hope that the biblical exegeses and commentaries within will become a helpful tool that brings to light the wonderful and remarkable way our God has made us in His image, after His likeness. Most important, it is my deep desire that the work within this book reveals the principles that God has established in order for us to walk with Him in intimacy, ongoing victory, and growing Sanctification.

Interim

WRITING STRUCTURE

Up to this point, we have been involved with typical biblical commentaries. Now, the structure of writing has been handled a little differently. From Part II through Part IV, I have used the Scripture itself as the title for each exegetical commentary, and I have called them "Subject Scriptures."

I have chosen this method in order to expound more specifically about a particular portion of Scripture. In addition, you will find that each exegetical commentary is an exclusive study within itself. Therefore, the exposition becomes an exclusive teaching and preaching tool of that portion of Scripture.

There will be some expositions that you can spend weeks studying. This is due to the in-depth subject matter within a particular portion of Scripture. This is not meant to detour you from simply reading through the book – you certainly can if you would like. However, this book has not been drafted to engage as a novel. The commentaries and exegeses are intended for theological application in the study of spiritual principles. Coming to understand these principles brings tremendous clarity for growing in triumph and holiness, as well as clarity for what is going on within and around us. It is my sincere hope that this work becomes a tool in equipping you for an exciting, Spirit-filled journey in understanding more of the Word of God.

PART II

Spiritual Laws
and Their Dynamics

CHAPTER 4

Our Old Man

ROMANS 6:6-7

PREFACE

Contained within the sixty-six Books of the Bible is God's Revelation to mankind and, in a lifetime of study, we only tap the surface of the unsearchable riches of His Word. His Word alone is what we who are born again desire to govern our entire life and, in His knowledge of our desire, He is ever ready to teach us everything needed for our life and living *(I John 2:27)*. Not one thing given to us within His Word is by mistake; all has a unique design and an excellent purpose. For this reason, the book of *Romans* plays a role unlike any other Book in the Bible. Due to the role it plays, many Scholars have proclaimed the Book of *Romans* to be the Mount Everest of the Bible. Within it, God has given us a behind-the-scenes look into the astonishing principles and spiritual Laws that govern Man.

These spiritual Laws are not a rigid set of rules to live by through our physical body. Spiritual forces can be Likened to gravity – though we do not see it, we walk within its forces every moment of our lives. Without gravity, our world would drift from the sun, the seas would turn to ice, and human life would cease to exist. Yet, gravity works with the confines of a Law – the Law of Gravity. When this Law is understood, we then have the knowledge to break free from its forces and discover more of God's creation.

Likened to the Law of Gravity, there are powerful forces at work right now and, though unseen, these forces function within their own Laws. Whether or not this is realized, we are affected by them every moment of our lives. The Law of Sin is one of them. The forces at work within this Law hold humanity in its grips until its power is broken by the most powerful Law – the Law of the Spirit of Life in Christ Jesus *(Rom. 8:2)*.

Christianity is not a based on performance through the physical; it is based on a relationship with God through Faith. This relationship begins with the knowledge of God's Ways and, when embraced through Faith, an intimate journey with our Creator begins.

Before we get started on this remarkable journey and because we are first investigating the principles of our old man, I would like to lay the groundwork for a better level of understanding. Therefore, I would like to first deal with the term, "the sin nature," and how this nature can affect us as Christians. Most Christians have never heard of this term before, but the Bible clearly bears it out. For example, in a literal translation of the *sixth chapter of Romans*, the Apostle Paul wrote the word "sin" seventeen times, thirteen of which have the definite article "the" before the word "sin." This speaks of "the sin," the original nature of sin passed onto all mankind due to the Fall of Adam *(Rom. 5:12; 7:23)*.

With the exception of Jesus, every person has been conceived in this nature of sin. This was an unavoidable fact for them, and all who will be born today and in the future. To one degree or another, every person is influenced by the sin nature from conception to natural childbirth and on until Salvation is received *(Psalms 51:5; Rom. 3:10)*.

Though this is a grim fact for the unsaved, it is irrefutable regardless of what one wants to believe. Nonetheless, it is this nature of sin that causes the action of sin *(Rom. 7:20)*. However, it must be understood that the sin nature is confined within the members of the physical body of each human, Saved or unsaved *(Rom. 7:23)*. It is only upon Salvation that the sin nature becomes incapacitated and remains incapacitated so long as Faith remains ever anchored in the Cross *(Rom. 7:25; 8:2; I Cor. 2:2)*. Once again, Jesus was not conceived of the seed of a fallen man. Therefore, Jesus was not born with this nature – *"...for that which was conceived in her* (Mary) *was of the Holy Spirit" (Matt. 1:20)*.

For years, in my own personal walk in Christ, I did not understand that my sinful thoughts and actions were due to the nature of sin. As a matter of fact, in the early years of my walk, I did not even know that there was a nature of sin and that there were dynamics that I needed to understand so that I could remain free from its ruling dominion. For this reason, let us look into a concise delineation between the action of sin and the nature of sin.

The action of sin is defined within the biblical Greek word *hamartano* (ἁμαρτάνω, NT: 264, ham-ar-tan'-o). It is defined as missing the mark, and so not share in the prize, i.e., to err, especially morally: – for your faults, offend, sin, and trespass.

The nature of sin is defined within the biblical Greek word *hamartia* (ἁμαρτία, NT: 266, ham-ar-tee'-ah). It is defined as full sin (properly abstract) – sin (-full). Literal translation describes "full sin" as "the sin." This directly references the actual nature of sin that all mankind is conceived in, and born with, as a direct result of Adam's Original Sin. Therefore, the full descriptive term, "the sin nature" is used throughout the draft of this book.

We find biblical reference disclosed by the Apostle Paul when he struggled with the sin nature prior to understanding the way of victory – *"²²for I delight in the Law of God according to the inward man, ²³and I behold another Law in my members, warring against the Law of my mind, and bringing me into captivity to the Law of the sin that [is] in my members"* (Rom. 7:22-23 – YLT).

To help bring clarity and application to this term, let us look into how the Apostle Paul first begins to reveal the principles behind it by writing – *"Knowing this, that our old man is Crucified with Him, that the body of sin might be destroyed, that henceforth we should not serve sin"* (Rom. 6:6). Within *Romans 6:6* we find the phrase *"body of sin."* However, it is written in a literal translation as "body of the sin," thus making clear reference to the nature of sin, not the action of sin. The Apostle Paul is saying to us that the body of sin is "the sin nature." Furthermore, this nature of sin was kept alive through the ways of our old man. The question is: after Salvation, can the sin nature revive and have dominion once again now that our old man is Crucified?

To qualify the reality of this taking place within the life of the Christian, let us look at the phrase *"might be destroyed"* in *Romans 6:6*. Due to the word *"might,"* we are given a certainty that the sin nature can revive. Also, as we examine the last portion of *Romans 6:6* – *"that henceforth we should not serve sin"* – we clearly see *"we should not serve sin."* This reveals to us another certainty that we can end up serving sin.

For further qualification, let us view another Scripture within passage context – *"Let not sin therefore reign in your mortal body, that you should obey it in the lusts thereof"* (Rom. 6:12). As we look into the beginning of *Romans 6:12*, we see – *"Let not sin therefore reign in your mortal body."* This gives us certainty that we can end up letting the sin nature reign in the physical members of our mortal body. As we look into the balance of *Romans 6:12*, we see *"that you should obey it in the lusts thereof."* This gives certainty that it is up to us not to obey the sin nature. Now the question is: how do we not let the sin nature reign in our physical body? As you delve further into the subject matter of this book, the answer to this question will become crystal clear.

In the overall scope of this book, we are heavily zeroing in on the *sixth and seventh chapters of Romans*. Within *Chapter 6*, the Apostle Paul reveals what takes place upon our Salvation. *Chapter 7:1-6*, the Apostle reveals our dynamic relationship with the Mosaic Law, while in *Chapter 7:7* the Apostle unveils that now born again, the purpose of the Law is to reveal. Within the balance of *Chapter 7*, with the exception of *verse 25*, we find a remarkable disclosure of Paul's struggle with the sin nature. *Verse 25* of *Chapter 7* reveals the doorway to his victory, thereby unveiling his magnificent freedom in the first *verses* of *Chapter 8*.

Though the entire book of *Romans* has a full scope chronology, this personal chronology within *Chapters 6 and 7* can bring comfort to all Believers who have struggled or are currently struggling with sin and the nature of it by coming to know that Paul went through the same struggle as a Christian. We must always understand that all of the Word of God is His Revelation to Man, and that it was the Holy Spirit that moved and superintended the Apostle Paul to write out, in detail, the fundamental principles we find in each of these *chapters*. It is a marvel that God has disclosed them through the Apostle Paul for us. Yet, for this reason, we can fully embrace the endeavor to gain insight and understanding as to what has happened in us and what is happening in us. Most importantly, this is so that we might come to walk in the way that He has established through Jesus Christ for us. Let us get started!

Romans 6:6 – Subject Scripture
Knowing this, that our old man is Crucified with Him, that the body of sin might be destroyed, that henceforth we should not serve sin.

Romans 6:6 – Portion I
"Knowing this, that our old man is Crucified with Him…,"

By the Apostle Paul beginning with *"Knowing this,"* he desires that each of us as Christians come to terms with knowing *"that our old man is Crucified with Him."* We are no longer forced to live by the Law through our flesh due to carnal thinking *(Rom. 7:2-6, 15-21; 8:10).* Now born again, we are free, and therefore have the opportunity to live by Faith *(Gal. 2:19-20; 3:11).* However, the ways of our old man are known through the carnal mind *(Rom. 7:14; 8:7; Eph. 4:22; Col. 3:9).* What does this mean?

Before Salvation, our old man had an avaricious desire to live by the Law, due to the work of the Law that was written in our heart. Our conscience did bear witness to that Law. Nonetheless, we were unable to live by that Law, so we continually experienced condemnation wherein our thoughts would either accuse or excuse us. This caused us to create our own standard of laws and methods to avoid the moral standard written in our heart *(Rom. 2:14-15).* However, because the strength of the sin nature is the Law, when we embraced the Law or any devised method in the attempt to attain some semblance of holiness, we remained under the evil reign of the sin nature *(I Cor. 15:56).*

Making matters worse, failure always led to greater self-efforts. Still, because the strength of sin is the Law, failure, bondage, and condemnation were the ongoing result *(Rom. 7:9, 15, 19)*. Therefore, now as Christians, we must put away the carnal thinking of our old man and truly come to understand what it entails to live by the Faith of the Son of God *(Rom. 7:25; Gal. 2:20; Eph. 4:17-32)*.

Living by the Faith of the Son of God means Faith is to remain in the Cross and forever leave behind any and all dependency on our old man with his carnal thinking and methods. This is literally what it means for us to deny ourselves and take up our cross daily *(Luke 9:23)*. This daily walk comes with the power of God and freedom resulting in abundant life, inexpressible joy, and ongoing rest.

Romans 6:6 – Subject Scripture

Knowing this, that our old man is Crucified with Him, **that the body of sin might be destroyed,** that henceforth we should not serve sin.

Romans 6:6 – Portion II
"...that the body of sin might be destroyed...,"

As we begin with Portion II, *"that the body of sin"* is written within a literal translation as "that body of the sin," which directly references the sin nature. Moving on in portion II, the phrase *"might be destroyed"* could be perceived as obliterated, meaning the sin nature was completely done away with upon our Salvation and was never again to be a problem. However, as we have learned in the preface, this is not the case. Furthermore, based on the premise that the Apostle Paul is dealing with the body of sin in his struggle *(Rom. 7:8-23)*, this view of being done away with would violate Scripture.

"Might be destroyed" is defined within the biblical Greek word *katargeo* (καταργέω, NT: 2673, kat-arg-eh'-o); from NT: 2596 and NT: 691; to be (render) entirely idle (useless), literally or figuratively.

In conclusion, upon Salvation, the sin nature has not been obliterated or done away with; it has been put down, made idle, incapacitated.

We can associate the phrase *"might be destroyed"* with another highly significant Scripture to help us understand the current position we are in while we wait for that Glorious Day of the Lord. We find this association within *1 John 3:8* – *"He who commits sin is of the Devil; for the Devil sinneth from the beginning. For this purpose the Son of God was manifested, that He might destroy the works of the Devil."* Within *1 John 3:8*, we find the associating phrase *"might destroy."* So let us look into the definition of this phrase and then bring the two together in a life application.

"Might destroy" – in reference to *1 John 3:8* – is defined within the biblical Greek word *luo* (λύω, NT: 3089, loo'-o); a primary verb; to "loosen" (literally or figuratively): – break (up), destroy, dissolve, (un-) loose, melt, put off.

Much disillusionment has arisen from not understanding these two phrases. For example, if we are born again, why can we find ourselves struggling once again with sin? And if Christ was triumphant on the Cross and the works of the Devil destroyed, why does the Devil still wreak havoc?

By *"might destroy"* in *I John 3:8,* we know that Jesus Christ has triumphed over all principalities and powers on the Cross through His death *(Col. 2:14-15)*. Therefore, "It is finished" *(John 19:30)*. Nonetheless, we see sin and death all around us, which clearly reveals that the *"works of the Devil"* have not been obliterated or done away with but triumphed over. Therein, they have been "broken," "wrecked," or "cracked," i.e., (especially) to sunder. Thus, through the finished work of the Cross, the Devil cannot do what he wants; his works, as well as his power, have limits and are under the direct Sovereignty of God *(Job 1:6-12; I John 3:8)*. God, for a season, allows the Devil to influence as the god of this world *(II Cor. 4:4)*, but the

Devil and those with him have boundaries. Within these boundaries, the world is under his broken government, limited influence, power and trickery. The unsaved individual remains openly susceptible to these. However, the eternal fate of the Devil and all principalities and powers are sealed, impossible for them to change. In the end, the Devil and Death and Hell will be the last to be thrown into the Lake of Fire *(Rev. 20:14-15).*

For all who are born again, our old man is Crucified with Christ, and the body of sin incapacitated; it has not been done away with *(Rom. 6:6; 7:9)*. Nonetheless, because the body of sin was incapacitated, we were released from its ruling dominion though it remains in our physical members *(Rom. 7:2, 23)*. Despite this, we must remain dead to the ways of our old man in order to keep the body of sin from reviving and the influence, power, and trickery of the Devil from deceiving us. Still, remaining dead is under our direct sovereignty regarding how we will maintain this *(Rom. 6:12; 8:13).*

The quandary is that we do not have the power in ourselves to remain dead, nor do we have the power to overcome the sin nature once it revives by our not remaining dead. This is not so with God, He is Sovereign, and thus has Power over the Devil at all times. Therefore, remaining dead to the ways our old man and his carnal thinking literally mean that we are to remain dead to the Law. How this is maintained is up to us; this is the sovereignty that God has given to us *(Rom. 6:17-18; 7:25; 8:1-4; Gal. 2:19-20).*

In this sovereignty, the problem we now have is that the enticements of living by the Law come in many forms, and remaining dead cannot be accomplished through any of them. Why? Because every other way besides Faith placed in Jesus Christ, and Him Crucified, are all carnal ways. Therefore, we must be careful not to engage them because the carnal mind is not subject to the ways of God *(Rom. 8:7).*

The death we seek while we live comes through Faith exclusively anchored in Jesus Christ, and Him Crucified *(Rom. 7:25; I Cor. 2:2; Gal. 2:19-20)*. Any other way will be motions of sins in the flesh, which are by the Law *(Rom. 7:5)* and, once again, the sovereignty for this choice is ours *(Gal. 5:4, 17)*. The final conclusion for the phrase *"might be destroyed"* is that, upon our Salvation, the body of sin has been incapacitated. It has not been abolished in terms of absolution. Yet it is our sovereign decision as to how we keep the body of sin down. God does not violate our sovereignty in regards to this matter *(Rom. 7:8-25)*.

Romans 6:6 – Subject Scripture

Knowing this, that our old man is Crucified with Him, that the body of sin might be destroyed, **that henceforth we should not serve sin.**

Romans 6:6 Portion – III
"…that henceforth we should not serve sin."

Portion III begins with the phrase *"that henceforth"* and refers to the first steps of Salvation and thereafter in our walk with Christ *(Col. 2:6-7)*. That is, we should never have to be under the ruling force of the sin nature, and as long as our Faith is ever resting in the Cross *(Rom. 7:25; I Cor. 2:2)*, the sin nature will remain incapacitated *(Rom. 6: 7)*. The terminology in the balance of *Romans 6:6 – "we should not serve sin"* – is clear, yet how do we who love God with all our heart, sometimes find ourselves overcome by sin, not serve sin?

It may be easy for some to say, "Just stop sinning." However, if that is all it took to overcome, Christ would not have had to come, and we would be perfected through our self-righteous works. Furthermore, if we found ultimate victory through our self-efforts, we would create methods of our own and eventually impose them upon others as the means for their victory. In any case, regardless of how deeply we search for another way, the warfare is spiritual *(II Cor. 10:4)*. Therefore, it is impossible for us to find what we are looking for apart from the way that God has established through Jesus Christ. For this reason, God has given us one way: through Jesus Christ, and Him Crucified, which is the meaning of "through Jesus Christ" *(Rom. 7:25)*.

Sin is powerful and there is literally nothing in us (that is, in our flesh) to perform the good we want to do in trying to resist the sin nature *(Rom. 7:8-11, 18)*. If we engage any method to resist sin or attain some idea of holiness apart from the victorious way of the Cross, we are literally reaching back through the carnal mind of our old man and engaging the letter of the Law *(II Cor. 3:6)*. The major problem with living by the Law is that the strength of sin is the Law *(I Cor. 15:56)*; thus, by doing so, we remain overcome by the very thing we are trying to overcome.

We are to remain dead to the ways of our old man because the carnal mind always wants to use the physical body as the means to resist sin, restrain it, or attain some sense of holiness. Although these ways seems right to our carnal mind, they are not only by the Law, they deny the power of the Holy Spirit *(II Tim. 3:5)*. As I have stated, for reasons of the sin nature, our physical body has been rendered useless in regards to spiritual matters, and therefore should not be utilized to deal with the intangibles of the sin nature. Overcoming has to be by Faith, and Faith exclusively exercised in Jesus Christ, and Him Crucified, plus or minus nothing *(I Cor. 2:2; Gal. 6:14)*. In this, sin and death will become dealt with, and the Spirit of Life will quicken our physical body in the likeness of Jesus being raised from the dead *(Rom. 6:3-5; 8:2, 11)*.

The Apostle Paul was freed from the body of sin upon his Salvation into Christ. However, prior to knowing the way of victory, when he was tempted by the thing he did not want to do *(Rom. 7:15,*

19), he tried to overcome through his own strength *(Rom. 7:9)*. This seemed right because he was familiar with the Law, being that the Law was all he knew, but he learned that trying to live by the Law revived the sin nature and created motions of sins in his flesh *(Rom. 7:5, 8-11, 23)*.

Like Paul, we are born again, and in the Spirit *(Rom. 8:9)*; all things have become new *(II Cor. 5:17)*. Though we know the ways of our old man, each of us is to endeavor to be renewed in the spirit of our mind by putting on the new man who, after God, is created in Righteousness and true holiness *(Eph. 4:23-24)*. Furthermore, we must understand that the new man's thinking comes from the Mind of Christ that we now have *(I Cor. 2:16)*, and the Mind of Christ always had the Cross before it *(Matt. 26:39; Phil. 2:5-8; Heb. 10:5-10)*

Though God's Grace is sufficient in the struggles we face, as long we exercise Faith in the Cross, the Holy Spirit can effectually help us put on the new man's ways of thinking, resulting in godly behavior and deeds unto the Will of the Father.

Romans 6:7 – Subject Scripture undivided
For he who is dead is freed from sin.

Verse 7 is significantly short, given that it is packed with a profound truth – *"For he who is dead is freed from sin."* Upon Salvation, our old man is Crucified with Him, and the body of sin incapacitated *(Rom. 6:6)*. In no uncertain terms, our old man is Crucified and that is that. However, known are the ways of our old man due to the carnal mind that remains with us for the time being *(Rom. 7:9, 14; Eph. 4:22; Col. 3:9)*. Therefore, the profound truth is: now that we are born again we must remain dead to remain free *(Luke 9:23; Rom. 6:7)* while we wait for the Trump of God to sound. At that time, we will be changed from our mortality by putting on immortality *(I Cor. 15:50-53)*. Until then, the carnal mind remains with us, and the nature of sin remains with us *(Rom. 7:14, 23)*. This is not to say the sin nature is the focal point because it is not to be. This is to say that, if we are not careful and do not remain dead to the ways of our old man, we can give occasion to the sin nature due to the carnal mind of our old man desiring to live by the Law *(Rom. 7:5; Gal. 5:4, 17)*. For this reason, the Cross is to be our focal point and pondering view for our life and living *(I Cor. 1:17-18; II Cor. 4:7-18; Gal. 6:14)*. This view for life and living comes from the Mind of Christ *(I Cor. 2:16)*, and this type of thinking comes from a renewed mind, the mind of the new man *(Col. 3:10-14)*.

In our desire to grow in Sanctification, it is easy to find that much of our walk with God can be going through the motions of trying to die to self, yet never finding the actual way to die to self and thus remain truly free from sin. It is imperative to understand this, so I would like to break it down another way to give a more in-depth perspective. The purpose for this greater perspective is that remaining dead is the foundation to remaining free and, as Christians, we inwardly know this because it is one of the fundamental truths of Biblical Christianity. So paramount is death while alive, it is impossible, while alive, to experience the likeness of Jesus' Resurrection unless this death comes first *(Rom. 6:3-5, 7; 7:25; 8:2; Phil. 3:7-11)*.

The Pauline Epistles hold much regarding this fundamental truth of death while alive, so I would like to use a couple of familiar Scriptures to narrow down my explanation – *"¹⁹For I through the Law am dead to the Law, that I might live unto God. ²⁰I am Crucified with Christ: nevertheless I live; yet not I, but Christ lives in me: and the life which I now live in the flesh I live by the Faith of the Son of God, Who loved me, and gave Himself for me" (Gal. 2:19-20)*.

Daniel E. Armour

Let us start with *Galatians 2:19* – "*For I through the Law am dead to the Law, that I might live unto God.*" In the beginning of *verse 19*, we find the following: "*For I through the Law am dead to the Law.*" This reveals that we see we must go "*through the Law*" to remain dead "*to the Law,*" but let us examine the word "*through*" in order to gain insight as to what Paul is saying.

"*Through*": A {1} – a function word used to indicate movement into one side or point and out at another and especially the opposite side of (e.g., drove a nail through the beam) {2}: by way of (e.g., right through the door) {3}: a function word used to indicate the passage from one end or boundary to another (e.g., a highway through the forest – a road through the desert) B {1}: – a function word used to indicate the passage into and out of a treatment, handling, or process (e.g., the matter has already passed through His hands).

As we personalize this to examine the application of the word "*through,*" it can be seen that it means to pass from one side to the other without stopping. If we do not know the way "*through the Law,*" we end up living by the Law without realizing what we are doing. We are born again and we have Faith, yet we can find ourselves struggling with something, and no matter how hard we try to overcome, we will stop in our walk on a continual search for some way "*through*" the problem.

The reason we are at a stop is because our effort was by the Law or some other method as the means to overcome. Although whatever method used may have been with good intentions, if the object for Faith is not understood, our only available resources were to combine our intangible willpower with our tangible human body. This is not what it means to remain dead. Furthermore, this is evidenced in our will taking first place instead of the Will of the Father. Though one might argue this and suggest his or her Faith was in Jesus while engaging the method, a biblical examination would conclude that

50

Faith was in the method even though he or she believed in Jesus. This is misplaced Faith. For this reason, the Apostle Paul writes – *"Examine yourselves, whether you be in the Faith…" (II Cor. 13:5).*

Misplacing Faith is easy to do if the Cross is not clearly understood for maintaining death while alive; Faith needs the proper object. This is the biblical truth *(I Cor. 2:2; Gal. 2:19-20).* The proper object to remain *"dead to the Law"* is the same as the answer needed to go *"through the Law."* The result will be as the Apostle Paul writes in *Romans 6:7* – *"For he who is dead is freed from sin."*

The answer is the Cross; our Faith must ever rest in the Cross. This is the proper object for our Faith *(Rom. 7:25; Rev. 12:11).* This is the way of Jesus, Who has made His Cross the way for us *(Gal. 6:14).* He died once for all; our death comes as we deny ourselves and place Faith in His death *(Luke 9:23),* even when it comes to His obedience of giving His life on the Cross *(Matt. 19:30; Phil. 2:5-8; Heb. 12:2).* As our Faith becomes anchored in Jesus Christ, and Him Crucified, we supernaturally die while alive and experience the benefits of what He has done on the Cross for us *(Rom. 6:3-5, 7).*

The only way to remain *"dead to the Law"* in order to go *"through the Law,"* resulting in *"For he who is dead is freed from sin,"* is through Faith alone. It is not by anything we can do through utilizing our flesh – it is by Faith, plus or minus nothing *(Rom. 8:10).* Once we come to embrace this magnificent Truth of Faith in Jesus Christ, and Him Crucified, we can experience the balance of *Galatians 2:19* wherein Paul writes – *"that I might live unto God."*

The Apostle Paul gives us open view into how he was able to live unto God in *Galatians 2:20* – *"I am Crucified with Christ: nevertheless I live; yet not I, but Christ lives in me: and the life which I now live in the flesh I live by the Faith of the Son of God, Who loved me, and gave Himself for me."*

51

Galatians 2:20 holds amazing insights within it; however, since we are dealing with *Romans 6:7 – "For he who is dead is freed from sin"* and thus qualifying that Faith must remain in Jesus Christ, and Him Crucified, in order to experience the likeness of Jesus' death and likeness of Him being raised, let us deal with the first portion of *verse 20 – "I am Crucified with Christ."* This remarkable statement is quite different from his statement in *Romans 7:9 – "For I was alive apart from the Law once; but when the Commandment came, sin revived, and I died."*

Paul's struggle with the sin nature disclosed in *Romans 7:9* is an altogether much different death than his testimony of triumph and freedom we see in *Galatians 2:20.* The death that came from Paul's struggle with the sin nature came as a result of him trying to live by the Law through his flesh. This is the sting of death that results in condemnation due the penalty of the Law *(Rom. 8:1-4).*

The Apostle was born again during his struggle with the sin nature; he had the desire to live for God, he had Faith, and he had willpower, but his Faith was misplaced *(Rom. 7:8-11).* Though Paul's intentions were good, his Faith was in his will working through his physical body in an effort to overcome. Paul did not know that his Faith needed to be placed in the proper object. As a result, during Paul's struggle, his Faith was applied to his flesh (his willpower and his physical body), and this is an illegal combination as it regards dealing with spiritual matters *(Rom. 8:10).*

The freedom and triumph to which the Apostle Paul is giving testimony in *Galatians 2:20* came as a result of living by Faith properly placed, wherein he states – *"I am Crucified with Christ: nevertheless I live; yet not I, but Christ lives in me: and the life which I now live in the flesh I live by the Faith of the Son of God, Who loved me, and gave Himself for me" (Gal. 2:20).* Within *Galatians 2:20,* we can see that the Apostle Paul is living *"by the Faith of the Son of God."*

Paul came to understand, through the Revelation of Jesus Christ *(Gal. 1:11-12)*, that while he was alive in his mortal body, he could not utilize his flesh (body-willpower) in dealing with spiritual matters of Sanctification; he had to die to the flesh. In order to accomplish this extraordinary task, he must *"live by the Faith of the Son of God,"* that is, the Faith of the Man, Jesus *(John 1:14-18)*, the Author and Finisher of Paul's Faith *(Heb. 12:2)*. The Apostle came to understand that this Faith – *"the Faith of the Son of God"* – shall ever have the Cross before it. This is qualified in the balance of *Galatians 2:20*, wherein Paul writes – *"Who loved me, and gave Himself for me"*. This reveals that not only did Paul's Faith rest in Jesus Christ *"Who loved me,"* but he also had his Faith anchored in Him Crucified, wherein he writes, *"and gave Himself for me."* Therefore, the proper object for Paul's Faith was Jesus Christ, and Him Crucified.

As we take on the mind of the new man *(Phil. 2:5)*, ever making the Cross our single view, that is, the day and night ponder of our life *(I Cor. 2:2)*, we will remain dead while alive, and remain free from sin and the sin nature *(Rom. 6:7)*. Wherein the ongoing result of the Apostle Paul living in this truth, he wrote – *"But God forbid that I should glory, save in the Cross of our Lord Jesus Christ, by Whom the world is Crucified unto me, and I unto the world"* (Gal. 6:14).

CHAPTER 5

The Purpose of The Mosaic Law

ROMANS 7:1

PREFACE

T hroughout our life, to one degree or another, we have come to form our own ideas as to what Law means to us. There are many Laws; to name a few, there are those that regulate society, there are those that keep the universe running as it does, and then there are biblical Laws. The most familiar is the Law of Moses. The Mosaic Law is Holy, and it is spiritual because it came directly from God *(Exod. 31:18; Rom. 7:12, 14)*, making it altogether much different than the obscurity of man-made laws by which we may have formed ideas about the Mosaic Law. Nevertheless, the Mosaic Law is the moral standard for mankind: it is our moral compass.

Because the Law is Holy, and spiritual, it shines its light of high moral standard on the heart of every human being; yet, before we received Salvation, the Law played a unique part in bringing us to Christ. The Apostle Paul unveils this wonderfully in *Galatians*

3:24-25 – "²⁴Wherefore the Law was our schoolmaster to bring us unto Christ, that we might be justified by Faith. ²⁵But after that Faith is come, we are no longer under a schoolmaster."

Before our Salvation we did not know, nor could we have ever come to understand, the spiritual principle of "schoolmaster" about the Mosaic Law. This inability to understand spiritual principles was due to the complete subjection to the carnal mind of our old man. Therefore, with no other resource to live by than that of our carnal mind, we ever tried to live by the Law through our flesh. Unable to do so, the Law had dominion over us, and in our constant failing to live up to the moral standard of the Law, it became our schoolmaster that brought us to Christ. As we accepted Christ, we were justified by Faith and given the Faith of Jesus Christ that we might ever live for God through Him *(Gal. 2:16)*.

Now that we are Saved, the Mosaic Law is no longer a schoolmaster to us *(Rom. 7:4-6)* because we have the opportunity to live by the Faith of the Son of God *(Gal. 2:19-20)*. Therefore, the high moral standard of the Law is a spiritual light that reproofs and instructs the way of life *(Prov. 6:23; Rom. 7:25)*.

The Law reveals the intangible because the Law is the truth *(Psalms 119:142)*, revealing every way of sin on the outside and within us *(Psalms 119:101, 104, 110, 115, 126)*. The light of the Law reveals everything including thoughts that are contrary to the Word and Ways of God so that we do not fall prey to the deceitfulness of sin or the nature of it. However, this Law is without coercion; it is no longer a schoolmaster to us who are born again. The profound and intended purpose of this Law for us who are in Christ is to reveal what is contrary to God; it does not force us to overcome, it reveals *(Rom. 3:20; 7:7)*. The quality of the Law is Holy *(Rom. 7:12)*; the principles and function of this Law are spiritual *(Rom. 7:14)* and are at work every moment of every day to reveal sin and the nature of it. This shows the Holiness of the Law *(Rom. 7:7, 12)*.

When the Law reveals sin, it is the Commandment that comes and compels us unto Righteousness *(Matt. 22:36-40; I Tim. 1:5)*. Though we will be dealing with the compelling principle of the Commandment in Chapter 8, *The Sin Nature & The Commandment*, it is because the Commandment was ordained to life that we have this remarkable principle that compels us when the Law reveals *(Rom. 7:10)*. Yet, due to the compelling of the Commandment, if we are not careful we can engage the ways of our old man *(Rom. 7:8-11)* and try once again to live by the Mosaic Law through our flesh. In these attempts to live by the Law, the Law will once again have dominion over us and, as a result, we will be required to live up to the whole of the Law *(Gal. 5:3; Jam. 2:10)*. When it becomes realized this cannot be accomplished through our works of self-righteousness, we will create laws unto ourselves *(Rom. 2:14-15)*, and eventually fade into complacency, believing defeat is the best we will experience while on earth, unless the way of victory becomes discovered and embraced *(Rom. 7:25; 8:2)*.

Without knowing the way of victory, although Saved, we will not understand the principles and function of the Law. Thus, the Law will be viewed in letter form as something to keep away from. In avoiding the Law, we end up living by it and, as stated, instead of allowing the Law to serve as a light, it will be served in letter form due to the compelling of the Commandment *(Rom. 7:9)*. The result will be a seemingly unbreakable cycle of failure without realizing why *(I Cor. 15:56; II Cor. 3:6)*. Therefore, we must remain dead to remain free from the dominion of the Law.

Romans 7:1 – Subject Scripture
Know ye not, Brethren, (for I speak to them that know the Law,) how that the Law has dominion over a man as long as he lives?

Romans 7:1 – Portion I
"Know ye not, Brethren, (for I speak to them that know the Law,)…"

As we begin *verse 1*, this portion makes clear that Paul is speaking to us who are born again and know the Mosaic Law. However, our relationship with the Law may be unclear and needs to be understood because the Law did not go away in our life after we received Salvation *(Rom. 7:25; 8:7, I Cor. 9:21).* Now that we are born again, the spiritual dynamics of the Law play a much different role. For this reason, the Apostle Paul, moved by the Holy Spirit, writes out those dynamics that each of us will embark upon in our walk in Christ.

Romans 7:1 – Subject Scripture
Know ye not, Brethren, (for I speak to them that know the Law,) **how that the Law has dominion over a man as long as he lives?**

Romans 7:1 – Portion II
"…how that the Law has dominion over a man as long as he lives?"

The term *"how that"* is prefacing something crucial to understand. The Apostle is bringing out the established functioning principle of the Law and *"how that"* it can have dominion over us once again if we function by the Law through our flesh. Furthermore, because the strength of the sin nature is the Law *(I Cor. 15:56),* when we try to live by the Law in any effort to do good, the sin nature is given occasion to revive *(Rom. 7:8-9, 21– NKJV).* Moving on, the

Apostle Paul reveals a principle that *"the Law has dominion over a man as long as he lives?"* When we were unsaved, we were under the dominion and penalty of the Mosaic Law and, due to our inability to keep the Law, our experience was sustained condemnation to one degree or another. For this reason, sustained condemnation, subtle looming doom, depression and suicide are so prevalent throughout the unsaved world today. However, though the pursuit to be free from these is the intent of every living soul, ultimate true lasting freedom cannot be found outside of Salvation in Jesus Christ.

Now then, the Apostle Paul is, in reality, asking us if we realize *"the Law has dominion over a man as long he lives?"* Therefore, the implied answer is: we know we must die to be free from the dominion and condemnation of the Law *(Rom. 6:7; 8:1-4; Gal. 2:19-20).* Paul is not referring to physical death; otherwise, we who are born again would have been without the hope of freedom while presently in our mortal bodies. This death, for us who are born again, came through Salvation in Jesus Christ wherein we became planted together in the likeness of Jesus' death, and dead to the Law by the body of Christ *(Rom. 6:3-5; 7:4).*

Yet, we must understand that the Law did not die because God's Law still rules over men. We became dead to the Law, but this does not mean we can live Lawless lives *(Matt. 7:21-23; I Cor. 9:21; Heb. 8:10-13; 10:16-17).* It means the motivation and dynamic of our life and living does not come from engaging the Mosaic Law to live by it through our flesh *(Rom. 7:5-6; II Cor. 3:6; Gal. 5:4).* If we try to live by the Law through our flesh, we will come under the dominion of the Law once again, and, therein, be required to fulfill the whole of the Law, which is an impossibility *(Rom. 8:3-4; Gal. 5:3-4; Jam. 2:10).* Therefore, we are not to engage the Mosaic Law with our flesh, but instead, our Faith is to remain in the Cross whereupon the Law was fulfilled and the Penalty Paid. This recognizes Christ is the end of the Law for Righteousness because we believe *(Rom. 10:4)*. Though, when understood, this can be written in many ways, the Apostle Paul sets the example by writing – *"...So then with the mind I myself serve the Law of God..." (Rom. 7:25)*.

When our Faith remains in Jesus Christ, and Him Crucified, because He kept the Law perfectly, yet Vicariously Paid the Penalty of our inability, we receive the benefits of what He has done for us. Therefore, the Righteousness of the Law remains fulfilled in us, and we are not Lawless *(Rom. 8:3-4)*.

Furthermore, as our Faith remains in the Cross, we become quickened by the Spirit of Life through His Law, the Law of the Spirit *(Rom. 8:2)*, ensuring us that we are about the Will of the Father, not our will *(Rom. 8:11-17)*. This keeps us from Lawlessness *(Matt. 7:21-23)*. We will learn about this Law in Chapter 11, *The Law of The Spirit of Life in Christ Jesus.*

After Salvation, if the Believer does not come to understand the Cross for Sanctification, condemnation will be unavoidable. For this reason, many today who are born again are experiencing sustained condemnation to one degree or another. Although there are many factors that can cause condemnation, it is most likely due to engaging the Mosaic Law in an unlawful way *(Gal. 5:4; I Tim. 1:9)*. By doing so, the experience is condemnation due to the Righteousness of the Law not remaining fulfilled within them. Although they may be Saved, they are under the dominion and penalty of the Law *(Rom. 8:1, 4)*.

To ensure we do not come under the dominion of the Law, as Christians, our life, motivation, and living must come from the power and presence of God *(Zech. 4:6; Rom. 8:2)*. This intimate relationship with God is not only free from condemnation, it is a place of rest. This is the desire of each of us who walk with Him. When we believe in Jesus, this place of intimacy can be experienced daily as we learn to walk with God in the way that He established through Jesus Christ.

Because Christ is the end of the Law for Righteousness to everyone who believes, when Faith remains in Whom He Is, and what He finished on the Cross, condemnation simply fades away, and the place of rest begins *(Rom. 8:1-4; Heb. 4:9-11)*. As Christians, we must understand that mankind was Redeemed through His Shed Blood, and the works of the Devil destroyed through His death on the Cross *(Col. 2:14-15; I John 3:8)*. For this reason, our Faith must have both Jesus Christ and the Cross. Therefore, as it was for our Salvation, it is for our Sanctification *(Rom. 10:9-10; Col. 2:6-7; I Cor. 1:17-18)*. As our Faith continues in Jesus Christ, and Him Crucified, we remain in the likeness of Jesus' death while we still live. With Faith properly placed, the Law no longer has dominion over us *(Rom. 7:25; Gal. 2:19-20)*.

It is in this place that we have taken our hands off of all that Jesus Christ has already finished through the Shedding of His Blood and death on the Cross and learn to believe that what He has done on the Cross is enough. In addition, because He is Risen, likewise, we are quickened by the same Spirit that raised Him from the dead and experience the likeness of His Resurrection while alive in this present evil world *(Rom. 8:2, 11, 14; Gal. 1:4; 6:14)*.

CHAPTER 6

The Woman, the Husband, the Law, and Adultery

ROMANS 7:2-3

PREFACE

T he "old man" spoken of in *Romans 6:6* and "the husband," in this analogy of *Romans 7:2-3*, are one in the same. However, the Apostle Paul makes a clear delineation between them because they have their own principles, yet these principles are inseparable. The principles of the old man deal with the unregenerate condition and the fallen carnal nature of the mind. The carnal mind does not know, nor does it want to know, the ways of God *(Rom. 8:7)*. Therefore, its sole desire is to live by the Law through means of the flesh *(Rom. 2:14-15; 7:14)*. The acute problem with this is that the strength of the sin nature is the Law *(I Cor. 15:56)*. As a result, the ways of the old man keep the sin nature alive through a cycle of self-efforts, failure, and condemnation *(Rom. 7:8, 9, 15, & 23)*.

The principles of the husband deal with a Law within himself, a principle of enforcement. This is the delineation Paul makes between the old man and the husband. The old man is a way of thinking *(Rom. 7:14; 8:7)*, and the husband is the enforcer of this way of thinking *(Rom. 7:2, 6)*. What becomes remarkable to see is that this delineation has a chronological order. Hence, *Romans 6:6* preceding *Romans 7:2*. There is a unique design behind this and, once it is seen, there is understanding as to why the Holy Spirit did not have the Apostle Paul put the two together.

In this remarkable analogy, the Apostle demonstrates that the woman and her husband are like the Christian and the Law, yet there is more. Within this analogy, the Apostle Paul unveils four staggering dynamics: the Law of Marriage, the Law Enforcement, the Principle of Apostasy, and the Principle of Spiritual Adultery. Before we become involved in the Subject Scriptures, let us look into the woman's biblical lineage and story of her life so we can gain some insight into her condition.

THE WOMAN'S LIFE

Her biblical lineage started with Adam. However, due to Adam's decision to eat from the Tree of the Knowledge of Good and Evil *(Gen. 3:6)*, evil was able to take eminent domain with the physical members of Adam's children. Therefore, the woman, through the seed of a fallen man, became conceived and shapen in iniquity while within her mother's womb *(Psalms 51:5)*. Because of this, she was born with a fallen nature – an old man with a carnal mind who became her husband upon natural childbirth *(Rom. 5:12)*. To make matters worse, her old man was all she was able to view life through and, because he had the knowledge of good and evil, the eyes of her mind were wide open to this knowledge *(Gen. 2:17; 3:5-24)*.

As she became older, possibly in her youth, she saw herself for the first time and became aware of everyone around her. At times, she would feel accepted. Other times, she would feel unpleasant rejection due to consciousness of herself and a sense of impurity because of her condition and the knowledge of good and evil *(Gen. 3:10)*. For this reason, her mind had an ever streaming view of judgments of herself and of others: some good, some bad, some insignificant, while other thoughts of judgment overwhelmed her *(Gen. 3:12-13)*. In addition to this frame of mind, she did not know that she could not feel love the way she was originally created and made by the One Who truly loved her – her One True Bridegroom – Jesus Christ.

Knowing she was going through this turmoil, her True Bridegroom wrote His Law in her heart as a moral compass, a light of purity and truth, ever pointing her to Him, and her conscience bore witness to that Law *(Rom. 2:14-15; Gal. 3:24-25)*. She desperately wanted the light to shine its purity and truth, but due to her being one flesh with the man she was forced to marry at childbirth, the light was seen dimly, making purity and truth obscure. Therein, her old man with his carnal mind dominated her thinking and used the dimming to reveal her inabilities, then condemned her for not being good enough. Still, she quietly treasured what purity and truth she could see.

Thinking she could overcome the condemnation that her old man was putting her under, she worked as hard as she could in order to reach the purity and truth of the light. Yet, in each of her efforts, her husband would come and force her to do more and more. However, the harder she tried the worse she became because of an evil that lived in her body. She knew nothing of this evil, and it thrived in all her efforts *(I Cor. 15:56)*. Unable to live up to all of the demands and not knowing what was going on within her, she experienced ongoing failure and condemnation and found herself doing things she hated. Seeing no way out, she began to accuse others or excuse herself and decided to make her own laws in order to avoid the purity and truth of the light in her heart *(Rom. 2:14-15)*.

Unable to avoid the purity and truth, nor able to live up to any law or method she or another created, the woman began to see her plight and condition, but also began to see the One Who Paid for all her failures and inabilities – her One True Bridegroom. Although not knowing the purity and truth in her heart was the beacon of light ever pointing to Him, she nonetheless accepted the forgiveness and love He Offered, and embraced His Truth. At last, she was made free.

Romans 7:2 – Subject Scripture
For the woman which has an husband is bound by the Law to her husband so long as he liveth; but if the husband be dead, she is loosed from the Law of her husband.

Romans 7:2 – Portion I
"For the woman which has an husband is bound by the Law to her husband so long as he liveth…;"

The title *"husband"* typifies the woman's old man with his dynamics that were embedded in her unregenerate condition at conception and childbirth *(Psalms 51:5; Rom. 5:12)*. As stated in the preface, the "old man" spoken of in *Romans 6:6* and *"the husband"* here in *Romans 7:2-3* are one in the same. The Apostle Paul clearly delineates between them because they have their own principles, yet these principles are inseparable. The old man is a way of thinking *(Rom. 7:14; 8:7)*, and the husband is the enforcer of this way of thinking. If one does not think through the ways of the old man, the husband has nothing to enforce.

The Law of Marriage

Let us investigate this first dynamic, the Law of Marriage – *"For the woman which has an husband is bound by the Law to her husband so long as he liveth,"* hence *"bound by the Law to her husband."* An example can be seen within natural marriage – when a man and a woman become married they become one flesh *(Gen. 2:24)*. Upon their marriage, a legal and binding document is created. Now married, there are two ways in which they can become free from each other: they can divorce, or one of them dies. Through either one of these two cases, one of them becomes free from the legal obligations of the marriage. In the case of spiritual Laws, one cannot simply decide to walk away and find freedom. Such is the case within the woman's life because of Adam's decision to partake of the Tree of the Knowledge of Good and Evil.

Due to Adam's sin, every person (with the exception of Jesus), was, is, and will be born into sin – the body of sin *(Rom. 6:6)*. Due to the dynamics surrounding the body of sin, Paul has unveiled the husband and the Law of Marriage in order to reveal a principle impossible to circumvent. Thus, every person (with the exception of Jesus), was, is, and will be married to this husband at childbirth, becoming one flesh with him upon natural childbirth *(Gen. 2:24; Psalms 51:5; Rom. 5:12; 7:21)*.

R̲omans 7:2 – Subject Scripture

For the woman which has an husband is bound by the Law to her husband so long as he liveth; **but if the husband be dead, she is loosed from the Law of her husband.**

R̲omans 7:2 – Portion II

"...but if the husband be dead,
she is loosed from the Law of her husband."

As we begin the balance of *Romans 7:2, "but if the husband be dead"* speaks of the woman's Salvation and marriage in and to her True Bridegroom. The result: *"she is loosed from the Law of her husband."* Upon this magnificent event, her old man became Crucified, the body of sin incapacitated, and her True Bridegroom gave her His Mind *(I Cor. 2:16).* Now, for the first time, the purity and truth of His Law in her heart was seen, and she realized that her True Bridegroom had already finished all that she was unable to do in all of her hard work. As she believed, the husband who was forced upon her at childbirth died because he had nothing to enforce. Now free from her former husband of bondage, she became espoused to her One True Bridegroom. All of this happened the moment she came to Him.

Although the woman is wonderfully espoused to Christ, He does not force His ways, and if she is not careful, she can once again become bound by the dynamics of her former husband of bondage. Let us investigate the second principle in this marriage analogy.

THE PRINCIPLE OF ENFORCEMENT

This ending portion of *Romans 7:2* reveals the second dynamic, the Principle of Enforcement – *"but if the husband be dead, she is loosed from the Law of her husband."* The Principle of Enforcement is found within *"the Law of her husband."* The husband has a principle at work within himself, which is not the same as the Law of Marriage. The terminology can be more easily understood from a literal translation, which writes, "the Law *of the* husband."

When we were unsaved, *"the Law of the husband"* was a continual enforcement of any effort we imposed to live by the Mosaic Law, God's moral standard for Man. We lived by the Law because the work of the Law was written in our heart and, due to our heart being uncircumcised, we could only see the Law as a set of rules in the letter form through our carnal mind. Therefore, we tried to live by the Law through our flesh.

Making matters worse, the dynamic of the sin nature also thrived in this environment because the strength of the sin nature is the Law *(I Cor. 15:56)*. In our unsaved condition, we had no other choice than that of carnal thinking; thus, all efforts were by the Law in one way or the other whether we realized it or not *(Rom. 2:11-15)*. The problem was that, not only did the husband enforce this type of thinking, our efforts also kept us under the dominion and ruling power of the sin nature.

Upon Salvation, all of these dynamics changed. Our old man was Crucified and we were no longer held under carnal thinking. In addition, our heart was circumcised in spirit with the circumcision made without hands *(Col. 2:11)*. This remarkable event allowed us to see through the letter unto the spiritual aspects of the Law *(Rom. 7:7, 14, 25)*. Now, with a circumcised heart and the ability to circumvent the carnal mind, the husband died because he has nothing to enforce. All of this happened upon our Salvation, yet reveals the chronology of *Romans 6:6* and *Romans 7:2-3*.

The dynamic Principle of Enforcement might be seen in the example of nuclear power. This type of power is confined beyond a highly restricted area within which are by-product contaminates. In an illegal attempt to reach the nuclear power, we will have to pass into the restricted area. However, because our efforts would be illegal, adrenaline kicks in and, regardless of the obstacles in our way, we will try as hard as we can to reach the nuclear power. Nonetheless, we will die due to the by-product contaminates, and therefore never reach what we were after.

The restricted area typifies the husband, the adrenaline typifies his authority (i.e., the principle of enforcement), and the nuclear power typifies the Mosaic Law. The nuclear power was not bad; it is made up of atoms as we are. Yet the way atomic energy was designed for its specific application is far too great for our human body. Therefore, it cannot be touched with our physical body.

One might argue the fact that the by-product contaminates will have killed us in our attempt to reach the nuclear power, yet the by-product contaminates are the associated by-products of the nuclear power. That is, when our intention of going after the nuclear power (Mosaic Law) turns into an attempt in our flesh, the effort is by the Law nonetheless. In the end, we will have entered into the restricted area (the husband). Now in the restricted area, our adrenaline (principle of enforcement) ensures that we never give up trying to reach the unattainable (the Righteousness of the Mosaic Law). Unable to do so, we will either use someone else's laws or continue to create other laws and methods of our own, all of which are man-made derivatives (carnal by-product contaminates) of the nuclear power (Mosaic Law). Though these are the by-product contaminates, the husband still enforces his law resulting in death nonetheless.

One might say: "All we need is legal clearance and the proper atomically impervious suit and then we would be able to reach the nuclear power." Their response would be right! However, there is only one legal clearance and one suit designed to withstand such effects, yet both must be used together. If one is used without the other, the by-product contaminates will cause death. The legal clearance is Jesus Christ, and the atomically impervious suit is Faith in His Cross – you cannot have one without the other or you will die. Why? As we have learned, we can have Faith in Jesus Christ, yet still experience death due to the by-product contaminates created in trying to live by associated methods of the Law.

When we combine Jesus Christ and the Cross, the entire legal means of attaining the nuclear power are now fulfilled, by which we are impervious to the dire effects of the nuclear power. Due to the our inability as humans, we cannot attain the unattainable, that is, it is humanly impossible to reach the moral perfection required by the Mosaic Law, and this is a two-fold problem. First, without reaching the required moral standard of the Mosaic Law, the result is death. Second, any attempt to reach the required moral standard of the Mosaic Law with the use of the human body will result in death. Therefore, reaching the required moral standard of the Mosaic Law is humanly impossible. In order to reach the Righteous requirements of the Law, Faith must remain in Jesus Christ, and Him Crucified. In this, we remain impervious to the dire effects of the Mosaic Law, or as Paul has revealed: Faith must remain in Jesus Christ, and Him Crucified, in order to go through the Law *(Gal. 2:19)*.

It was for this purpose that Jesus Christ Shed His Blood and Vicariously Paid the Penalty for us through His death on the Cross. Christ is now the end of the Law for Righteousness to everyone who believes. Therefore, when we who believe place our Faith in Jesus Christ, and Him Crucified, the Righteousness of the Law remains fulfilled within us *(Rom. 8:4)*. Therein, we pass through the restricted area legally, and the husband cannot enforce because we are not doing anything illegal. By passing through the restricted area legally, the Mosaic Law becomes an ongoing light that reproofs and instructs the way of life *(Prov. 6:23; Rom. 7:25)*.

If we attempt to re-engage the Mosaic Law unlawfully to live by it through our flesh, the Law of the Husband – the Principle of Enforcement – will take place *(Rom. 7:9)*. Once in place, we have become legally bound to live up to the whole of the Mosaic Law *(Gal. 5:3; Jam. 2:10)*. This is the binding Law of the Husband because he is the enforcer. Therefore, if we do not think carnally in regards to Sanctification, we will not go after the Law unlawfully. The result is that the sin nature will remain incapacitated, the husband will have nothing to enforce, and we will remain free.

THE PRINCIPLE OF APOSTASY

The third dynamic is that of apostasy. In addition to the husband being a Law enforcer, he is also the apostatizing husband, forcibly leading all who decide to live by the Mosaic Law, away from Saving Faith. We might say that this dynamic of apostasy is a by-product of his true position which is that of Law enforcement. If we try to live by the Law through our flesh, then by default we are apostatizing; if we do not turn from trying to live by the Law, the husband's Principle of Enforcement will continue in order to ensure complete apostasy *(Gal. 5:4; Phil. 3:18)*.

Our Salvation is based upon believing in Jesus Christ, His Atoning Blood and Sacrifice, and His Resurrection *(John 3:16; Rom. 10:9-10)*. Now that we are Saved, our growth in Sanctification comes through Faith in Whom He is and what He has finished on the Cross, plus or minus nothing *(Rom. 7:25; I Cor. 2:2; Gal. 2:19-20; 6:14)*. Trying to live by the Law is based on works of self-righteousness. The final result of those who fully and knowingly embrace this manner of lifestyle is a falling from Grace and eventually becoming enemies of the Cross of Christ *(I Cor. 1:18; Phil. 3:18)*.

Romans 7:3 – Subject Scripture
So then if, while her husband liveth, she be married to another man, she shall be called an adulteress: but if her husband be dead, she is free from that Law; so that she is no adulteress, though she be married to another man.

Romans 7:3 – Portion I
"So then if, while her husband liveth, she be married to another man, she shall be called an adulteress…:"

By the Apostle beginning *Romans 7:3* with *"So then if,"* he is bringing out a reality. *"So then if"* the woman attempts to re-engage the Mosaic Law unlawfully, by trying to live by it through her flesh, the husband who was dead will live again, and because she was born again, espoused to Christ *(II Cor. 11:2)*, she will be in adultery. The potential for this is seen in the terminology – *"So then if, while her husband liveth."* This terminology comes from the inseparable phrase "while liveth," and is defined in biblical Greek within the word *zao* (za/w, NT: 2198, dzah'-o); a primary verb; to live (literally or figuratively): – life (-time), (a-) live (-ly), quick.

THE PRINCIPLE OF SPIRITUAL ADULTERY

This staggering principle of spiritual adultery can be accurately revealed within *"zao,"* and it can be viewed as this: *"So then if"* the woman, now born again and espoused to Christ, unlawfully decides to engage the Mosaic Law by trying to live by the Law through her flesh, the husband, who was dead, is brought quickly to life within the time of engagement. This is the time in which she tried to live by the Law. Thus, she is in adultery during this time of unlawful engagement. Conversely, if she turns to the ways of her True Bridegroom through Faith, the former husband dies, and she is no longer in adultery. This can be seen in the balance of *Romans 7:3* – *"but if her husband be dead, she is free from that Law; so that she is no adulteress, though she be married to another man."*

Romans 7:3 – Subject Scripture
So then if, while her husband liveth, she be married to another man, she shall be called an adulteress: **but if her husband be dead, she is free from that Law; so that she is no adulteress, though she be married to another man.**

Romans 7:3 – Portion II
**"…but if her husband be dead, she is free from that Law;
so that she is no adulteress, though she
be married to another man."**

Beginning this remarkable portion with *"but if her husband be dead,"* we see the Grace of her True Bridegroom if she had fallen into adultery. Yet, now in love with her One True Bridegroom, He is showing her of the condition that she had been born into due to her lineage. As she listens to Him speak of His Love for her, she comes to realize more clearly, Whom He really Is, and the magnitude of what He has done for her through the Shedding of Blood, and death on the Cross. As He continued to share in His loving care, He shows her that He gave to her His Faith and His Mind, and reveals to her that if she ponders His Amazing Love which was displayed on the Cross for her, He will live through her while she waits for His return,

74

whereupon He will consummate their marriage. At last *"she is free from that Law; so that she is no adulteress."*

This serious indictment of adultery is qualified by *"she be married to another man,"* clearly unveiling that she was married to her One True Bridegroom upon her coming to Him and receiving Salvation. *"So then if"* the woman tries to live by the Mosaic Law or any law through her flesh after she has received Salvation, she will fall from the Grace of her True Bridegroom *(Gal. 5:4)* – the One Whom cleansed her and presented her to Himself as a chaste virgin through His Shed Blood and death on the Cross.

Though we may understand adultery in terms of the woman being married to Christ and the husband now living again; we must understand that the Apostle Paul is ultimately revealing the Christian and the Mosaic Law. If the woman tries to live by the Mosaic Law through her flesh, it becomes adultery. Moreover, if she actually goes after the Mosaic Law to live by it through her flesh, she is required to live up to the whole of the Mosaic Law *(Gal. 5:3; Jam. 2:10)*, and the husband will come quickly to life in order to enforce this type of carnal thinking, which is of her old man.

As Christians, we deal with the spiritual, and the principles in place are spiritual Laws. They are like gravity; though it is not seen, gravity is an invisible force working within an established Law that is walked within every moment of every day. Gravity is all around us – we can let go of a feather and it falls gently to earth, yet we can be killed if we violate its Law. Spiritual Laws are similar to gravitational Laws. However, their power is experienced differently, depending on how we engage their dynamics. Likewise, the Mosaic Law handled properly can be a light unto our path *(Prov. 6:23; Rom. 7:7, 25)*, but it can bring death if handled improperly *(I Cor. 15:56; II Cor. 3:6)*. To take the idea further, when a Christian engages the act of sin, death comes and he or she can feel it. Whatever the place was before the personal fall, it is most often looked back upon as a much better place. This feeling of death is real, and the events going on within this setting are spiritual, as is the joy that follows when he or she is renewed. The point is that these principles are spiritual and they are real – they are not carnal *(II Cor. 10:4)*.

CHAPTER 7

The Christian's Relationship
To the Law

ROMANS 7:4-7

PREFACE

There are many views about the Law, yet there are three remarkable aspects that can be seen within the Word of God. First, due to the Fall of Adam, God gave the Law to reveal the acceptable moral code for mankind. Second, Man's fallen condition was revealed due to the inability to live up to the moral standard of the Law *(Rom. 3:20)*. Third, the Mosaic Law was the dispensational stop-gap measure for mankind before the Cross. Ending this dispensation, God, in His Love, came to satisfy the full demands of the Law by Vicariously Paying the Penalty of Man's inability to meet the moral obligations of the very Law that He gave *(Rom. 8:3-4; Col. 2:13-15; Heb. 10:9)*.

The exponential quandary is, the more time that elapses from the Fall of Adam, the greater the degree of difficulty in accepting the reality of the Fall. Adding to this difficulty is the increase of knowledge. Through knowledge, fallen Man demands that God be replaced with evolution, the Big Bang, and every other thing that would enable Man to replace God in his belief system – the ultimate goal in eliminating God from the equation altogether. This is the plight of fallen Man.

However, God's Law is the unchangeable moral code for mankind, and without meeting the requirements of this code, for the Christian, the result is unavoidable condemnation at best. All of this sounds grim, but the Law is actually part of the greatest love story ever told, and those of us alive today are living in the midst of it.

God knew what it would take to create man in His image, after His likeness, and He resolved the full scope of His plan for man before He initiated the magnificent events of forming man; and breathing into his nostrils the breath of life. God knew of the potential for Adam to fall; thus, the Cross was foreordained before the foundation of the world *(I Pet. 1:18-20)*.

This foreordained plan of the Cross would not only become the greatest display of God's wisdom, much greater than creation as we see it, but would also reveal His endless love toward Man. God did not design the Fall – it is because of God's Love that He created Adam with free will. The Fall came through Adam's decision to violate the command of God. Though this story would carry on through each dispensation until the end of time as we know it, without some type of moral compass, mankind would not understand their fallen condition. Because of all of this, the Law was given.

Although the purpose of the Law could not be fully understood in the dispensation of time up to the Cross, the Law nonetheless revealed Man's fallen condition, which pointed him to his Creator. As the revelation of sin was seen, so was the Righteousness of God;

thus, the shedding of blood was the only acceptable sacrifice for the remission of sins prior to the Cross. Still, the blood of animals did not cleanse the conscience during the dispensation of the Mosaic Law before the Cross *(Heb. 9:9)*. Nevertheless, the Old Testament sacrifices were acceptable unto God because they were types and shadows of His foreordained plan of the Cross.

Now, through the Shedding of His Own Blood and His death on the Cross, the Penalty of Man's inability to keep the Righteous Requirements of the Law has been Paid once for all *(Heb. 10:9-14)*. For this reason, through the Cross, the Old Testament types and shadows have been done away with. Now, Christ is the end of the Law for Righteousness to everyone who believes *(Rom. 10:4)*.

Does this mean the Law has been done away with? Certainly not! *(Heb. 7:12-28; 8:10-13)*. What was our schoolmaster that brought us to Christ *(Gal. 3:24-25)* is now a light that reveals and instructs the way of life *(Prov. 6:23)*, ever pointing us to God through Jesus Christ, and Him Crucified *(Gal. 2:19-20)*. Our relationship with the Law begins and ends with the Cross *(Rom. 7:4-6; Col. 2:13-15)*. As the Cross becomes the center piece of our Faith, the Righteousness of the Law remains fulfilled in us *(Rom. 8:3-4)*. For this reason, the Law is no longer to be served through our flesh. It cannot be. It is served with our mind *(Rom. 7:25)*. It is our moral compass, ever pointing us to Jesus Christ and His Cross for what He has done to satisfy the Law and Pay the Penalty of our inability through His Shed Blood and death. As Believers, this is our relationship with the Law.

Romans 7:4 – Subject Scripture
Wherefore, my Brethren, you also are become dead to the Law by the body of Christ; that you should be married to another, even to

Daniel E. Armour

Him Who is raised from the dead, that we should bring forth fruit unto God.

Romans 7:4 – Portion I
"Wherefore, my Brethren,
you also are become dead to the Law by the body of Christ…;"

The Apostle Paul writes, *"Wherefore, my Brethren,"* and brings the analogy of the woman, the husband, and the Law back to all of us who are Saved. Then in *Romans 7:4*, the terminology *"you also are become"* is deliberately penned as such in order to let us understand the past, present, and future tense in what happened upon our Salvation, what is now taking place, and what we are becoming. Meaning, if we find that we are struggling with the sin nature, our Salvation is not in jeopardy as long as we continue in Christ *(Rom. 5:20-21)*. Yet, in our struggle to continue on in Christ, we are becoming Overcomers, learning obedience of Faith, and growing in the knowledge of this *(Rom. 16:26)*, even though we may struggle at times with sin or the nature of it.

As Christians, we can never justify the actions of sin or engaging thoughts of sin *(Rom. 6:1-2)*. We have been called to holiness *(I Pet. 1:16)*, and we have been called to Sanctification *(Rom. 6:12; 8:13; II Pet. 1:5-8)*. The Gospel is not demanding perfection from us *(I John 1:9-10)*, but we cannot stay in habitual sin if we fall into sin *(I John 3:6-9 – NT: 264 – action of sin, to miss the mark, trespass)*.

Therefore, until we are changed at the Trump of God or we die a physical death, the sin nature will remain in our physical members *(Rom. 7:23, 25)*. To say we are without the sin nature makes us liars *(I John 1:8 – NT: 266 – the sin, not the action, but the nature)*. Ultimately, we are to learn what it takes to keep the sin nature incapacitated, yet in this learning process, though we may fail at times, we are learning to overcome. Once again, the terminology *"you also are become"* is deliberately penned as such in order to let us understand the past, present, and future tense in what happened at Salvation, what is now taking place, and what we are becoming.

The terminology *"dead to the Law"* means that our old man is Crucified with Him *(Rom. 6:6)*. Thereby, we are dead to the Law and out from under the eternal consequences of the Law *(Col. 2:12-15)*. However, if we engage the Law or any method created by ourselves, someone else, or an Angel whereby we try to gain triumph and holiness *(Gal. 1:6-9; Col. 2:8, 20)*, the result will be death, bondage, and condemnation due to experiencing the demands and penalty of the Law.

Moreover, it must be understood that the power of the sin nature is the Law *(I Cor. 15:56)*. When the Law is viewed as the letter (enforced as a strict set of rules to live by), it will be engaged, giving the sin nature occasion to revive *(Rom. 7:8)*. If this becomes the case, not only have we fallen from Grace in our effort to live by the Law *(Gal. 5:4)*, we will find that our willpower working through flesh is woefully insufficient to overcome the power of the sin nature *(Rom. 7:9, 15, 18, 23)*. Therefore, we are to remain dead to the Law so that the sin nature is not given occasion to revive. For this reason, we cannot use our old man's carnal thinking in any way or form to live for God. Instead, we are to view the Law in spirit wherein we will ponder where and how the Law was fulfilled and the Penalty Paid *(Rom. 7:25; 8:3-4)*.

We have become dead to the Law, but this is contingent upon remaining planted in the likeness of Jesus' death while we live *(Rom. 6:3-5; Gal. 2:19-20)*. Still, to understand death as we live, death means we have no strength within ourselves. Our body is dead because of the sin nature *(Rom. 8:10)*, and therefore we cannot use our physical body to overcome. In this, we learn that full dependency must be on God through Jesus Christ, exclusively Jesus Christ, and Him

Crucified *(Rom. 7:25)*. This exclusive dependency gives the Holy Spirit the liberty to empower us to live for God the way He desires. Outside of this dependency, it will be the way we desire, and we cannot do what we want *(Gal. 5:17)*.

The dynamics of remaining *"dead to the Law"* come through Faith alone. Many Christians have Faith in Jesus Christ but remain under condemnation due to not understanding their relationship with the Law. Regardless of how hard they have tried, they have found no way out from under this heavy burden. This is simply due to misplaced Faith. In other words, though they believe in Jesus Christ, ongoing condemnation evidences that their Faith is resting in their self-efforts. These self-efforts, no matter how they may be perceived, are by the Law, which simply means that they have not remained dead to the Law by the body of Christ. This is not said from a judgmental heart, but a heart broken for those trapped in such a position.

Properly placed Faith means that the object of our Faith must always and ever be Jesus Christ, and Him Crucified *(I Cor. 2:2)*. Although this racks the theology and belief system of our mind at first, this is the only way to remain dead while alive in our present mortal body *(Gal. 1:4; 2:19-20; 6:14)*.

There are many benefits that come through properly placed Faith. One of them is remaining *"dead to the Law,"* yet in doing so, the result is the ongoing experience of remaining in the likeness of Jesus' Resurrection *(Rom. 6:3-5; 8:11, 14)*. For this reason, the Apostle Paul wrote – *"¹⁰That I may know Him, and the power of His Resurrection, and the fellowship of His sufferings, being made conformable unto His death; ¹¹If by any means I might attain unto the Resurrection of the dead" (Phil. 3:10-11).*

As stated earlier, *Philippians 3:11,* is not speaking here of our future Resurrection as Saints. It speaks of our experiencing the power of Jesus' Resurrection while alive in this present evil world, and the Apostle Paul reveals the way in which this is attained in *verse 10* – *"That I may know Him, and the power of His Resurrection, and the fellowship of His sufferings, being made conformable unto His death."*

Very simply, because we live in our present mortality, we must be made conformable unto Jesus' death, in order to experience the power of Jesus' Resurrection *(Rom. 6:7; 8:11).* How is this death possible while we live? Although it is not possible to return to the events of the Cross, the benefits of the Cross are supernaturally made manifest to us as we place Faith in Jesus Christ, and Him Crucified *(Rom. 7:25; 8:2; I Cor. 1:17-18; 2:2).*

Ultimately, this is the Resurrection life we are deeply looking for, and resting our Faith in Jesus Christ, and Him Crucified, is the only way to find it. This is the Faith of the Son of God wherein we can live *(Gal. 2:16-20; 6:14)* and experience the Spirit of Life effectually leading us unto the Will of the Father *(Rom. 14-17).* As we walk in this truth, we enter His rest *(Heb. 4:3, 10)* and we come to realize this is the victorious way of the Cross wherein we remain *"dead to the Law"* and alive unto God in Christ.

The language, *"by the body of Christ"* in the ending balance of *Romans 7:4* portion I, gives us tremendous insight into the enormity of the Fall and what God had to do to Redeem mankind back unto Himself. Though it is not fully possible to comprehend God coming from Eternity into time *(John 1:14),* God was made in the fashion and likeness as a man, yet He was not conceived through the seed of a fallen man – *"20...for that which is conceived in her* (Mary) *is of the Holy Ghost. 21And she shall bring forth a Son, and you shall call His Name JESUS: for He shall save His people from their sins. 22Now all this was done, that it might be fulfilled which was spoken of the Lord by the Prophet, saying, 23Behold, a Virgin shall be with Child,*

and shall bring forth a Son, and they shall call His Name Emmanuel,
which being interpreted is, God with us" (Matt. 1:20-23).*

For God to become the Only Acceptable Sacrifice in order to Redeem fallen Man and destroy the works of the Devil, His body had to be as Adam's was prior to Adam making the decision to partake of the Tree of the Knowledge of Good and Evil *(I Cor. 15:45)*. The first Adam was made a living soul, created in the image of God, after His likeness *(Gen. 1:27; 2:7)*. However, through Adam's disobedience, the sin nature entered into the human race *(Rom. 5:12)*. Therefore, the Man, Jesus, was not conceived through the seed of a fallen man, for that which was conceived in Mary was of the Holy Ghost *(Matt. 1:20)*.

The last Adam (Jesus) came in the likeness of sinful flesh. Still, He was apart from sin in order to rectify the consequences that came through the disobedience of the first Adam *(Gen. 3:15; Rom. 8:3; Heb. 4:15)*. No man could have ever gone to the Cross other than God Himself *(I John 4:16)*. God came from Heaven to Earth to do what no man would be able to do through life or death *(Col. 2:12-15; I John 3:8)*, and He did this remarkable work in the likeness of sinful flesh *(John 1:1, 14; Phil. 2:5-8; II Tim 2:5)*.

Although thousands have died upon a cross, for our Thrice Holy God to have known the magnitude of the Fall prior to the creation *(I Pet. 1:18-20)* and then form the remarkable plan of the Cross, knowing that His creation would Crucify Him upon it, is much different. A human view should reveal that it is difficult for any person to run his or her own life smoothly, let alone perfectly. It is humanly impossible. Furthermore, there are some very intelligent people who have found themselves in dire trouble through just one mistake. Not so with God. God knows the beginning of time to the end of time and every thought of every man, woman, boy, and girl, including every one of their hurts, pains, and everything associated with their life and living. Still, He came into the world because He Loved us, and died on the Cross for every Sin *(John 3:16)*. No human could bear the magnitude of this, nor the associated seen and unseen powers of darkness. He still laid His life down for us – no man took it from Him *(John 10:15-18)*.

Jesus Christ and His Obedience unto death, even the death of the Cross, were the Perfect and entirely Sinless Sacrifice *(Heb., Chptrs 9-10)*. After receiving Salvation, the awe striking magnitude of this once for all Sacrifice can slip from our view, so we must be careful not to allow anything to take second place to the tremendous cost of what God had to do in order to make right the consequences of Sin.

In His sinless body, Jesus Vicariously Paid the Penalty of the Law and condemned sin in the flesh – *"³For what the Law could not do, in that it was weak through the flesh, God sending His Own Son in the likeness of sinful flesh, and for sin, condemned sin in the flesh: ⁴That the Righteousness of the Law might be fulfilled in us, who walk not after the flesh, but after the Spirit" (Rom. 8:3-4)*.

Therefore, we who believe are delivered from the Law *"by the body of Christ."* However, if we are experiencing condemnation, it reveals that we are walking after the flesh. That is, we are trying to live by the Law through our flesh in some way, and because of this effort we are experiencing the associated penalty of the Law *(Rom. 8:1 & 4)*.

Conversely, as we learn to walk after the Spirit, by learning to exercise Faith in Whom He Is, and His triumphant Atoning Sacrifice on the Cross, the Righteousness of the Law remains fulfilled within us *(Rom. 8:1-4)*. The result of walking after the Spirit is condemnation fading away because we have become delivered from the effects and associated penalty of the Law *"by the body of Christ."* This is the power of the Cross *(I Cor. 1:17-18)*.

Romans 7:4 – Subject Scripture
Wherefore, my Brethren, you also are become dead to the Law by the body of Christ; **that you should be married to another,** even to Him Who is raised from the dead, that we should bring forth fruit unto God.

Romans 7:4 – Portion II
"…that you should be married to another…,"

This second portion of *Romans 7:4* reveals that each of us who are born again has become espoused to Christ. Just as the woman who typifies the sinner in *Romans 7:2*, we who have received Jesus Christ as Lord and Saviour have become cleansed, presented as chaste virgins, and espoused to Christ *(II Cor. 11:2)*. Our Marriage to Christ is to become consummated prior to His Second Coming *(Rev. 19:7-9)*.

For now, our True Bridegroom has shown us His Love through His Cross; He alone has Redeemed His Fallen Bride back unto Himself. No greater Love has ever been known. No greater Love has ever been shown than that of Jesus Christ, and His Vicarious Shed Blood and death on the Cross. The effects and benefits of this are available for each of us today as long as our Faith remains in Him, and His Sacrifice *(Rom. 7:25; I Cor. 2:2)*. God is Love, and His Love has become revealed on the Cross – there is no other place to look *(Gal. 2:20)*. Herein, the Author of Hebrews writes – *"Looking unto Jesus the Author and Finisher of our Faith; Who for the joy that was set before Him endured the Cross, despising the shame, and is set down at the Right Hand of the Throne of God" (Heb. 12:2)*.

When *Hebrews 12:2* becomes properly understood, it reveals that Jesus Authored Faith as the Man, Jesus, and finished Faith on the Cross as the Man, Jesus. This is the Faith of the Son of God given to us upon Salvation *(Gal. 2:16, 20, 24-25; Phil. 3:9)*, and it shall always have the Cross before it. To be married to such a Bridegroom, we should look to no other place for the power to restrain evil, live life, and grow in holiness *(Gal. 6:14; Rev. 12:11)*.

Romans 7:4 – Subject Scripture

Wherefore, my Brethren, you also are become dead to the Law by the body of Christ; that you should be married to another, **even to Him Who is raised from the dead,** that we should bring forth fruit unto God.

Romans 7:4 – Portion III
"…even to Him Who is raised from the dead…,"

This magnificent third portion of *Romans 7:4* proclaims the absolute sinlessness of the Man, Jesus. Had Jesus sinned in any way, thought, or deed, He would not have been raised from the dead and the catastrophic results would be eternal hell for all mankind. Although this is shocking to think about, the outcome was resting upon Jesus and His purpose as a man. However, there is nothing about the Divine Nature and Attributes of our Thrice Holy God that demands an outcome. In this, failure is not in God because God is Love, and Love never fails *(Acts 2:24; I Cor. 13:8; Heb. 6:18-20)*. This amazing wisdom of God was shown openly on the Cross for us *(Col. 2:13-15; I Pet. 1:18-20; I John 3:8)*, and all that was done was done and accomplished in Love with meekness and humbleness of Heart and Mind *(Matt. 26:39; Phil. 2:5-8; Heb. 10:5-10)*.

Upon the Cross, after Jesus said, *"It is finished"* (John 19:30) Luke tells us that Jesus then *"gave up the ghost"* (Luke 23:46). No man took His life; only He, as God, had the Power to lay down His life and take it back up again *(John 10:17-18)*. This could be done because He had accomplished all things on the Cross as the Man, Jesus, in His

Sinless body *(John 19:28)*. Therefore He, as God, *"gave up the ghost"*; that is to say, to breathe His last with His physical body *(to breathe His last – NT: 1606; from NT: 1537 and NT: 4154 – to expire)*. Thus, He, as God, gave up the ghost to His human body and, by doing so, this clearly signifies His Deity.

If, at that time, natural eyes were opened to the remarkable unseen reality of the Man, Jesus, giving up the ghost of His humanity, they would have seen Christ Jesus alive and victorious, never ceasing to be God. Triumphant through the death of His humanity on the Cross, He descended into the lower parts of the earth, into Paradise (Abraham's bosom). Yet God, Christ Jesus unchanged, did not ascend to God the Father before He Preached from Paradise unto the spirits in the burning side of Hell *(John 20:17; I Pet. 3:18-20)*, as we can see in the literal account of Lazarus *(Luke 16:19-31)*. After He Preached to the spirits in the burning side of Hell, He then led the Old Testament Saints out from that region *(Eph. 4:8-10)*. Although there is so much that took place in the three days of events after His death on the Cross, in everything, His Will was divested unto the Will of the Father. Therein, God raised Him up on the third day *(Acts 10:40)*.

Romans 7:4 – Subject Scripture
Wherefore, my Brethren, you also are become dead to the Law by the body of Christ; that you should be married to another, even to Him Who is raised from the dead, **that we should bring forth fruit unto God.**

Romans 7:4 – Portion IV
"...that we should bring forth fruit unto God."

This firth portion ends *Romans 7:4*, revealing what can be accomplished through Faith in His Son, and what He has done through His Cross. As Christians, our ultimate fruit unto God is a life of overcoming through His Spirit *(Rom. 8:13)*. This fruit is produced as we learn to die while we live *(Phil. 2:5; 3:7-11; II Cor. 4:10-11)*. For many it has meant, and even means today and the days to come, physical death, yet this will be their testimony: *"And they overcame him by the Blood of the Lamb, and by the word of their Testimony* (Jesus Christ, and Him Crucified *[Gal. 6:14]*); *and they loved not their lives unto the death" (Rev. 12:11)*. When our testimony becomes Jesus Christ, and Him Crucified, the power of God will help us do what needs to be done so that we may bring forth fruit unto God.

Romans 7:5 – Subject Scripture
For when we were in the flesh, the motions of sins, which were by the Law, did work in our members to bring forth fruit unto death.

Romans 7:5 – Portion I
"For when we were in the flesh…,"

The phrase *"in the flesh"* is referring to both the Saved and unsaved individual. This, in its simplest form, means to apply willpower to the physical human body through carnal thinking, whereby the individual tries to live for God. This was our constant state of mind before we received Salvation. In this condition, as it regards trying to live a good life, we only had our carnal mind and its primary impulses on which to rely. The resonating catalyst for this endeavor, due to the unregenerate dynamics, was to live by the Law written in our heart because our conscience bore witness to that Law. Unable to live up to that Law, we continually experienced condemnation to one degree or the other, wherein our thoughts either accused us or excused us, causing us to create or follow another standard of laws in order to avoid the moral standard in our heart *(Rom. 2:14-15)*. This was an unbreakable cycle until Salvation and, for this reason, the entire unsaved world functions with this mindset at the base of their thinking regardless of their financial, religious, or social status.

After Salvation, the phrase *"in the flesh"* is widely used. However, the mere core equation of our walk, now that we are born again, is either a walk after the flesh or a walk after the Spirit *(Rom. 8:1, 4)*. A life application may look like this: If my walk is after the flesh, to one degree or another, bondage and condemnation will be my experience due to my efforts of trying to live by the Law *(Rom. 7:15, 23; 8:1)*. Flat out, I cannot live by the Law without reaping the associated consequences of trying. Just two of these associated consequences are condemnation and strengthening the sin nature. When I try to live by the Law, condemnation is experienced because of the non-fulfillment of the righteousness of the Law in my life. As a result, the sin nature is not only given occasion to revive, but it is strengthened the harder I try *(I Cor. 15:56)*.

So then, if I am experiencing condemnation and bondage, it simply reveals that my walk is after the flesh. This is a miserable place for me to be, and I would be experiencing this because my Faith is in something other than the Cross. This does not mean that I have lost my Salvation; this reveals my Faith is misplaced *(Rom. 7:9, 15, 23; 8:7)*.

On the other hand, if I am walking after the Spirit, this means the Holy Spirit is leading me; therein, I am walking after His leading. However, the only way I can walk this walk is to determine that the Cross shall ever be the view of my motives and thoughts, and thereby my life *(Rom. 7:25; I Cor. 2:2; Gal. 2:19-20, 6:14)*.

In conclusion: as I make the decision to place my Faith in Jesus Christ, and Him Crucified, I will begin to experience the Spirit of Life quickening me unto the Will of the Father *(Rom. 8:2, 11-17)*. As I walk after the Spirit, this does not mean that I will not fail – at times I might. However, when I am truly walking after the Spirit and I fail, condemnation will not be associated with my failure, but quite the opposite. Instead of condemnation, there will be a conviction wherein I will repent and make the unwavering decision in trusting God for His help as I grow in Sanctification. Herein, I will have the clarity of mind, free from the whirlwinds of darkness that come from condemnation, to get up and continue on after the Spirit. As my decision towards the Cross turns into determination and my will follows my decision, I will grow in the knowledge that determination is for my Faith. I will be determined to keep my Faith in the Cross when tempted by sin. As I experience the ongoing results of properly maintaining my Faith, I will come to realize this is the good fight of Faith *(I Tim. 6:12; II Tim. 4:7)*. In this place, the past tense of *"were in the flesh"* is exactly that – past tense.

Romans 7:5 – Subject Scripture

For when we were in the flesh, **the motions of sins, which were by the Law,** did work in our members to bring forth fruit unto death.

Romans 7:5 – Portion II
"...the motions of sins, which were by the Law...,"

This portion of *Romans 7:5* qualifies a remarkable truth. By the Apostle Paul beginning with *"the motions of sins,"* he has chosen an unusual set of words. Nonetheless, he is referring to our functioning in the flesh. Let us once again apply a life application for this portion.

As a Believer, if I do not know the way of victory, I will continue to fall *(Rom. 7:9, 15)* and, due to failure, I will experience condemnation. Herein, it is entirely possible for me, in this condition, to try harder and harder to overcome using my human strength by one or many methods. These methods are ultimately laws devised by myself or the mind of another. Yet because the strength of the sin nature is the Law *(I Cor. 15:56)*, I will remain under the evil reign of the sin nature. The result will be the sin nature manifesting through my physical body producing *"the motions of sins."*

If I continue in the Law this way, I will remain in this condition and the motions of sins, which are by the Law, will be ongoing due to the sin nature thriving within this environment. Though I might not think that I am improperly functioning in the Mosaic Law, if I try to live by it or any type of law or method that causes me to use my willpower in conjunction with my physical body to deal with spiritual matters of Sanctification, it is, in and of itself, a law embedded in the Law.

The Apostle Paul is speaking of what once was due to our unregenerate condition. We are no longer forced into the confines of our carnal mind, producing this endless cycle. We have been given a new way to live through Faith. Thus, Paul describes this cycle in the past tense: *"the motions of sins, which were by the Law."*

Romans 7:5 – Subject Scripture
For when we were in the flesh, the motions of sins, which were by the Law, **did work in our members to bring forth fruit unto death.**

Romans 7:5 – Portion III
"...did work in our members to bring forth fruit unto death."

Beginning with *"did work in our members"* in this portion, the Apostle Paul is revealing that the sin nature did work through the physical members of our human body in order to produce acts of sins that result in death. All of this was due to trying to live by the Law *(Rom. 7:8-11)*. However, this still remains a reality for many Christians.

This type of reality is due to the efforts of trying to live by the Law instead of going through the Law *(Gal. 2:19)*, and because the strength of the sin nature is the Law *(I Cor. 15:56)*, the sin nature is able to apprehend his or her physical body to work in and, thus, manifest its control *(Rom. 7:15, 23)*. For this reason, our body is dead because of the sin nature *(Rom. 8:10)*; for us who are Saved, our physical body has become rendered ineffective as it regards using it to overcome the sin nature and grow in Sanctification *(Rom. 7:18)*.

It is quite amazing to come to terms with this truth, however, if we could utilize our own strengths, (intellectual or otherwise), in order to overcome, grow in Sanctification, and thereby live for God, we would not need to depend on God. As Christians, we know this, yet the spiritual realm that surrounds us is significantly more powerful than we can ever realize for now. Because of this, God has given Believers the way to live victoriously within our current environment *(Rom. 8:2; Gal. 1:4; 6:14)* because our power is woefully insufficient. This is ultimately what we need to learn.

The ending portion of *Romans 7:5 – "to bring forth fruit unto death"* – reveals that, if our Faith is in any other "thing" apart from Faith in Jesus Christ, and Him Crucified, for growing in Sanctification, our efforts will in no uncertain terms be by the Law. Therein, the sin nature will have the legal means to work in and through our physical body so it can *"bring forth fruit unto death."*

Thus, if we try to live by the Law, we will experience the wages of sin, the sting of death *(Rom. 6:23)*. In this condition, the sin nature will reign in our physical body, yet the war waged will be taking place in our mind *(Rom. 7:23)*. This type of lifestyle produces continual fruit unto death, all due to the Law of Sin, which resides within our members.

Romans 7:6 – Subject Scripture
But now we are delivered from the Law, that being dead wherein we were held; that we should serve in newness of Spirit, and not in the oldness of the letter.

Romans 7:6 – Portion I
"But now we are delivered from the Law…,"

By the Apostle beginning with *"But now,"* he is letting us know that the role of the Law now has a much different dynamic for us who are Saved *(Rom. 7:7, 25).* The balance of *"we are delivered from the Law,"* in no uncertain terms, reveals a truth. Regardless of the circumstances, tangible or intangible, those of us who are born again are delivered from the Law. However, there are many Christians today who are under condemnation and do not know why and, without the knowledge for freedom, their life can be spent searching for the answer in all the wrong places.

As Christians, we are delivered from the Law by the body of Christ. So then if there is condemnation, it simply means that Faith is in some "thing" other than the Cross. Therefore, due to misplaced Faith, the Righteousness of the Law is no longer fulfilled within the life of the one who has his or her Faith in self-efforts. This does not mean that he or she is no longer Saved – it simply means that condemnation is experienced due to the non-fulfillment of the Law in his or her own life.

Let us once again view *Romans 8:3-4* in order to qualify this – *"³For what the Law could not do, in that it was weak through the flesh, God sending His Own Son in the likeness of sinful flesh, and for sin, condemned sin in the flesh: ⁴That the Righteousness of the Law might be fulfilled in us, who walk not after the flesh, but after the Spirit."*

Romans 8:3, reveals that the Law was inadequate in giving us the ability to reach the moral standard that God requires for our life. This has not changed now that we are born again; the Law is still inadequate in giving us the ability through our flesh to keep the Righteousness of the Law fulfilled in us. For the purpose of the Cross *(Heb., Chptrs 9-10),* Christ is the end of the Law for Righteousness to everyone who believes *(Rom. 10:4).* For this very reason, our Faith must rest in Whom Jesus Christ is, and where and how the Law was fulfilled, Satisfied, and Paid in Full. Our Faith must rest in the Cross.

Romans 8:4, qualifies *Romans 8:3.* Yet, as we can see in *verse 3,* the Righteousness of the Law remaining fulfilled in each one of us is contingent upon our own personal decision to walk after the Spirit. However, walking after the Spirit is accomplished only if one is led by the Spirit, and this is contingent on properly placed Faith. Thus, the sovereignty to choose where Faith is to be placed is up to each of us.

The bottom line is *"we are delivered from the Law."* If a Christian comes under condemnation, it simply means that his or her Faith is in some "thing" other than the Cross. As he or she makes the determining decision to maintain Faith in the Cross, the Righteousness of the Law will be fulfilled in his or her life. Guilt and condemnation simply fade away. In addition, the Spirit of Life in Christ Jesus will make that Christian free from the Law of Sin and Death – this is the Law of the Spirit of Life *(Rom. 8:2).*

Romans 7:6 – Subject Scripture
But now we are delivered from the Law, **that being dead wherein we were held;** that we should serve in newness of Spirit, and not in the oldness of the letter.

Romans 7:6 – Portion II
"...that being dead wherein we were held...;"

This portion of *Romans 7:6* speaks of the dynamic consequences of original sin, that is, the consequences of Adam's decision by partaking of the Tree of the Knowledge of Good and Evil *(Gen. 3:6-9)*. It is most difficult for we who are Saved to understand these consequences, let alone the invisible principles going on within and around each human being, Saved and un-saved. Because of this, *Romans* plays a most astounding role within which the Apostle Paul specifically unveils the dynamics that held us due to Adam's decision. These are the principles of the old man with the body of sin in *Romans 6:6*, and the principles of the husband and his Law of Marriage and Enforcement in *Romans 7:2*. Though they are one and the same, their principles are inseparable. The old man is a way of thinking, and the husband is the enforcer of that way of thinking. By the Apostle Paul writing *"that being dead wherein we were held,"* he is letting us know that, due to the Cross, we are no long held by those things that caused us to believe contrary to the ways of God and then enforced that way of belief. As Christians, we have been given the Mind of Christ with the opportunity to live by Faith.

Romans 7:6 – Subject Scripture
But now we are delivered from the Law, that being dead wherein we were held; **that we should serve in newness of Spirit, and not in the oldness of the letter.**

Romans 7:6 – Portion III
"...that we should serve in newness of Spirit, and not in the oldness of the letter."

As we begin this third portion of *Romans 7:6*, we see *"that we should serve,"* yet it is clear that we are to *"serve in newness of Spirit."* Therefore, let us look into the proper New Testament application of *"serve"* that will help bring us understanding. *Philippians 4:13* is a great example – *"I can do all things through Christ which strengtheneth me."*

Although it is easy to run off in the concept that *"I can do all things,"* I must acknowledge that I can only do all things *"through Christ which strengtheneth me."* Therefore, I must first be strengthened by the Holy Spirit before I can do all things, and thus properly serve.

Let us take the idea further by looking into *Romans 7:18* – *"For I know that in me (that is, in my flesh,) dwells no good thing: for to will is present with me; but how to perform that which is good I find not."*

Notice within *Romans 7:18* that the Apostle Paul addresses his – *"will"* – and he references his will, with – *"perform."* As we have learned, our will begins in the subjective position (i.e., the intangibles of our mind); however, it can end up in the objective position (i.e., performance in our body). Meaning, there is nothing in us (that is in our flesh) that can be utilized to perform by which we may get the idea that we are serving.

Within *Romans 7:18*, the Apostle Paul is literally saying that he has the willpower, but there is nothing within the tangible makeup that he lives within to deal with the intangibles of the spiritual realm. So then, how is he to perform or, for that matter, do all things? Though it should be obvious that tangible things cannot adequately deal with spiritual things, it is most difficult to walk out after becoming born again. Nonetheless, as it was with Paul, it is with us in our desire to serve; we must make sure we are not performing in the flesh. We simply cannot use our physical body in order to perform any good service for God apart from the quickening of the Holy Spirit *(without God – Rom. 7:15; with God – Gal. 6:14)*. Therefore, by the Apostle writing *"serve in newness of Spirit,"* he is speaking of that which comes through remaining in the likeness of Jesus' death *(Rom. 6:3-5, 7)* wherein the likeness of Jesus' Resurrection takes place *(Gal. 2:19-20)* so that we can *"serve in newness of Spirit."*

As we close in on the end of *Romans 7:6*, the Apostle writes, *"and, not in the oldness of the letter."* Though obvious at first glance, this means that we should never view the Law in any other way than for its purpose and function, which is to reveal God's high moral standard for us. The Law is our moral compass; it is a spiritual light that reproofs and instructs the way of life *(Prov. 6:23)*. If we view the Law as a set of rules, the view will be through the carnal mind of our old man who views the Law in letter form. Therein, we will find ourselves serving *"in the oldness of the letter,"* which is nothing less than motions of sins in the flesh by the Law *(Rom. 7:5)*.

As Christians, we have a deep desire to live for God – this makes us susceptible to lean on even the smallest of laws and methods. If we lean on any one of them, our Faith will be placed in the law or method that is leaned on. We will then be functioning in the flesh even though we believe in Jesus; therein, our will and its power take the place of what could otherwise be the effectual power of God working in us.

Regardless of how subtle the effort of living by the Law or any law may appear, it ultimately becomes a form of godliness, but denies the power of God *(I Cor. 1:17-18; Phil. 3:18-19; II Tim. 3:5)*. Many Christians are functioning in the oldness of the letter, most often without realizing it. As I have stated in many ways previously, the ways of living by the Law may not be obvious. Instead, they can be very subtle, and the world system is built on such ways with much of the Church adopting them. For example, we can be led into trying to find our purpose in life, believing that by doing this we can then engage what we think is our purpose. However, this is in direct conflict with the Word of God and the way in which He has created us.

In the beginning, God created Man in His image, after His likeness so the He would have the opportunity to fellowship with us, for us to see in likeness what He sees, to know in likeness what He knows, and to love in the likeness of Him. Yes, God creates and thus we create, but we must remember that God creates in absolutes. He alone created both seen and unseen existence from nonexistent materials. Man cannot do this.

Due to the Fall of Adam, the view, the knowledge, and the love we have are known through a glass, darkly *(I Cor. 13:12)*. We do not truly know how to see, how to know, and how to love. For this reason, we are incapable of finding the purpose in which we can "do something." Although we have a purpose, this purpose is to know Him – that is all and that is it *(John 6:28-29; Phil. 2:5; 3:7-11)*. In this, He alone will move us and, before we know it, we will be walking out our purpose, yet it will be in Him *(Rom. 8:2)*. It does not work the other way around, and there is no other way around this *(Gal. 5:17)*.

Though a lengthy exposition, we are staying with the idea of properly "serving" in order to nail home its proper application now that we are born again. The reason for this is that we link up with the flesh naturally, and serving in newness of Spirit can be, though easily rolling of the tongue, difficult to learn to walk in. We are humans walking by Faith.

If we look around, we can see that everything about this world system is striving. Yes, in this striving, we can stay as busy as we want to and, because we believe in God, we can place our Faith in all of the good efforts we desire. However, it does not mean that we have found our true purpose whereby we can serve.

It is inherent within us as Christians to do something. There is need everywhere, yet it is very important that we do not get our intentions mixed up in our desire to grow close to God and walk with Him. What I mean is that the Word of God reveals what is required of us who believe – *"²⁷Labour not for the meat which perishes, but for that meat which endures unto Everlasting Life, which the Son of Man shall give unto you: for Him has God the Father sealed. ²⁸Then said they unto Him, What shall we do, that we might work the Works of God? ²⁹Jesus answered and said unto them, This is the Work of God, that you believe on Him Whom He has sent"* (John 6:27-29).

What a remarkable set of Scriptures! All that is required is that we believe on Him Whom He sent – this is all that is required, and there is a very good reason for this. Because of the way in which God has created us, we see need, we know of need, and we desire to fill the need by helping. However, unless we are moved by the Spirit and not by the purpose, we will be outside the Will of the Father and, in no uncertain terms, be serving in the oldness of the letter, regardless of how good any effort appears.

We must be moved by the Spirit first and then any doing will be unto the Will of the Father *(Rom. 8:11-17)*. It is easy to do something and then add God to the endeavor all the while thinking God is involved because we believe in Him. This is not said to be condemning; it is simply the quandary we can find ourselves in due to the dynamics going on within and around us. Nonetheless, all that is required from God is that we believe on Him Whom He sent!

As we look within *John 6:28*, we see the question proposed to Jesus – *"...What shall we do, that we might work the Works of God?"* This is a most astonishing question indeed, a question the desiring Christian is most likely asking. For our sake, Jesus gives us the most remarkable answer – *"...This is the Work of God, that you believe on Him Whom He has sent"* (John 6:29).

This answer is remarkable in the sense that He knows we want to do something, but it is also amazing that He would associate

"Work" with *"believe,"* yet at times it is work to believe. It is much easier to serve in the oldness of the letter than to determine to take a stand in Faith and believe that what Jesus Christ has finished on the Cross is enough. Nonetheless, it would be within this Revelation that the Apostle Paul was taught the Truth of the Cross *(Rom. 16:25-27; Gal. 1:11-12)*. This laid the parameter for the Faith, (that is, properly placed Faith), thus, the full meaning of *"...believe on Him Whom He has sent."*

Once the Apostle Paul came to understand that Faith must rest exclusively in Jesus Christ, and in the manifold events accomplished through Him Crucified, this way of believing might have been plenty of work at first. However, this was the good fight of Faith, which is vastly different than serving in the oldness of the letter. Furthermore, now having the tremendous responsibility in bringing this Message forth, he stood against everything that would detour him from functioning in Faith anchored in Jesus Christ, and Him Crucified *(I Cor. 2:2; Gal. 2:11)*. For this reason, the Apostle writes – *"²³But we Preach Christ Crucified, unto the Jews a stumblingblock, and unto the Greeks foolishness; ²⁴But unto them which are called, both Jews and Greeks, Christ the Power of God, and the Wisdom of God" (I Cor. 1:23-24)*.

Moreover, knowing the way of victory is through Christ's finished work, he writes – *"But God forbid that I should glory, save in the Cross of our Lord Jesus Christ, by Whom the world is Crucified unto me, and I unto the world" (Gal. 6:14)*.

Therefore, in regards to serving, that is, the question proposed to Jesus – *"...What shall we do, that we might work the Works of God?" (John 6:28)* Had Jesus answered the question any other way other than *"...believe on Him Whom He has sent" (John 6:29)*, it would have been contrary to Whom He Is and why He came.

One may have accomplished a lot in life. A man or woman may have many collegiate degrees and have helped solve world hunger, but was it accomplished in the flesh, or was it accomplished through the Spirit, and thus within the Will of the Father?

God's Divine Attributes are Truth, Justice, and Judgment. God is Love – this is His Divine Nature *(I John 4:8, 16)*. Therein, He has not created us to do anything based on an innate feeling to do something because we desire to fulfill a purpose for Him. As a result, it is imperative that we are led by the Spirit so that we can properly serve *(Rom. 8:14)*.

As we look upon the ceremonies exercised by so many other religions, it is easy to see that they are living by the Law, and we know to steer away from these. However, many other ways, though not traditionally ceremonial, can be engaged. Those who engage this way of living unknowingly unleash sin and death within themselves and are once again overcome by the very power of the sin nature they are trying to overcome. There is no getting around the fact because the strength of the sin nature is the Law *(I Cor. 15:56)*. Therefore, if we do not take back up what has been taken out of the way through the Cross, but instead place our Faith in the Cross, the sin nature cannot revive, and we will *"serve in newness of Spirit, and not in the oldness of the letter."*

Romans 7:7 – Subject Scripture
What shall we say then? Is the Law sin? God forbid. No, I had not known sin, but by the Law: for I had not known lust, except the Law had said, You shall not covet.

Romans 7:7 – Portion I
**"What shall we say then? Is the Law sin?
God forbid. No, I had not known sin, but by the Law…:"**

The Apostle Paul states in *Romans 7:6*, *"But now we are delivered from the Law...."* Here in *Romans 7:7*, the Apostle is also letting us know that the Law did not go away in our lives now that we are delivered from the Law. Quite the contrary. The Apostle Paul is helping us understand the role the Law now plays in our Christian life. Thus, *"What shall we say then? Is the Law sin? "God forbid. No."* The Law went from our schoolmaster to light; it is our moral compass now that we have received Salvation *(Rom. 7:25; 8:3-4)*. For this reason the Apostle writes – *"I had not known sin but by the Law."*

The Apostle Paul's statement *"I had not known sin"* in a literal translation addresses *"sin"* as "the sin," which speaks of the nature of sin, not the action of sin. This makes the statement quite astonishing. The Apostle is saying that he had not known the sin nature *"but by the Law."*

The Apostle knew that he had been made free from the sin nature upon his Salvation into Christ *(Rom. 6:6-7)*. However, prior to understanding the Cross for his Sanctification *(Rom. 7:15, 23)*, he did not understand how to live exclusively by Faith (that is, Faith properly placed).

Due to this quandary, though Paul was Saved, he could not remain dead to the Law, and thus he tried to live by the Law that he knew so well *(Phil. 3:4-7)*. Therein, the nature of sin that had become incapacitated upon his Salvation into Christ, revived once again *(Rom. 7:9)* – the Law revealed this. Prior to Paul's Salvation, the Law had a purpose; it was a schoolmaster to bring him to Christ *(Gal. 3:24)*. Now born again, Faith has come and the Law is no longer his schoolmaster *(Gal. 3:25-29)*. The Mosaic Law is now a spiritual light that reproofs and instructs the way of life to him and, for this reason, the Apostle Paul writes – *"I had not known sin but by the Law."*

Romans 7:7 – Subject Scripture
What shall we say then? Is the Law sin? God forbid. No, I had not known sin, but by the Law: **for I had not known lust, except the Law had said, You shall not covet.**

Romans 7:7 – Portion II
"...for I had not known lust, except the Law had said, You shall not covet."

As we begin the second portion of *Romans 7:7*, by the Apostle Paul writing *"I had not known lust,"* it should be noted that Paul is addressing the heart and thoughts of the mind: the intangible. Paul had not known the intangible power of lust *"except the Law had said, You shall not covet."*

Prior to Paul receiving Salvation, he viewed the Law as a set of rules in letter form, and he lived by them through his flesh *(Phil. 3:6)*. Now that he is born again, though delivered from the Law, he is not without the Law; that is, he is not Lawless *(Rom. 7:22, 25; I Cor. 9:21)*. He now knows and is teaching each of us that the Law has a unique function: it reveals the intangible images of the heart, and the thoughts of the mind.

For the sinner, as stated, the Law is a schoolmaster to bring him or her to Christ so that he or she might be justified by Faith, but after that Faith has come, and he or she is no longer under a schoolmaster; Christ is the end of the Law for Righteousness as long as he or she believes *(Rom. 10:4)*.

Therefore, unto us who believe, the Law reveals the intangible because the Law is the truth *(Psalms 119:142; Rom. 8:27; Heb. 4:12)*, revealing every facet of sin on the outside and within us *(Psalms 119:101, 104, 110, 115, 126)*. The Law reveals everything, including thoughts that are contrary to God's Holy Word, so we do not fall prey to the deceitfulness of sin or the nature of it.

The Law reveals, but the Law is without coercion – meaning the profound and intended purpose of the Mosaic Law is to reveal the high moral standard that God desires for us. However, in revealing this magnificent moral standard, the Law has no choice but to reveal sin. Still, it does not force us or move us to overcome – it reveals. The quality of the Law is Holy *(Rom. 7:12)*, the principle and function of the Law are spiritual *(Rom. 7:14),* and this function of the Law is at work every moment of every day to reveal sin and the nature of it. In this, we see the Holiness of the Law and its purpose for us who are born again; the Law is our moral compass that lights and instructs the way of life.

CHAPTER 8

The Sin Nature and the
Commandment

ROMANS 7:8-24

PREFACE

Unlike those who are unsaved, we who have received Salvation have become acutely aware of sin around us because our old man is Crucified, the body of sin incapacitated, the husband has died, and our sin has become washed away through the Atoning Shed Blood of Jesus Christ. Now, with the clarity to see through a clean heart and a cleansed conscience, we no longer want to sin *(Rom. 7:22; Heb. 10:22)*. In learning to overcome when faced with sin, we must come to understand the war we are in and the way God has established through Christ as the means of triumph over the world, the flesh, and the Devil.

I previously stated that the Law is light, bringing clarity and understanding to the way of life *(Prov. 6:23)*. Because of this, the Law reveals sin. Though the Law does not force us, we are not left to fend for ourselves when it shines its light on sin. When the Law reveals sin, the Commandment (which was ordained to life) comes as a constituent, authorizing the principle truth of the Law, and directing us to God.

As we have seen in *Romans 7:7,* the Apostle Paul unveils the spiritual principle of the Law and how it now reveals to us who are born again *"...I had not known sin but by the Law."* Although Paul unveils this remarkable principle of the Law, he facilitates a platform in order to unveil the specific spiritual principle of the Commandment: to compel.

The compelling principle of the Commandment can be a difficult principle to wrap our mind around. Nonetheless, this spiritual principle is real, and the Apostle Paul goes into great detail in order to unveil his discernment, as we come to see. When this principle is discerned and seen, it can become a magnificent piece of the puzzle for understanding what is going on within and around us as we make our way through this present world we live in. Let us begin looking into this principle by first viewing its description from within *Proverbs 6:23 - "For the Commandment is a lamp; and the Law is light...."* Scripture is so remarkable!

Here we see within *Proverbs 6:23* that the Commandment is a lamp; the difference between a light and a lamp is that the lamp is a vessel for the light. As we continue to view this in a tangible application, we might remind ourselves that we can have a lamp with no light - a lamp holds the light. For example, when we go on a journey, we take the lamp; when the lamp is lit, the light shines. Still, the lamp is only a lamp. The lamp is simply holding the light now revealing obstacles and detours on the road that need to be avoided. For this reason, we would take a lamp on a journey. To carry this idea further, when we go on a journey, we must know how to stay on the main road when the light of the lamp reveals an obstacle. Otherwise, we may become detoured.

In spiritual application, the Commandment is the lamp holding the Law that shines its light, and we are holding both of them within our heart and mind *(Heb. 8:10-13; 10:16-17)*. The journey we are on is life itself. The obstacle is the dynamics of evil and the sin nature; the detour is the way of sin (carnal, the flesh), and the light of the Law is shining on all of this. However, unlike manmade lamps, there is a remarkable characteristic about the lamp that we are holding. The lamp we are holding is Holy, and just, and good, and was ordained to life *(Rom. 7:10, 12)*; it directs us into the way of life by an expressed action: compelling unto Righteousness *(Mark 12:30; Rom. 7:9-10; 10:9-10)*. This remarkable characteristic of the lamp comes to help us when the light reveals any obstacle. However, this is where we can get into trouble.

The main road we are to stay on goes right – it is for the sheep and it is God's way. The detour goes left – it is for the goats, and it is the way of sin *(Matt. 25:32-33)*. God's road is walked upon through the Mind of Christ, wherein the decision will be made to place Faith properly, and determination resonates, our will following *(I Cor. 2:2)*. Herein, all strength needed comes from God *(Rom. 8:2, 11)*.

The detour is walked through the carnal mind by making a decision to apply our will to our physical body *(Rom. 7:18; I Cor. 15:56)*, thereby resonating willpower to rely on, even though we believe in God *(Rom. 7:5, 8-11)*. Therefore, if we are not careful, we may take the detour when the light reveals an obstacle.

How is it possible for us to take the detour? Although the main road we are on is an open view because the light is shining upon it, when the light shines on an obstacle in the way, we can take the detour due to the characteristic of the lamp and our desire to stay on the main road. It is quite a paradox, but very true and can be viewed as this:

When the light (the Law) reveals an obstacle (the sin) the remarkable characteristic of the lamp (the Commandment) will compel us unto Righteousness. However, because we may not know where our Faith is to be properly placed, our desire to live for God will cause us to think carnally *(Rom. 7:14; 8:7)*, wherein the decision will be made to use our physical body in order to deal with the obstacle. Therein, we will enter the detour, by engaging our flesh. Remember, we are in the spirit – our body is dead, unable to be used *(Rom. 8:10)*. Therefore, without realizing what we have done because it is so natural, we have taken the detour, thinking it was a good way. Now, with our will being manifested in our body, we have left ourselves with no other available strength in the detour but natural strength. Thus, willpower resonates and backs up our decision even though we believe in God.

Despite making the decision to maintain course on God's road sounding easy, the world and the Devil have presented things in such a way that making a decision to take the detour seems to be the right road to take. Nonetheless, it is the wrong road because will applied to our body resonates willpower, which results in our own strength. Thus, by default we take the detour. Our will must follow the resonating decision that would properly keep us on God's road and, therefore, when this decision is made, determination maintains it and our will does not resonate into our body as willpower. We remain on God's road by His strength, His love, His power, and His Spirit.

The difference between will and determination is also a difficult paradox to wrap our mind around, nonetheless, it is paramount we understand that our walk of Faith follows our decision *(Rom. 7:25)*. When we truly examine our belief and decide to accept the truth that what Jesus Christ has finished on the Cross is enough, the Holy Spirit then has the liberty to quicken our mortal body by the same Spirit that raised Jesus from the dead *(Rom. 8:11)*. Once this is experienced, we then determine to maintain this decision *(I Cor. 2:2)*. For this reason, determination is powerful – it maintains our decision, yet all strength in all we do is exclusively through the Spirit of God. All Glory goes to God.

However, before this truth becomes known, the detour always seems the good way to go. When the decision is made to take the detour, our will is evidenced as it becomes applied to our body, whereby our Faith falls into self-efforts even though we believe in God.

The acute problem with taking the detour is that all things done in the flesh are motions of sins in the flesh, which are by the Law. This revives the sin nature, and ever strengthens its power the harder we try to walk in the detour. The Apostle Paul comes to understand this, wherein he writes – *"8But sin, taking occasion by the Commandment, wrought in me all manner of concupiscence. For without the Law sin was dead. 9For I was alive without the Law once: but when the Commandment came, sin revived, and I died. 10And the Commandment, which was ordained to life, I found to be unto death. 11For sin, taking occasion by the Commandment, deceived me, and by it slew me" (Rom. 7:8-11).*

Romans 7:8-11 are the Apostle Paul's opening statements that set the stage as he begins to disclose the struggle he once had with the sin nature. This struggle played a significant role, as most often pain and suffering do, for it is within these trials that desperation forms a journey. This was Paul's experience wherein he was taught by the Revelation of Jesus Christ how to stay on the main road *(Gal. 1:11-12)*. Though we do not know the details of all that went on during this extraordinary Revelation, we do know that the Apostle Paul had been given the expansive responsibility in delivering what he had been taught. Therefore, as it regards this astonishing struggle, he begins with *verses 8 through 11* in order to unveil the spiritual principles by which this struggle began, thereby bringing to light the difference between the principles and function of the Law, and the principles and function of the Commandment.

As we poise ourselves to learn about the difference between the Law and the Commandment, we can begin to see Paul is unveiling that, because the Law is Holy, and it is spiritual, it truly reveals *(Rom. 7:7, 14)*. Because the Commandment is Holy, and just, and good, and was ordained to life, it truly compels unto Righteousness *(Mark 12:30; Rom. 7:10; I Tim. 1:5)*.

By the Apostle bringing out the dynamics of the Law and the Commandment in this particular way, we can come to understand that it is during this compelling that it becomes possible to make the decision to combine our will with our body. This combination is simply willpower motioning our flesh, which is the detour wherein the sin nature revives and apprehends us.

Paul is also teaching us that the Law is not bad in revealing, and the Commandment is not bad in compelling. It is because these principles were not known when he first engaged this struggle that he made the illegal combination wherein his struggle began. Though his intentions were to stay on the main road, these very intentions are what caused Paul to take the detour when the Commandment compelled him because he did not know where his Faith was to be placed.

In the case of the example regarding the main road verses the detour, Paul tried to use his willpower and physical body in order to stay on the main road. Still, Paul could not walk upon the main road with this application *(Zech. 4:6; Rom. 7:18; 8:10)*. Once again, will always follows the decision; if the proper decision is not made, by default, will is applied to the physical body. Thus, all power will be human power. Such was the case with Paul, even though he believed in God.

What then was Paul to do with his willpower? Nothing! We must remember that Paul's will (as is ours) was meant for his physical body. Therefore, Paul's will, as he learned and as we must learn, had to become subservient to the proper decision. This decision was to always do the Will of the Father. Therefore, as it was with Jesus, the decision must always be the Cross *(Matt. 26:39; Luke 9:23; Phil. 2:5)*. Otherwise, our will takes first position and then defaults into our body *(Rom. 7:9)*. For this reason, determination is meant for Faith *(I Cor. 2:2)*; it is meant to back our decision and maintain Faith in the Cross. Once the Apostle Paul came to understand this, he would write – *"Fight the good fight of Faith, lay hold on Eternal Life, whereunto you are also Called, and have professed a good profession before many witnesses"* *(I Tim. 6:12)*.

It is important for us to understand that though the Law is light that reveals and instructs the way of life, the Law is without coercion – it did not force Paul, and the Law does not force us in the way of life. It was when the Law revealed the obstacle (the sin) that the Commandment came and compelled Paul unto Righteousness. As it was for Paul, this compelling is the catalyst wherein we have the opportunity to make the decision to place Faith properly. Once Faith becomes properly placed, determination maintains the decision for Faith.

Paul's dilemma was that he did not understand the principle of the Commandment, nor did he understand where to place his Faith. Therefore, he kept taking the detour, which evidenced his will and not the Will of the Father. The scope of all of this will become much easier to see as we get further into the Subject Scriptures of this chapter.

Defining the dynamics of spiritual Laws and expounding upon them may appear tedious and complex because we are in time, but the reality of events is taking place in the intangibles of the mind, soul, and spirit instantaneously outside of time. The intangibles appear in time by defining and clothing them with words. Conversely, by reading or hearing words and definitions, they leave time when entering into the intangibles of the mind and spirit.

These dynamics are going on within our life each day. Nonetheless, given that the Apostle Paul has disclosed them for us, he also writes for those who seek – *"But strong meat belongs to them that are of full age, even those who by reason of use have their senses exercised to discern both good and evil"* (Heb. 5:14).

Before we become fully involved in the Subject Scriptures following this preface, I would like to lay the groundwork for them in order to give every opportunity for you to gain greater insight within the Subject Scripture expositions. Therefore, let us start the preface insight with *Romans 7:8 – "But sin, taking occasion by the Commandment, wrought in me all manner of concupiscence."* The Apostle Paul begins his disclosure in *verse 8* by writing *"But sin."* Here as well, *"sin"* is written in a literal translation as "the sin," thus speaking of the sin nature. As we move on in *verse 8*, we see how the sin nature was able to revive within Paul's physical body, *"taking occasion by the Commandment."* This unveils that it is by the Commandment that the sin nature is given the opportunity to revive. The result of sin reviving is seen in the following portion of *verse 8*, wherein Paul writes *"wrought in me all manner of concupiscence."* That is, once sin was able to use the Commandment and revive, the evil began manifesting. In view of this, it becomes quite staggering to think that the nature of sin has some way in using the Commandment to revive.

Though we have touched on this previously, once again, the Commandment is not bad *(Rom. 7:12)*. It is because the Commandment was ordained to life that we are experiencing a compelling unto Righteousness when the Law reveals. However, if the knowledge of where to place Faith is not known, Faith will be placed within our own self-efforts, and the sin nature will revive even though we believe in God. For this reason, the Apostle Paul begins the disclosure of his struggle by laying out this principle, and then begins to unveil the difference between the principle of the Law and the principle of the Commandment in *Romans 7:9*. He writes – *"For I was alive without the Law once: but when the Commandment came, sin revived, and I died."*

The first portion of *Romans 7:9* – *"For I was alive without the Law once"* – reveals that the Apostle Paul was made alive without the Law or any type of performance on his part and continued in this life until he tried to perform. Paul was delivered from the Law upon his Salvation into Christ. However, he did not know the Law was now light that he could not touch with his flesh. Therefore, he continued in this freedom until the Law shined its light on sin. Once sin became seen, the Commandment came and compelled him unto Righteousness. Still, not knowing the way of Sanctification, he made the decision to touch the Law. This is qualified as we look into the last portion of *verse 9* – *"but when the Commandment came sin revived, and I died."* This reveals that it was not the Law by which the sin nature revived, but it was *"when the Commandment came"* that sin revived, wherein his life of freedom ended, and he died. Paul did not die physically, he experienced the sting of death as he became captive to the sin nature *(Rom. 7:23)*. Under the captivity of sin, he found himself doing the things he did not want to do and did not understand why. For this reason, he wrote – *"For that which I do I allow not: for what I would, that do I not; but what I hate, that do I"* *(Rom. 7:15)*.

There are two independent yet dependent principles actually going on: the Law revealing, and the Commandment compelling. Due to these inseparable principles, we can see that there is a gap or place of decision – a "time gap" (so to speak), wherein deception can occur by that which is good *(Rom. 7:8-11, 13, 21)*. Though the terminology "time gap" may sound somewhat odd, nonetheless, it is this place between the Law revealing and the Commandment compelling that a decision must be made.

All of this is in the realm of the intangible and happens in an instant, yet it is crucial for us to understand so that victory can take place at the core initiation of sin revealed. Each of us experiences the Law revealing and the Commandment compelling throughout each day, whether we realize it or not. It is a dynamic that cannot be circumvented.

As we come (even in part) to understand these principles, we will further begin to understand the magnitude and importance of making the Cross the object of our Faith, as the Apostle Paul had done through his life once the way of victory was revealed and taught to him *(I Cor. 2:2; Gal. 1:11-12; 2:19-20; 6:14)*.

Making the Cross the way of life is not intended to be a laboring effort. Yes, maintaining Faith in the Cross is the good fight of Faith, but it is when the Cross is seen and embraced as the only way for growing in Sanctification, that thankfulness, through humbleness of mind, molds and shapes our approach and walk with God as we experience His power and presence *(Rom. 7:25; 8: 11-17)*.

When Paul references the Cross, he is not referring to the wooden beams – he is referencing Jesus Christ, and the events that surround His Vicarious, Atoning, and triumphant Sacrifice at the Cross through His death. The profound purpose of the Cross will become more easily seen as we work our way through Paul's struggle.

Now then, at the very initiation of sin revealed due to the principles of the Law, the Commandment comes, thereby creating a "time gap" or place of decision. However, there is nothing within us (that is, in our flesh) to perform the good we want to do in our desire to overcome *(Rom. 7:18; 8:10)*. This literally means, regardless of our desire to overcome and the measure of Faith we may have, if our Faith is not properly placed, willpower working through our flesh will be woefully insufficient to overcome the power of the sin nature. This was the Apostle Paul's experience *(Rom. 7:15, 19, 23)*. It is remarkable that the Bible discloses such a struggle. As we get involved within the following Subject Scriptures, we will see what Paul discovered about this "time gap" that allowed him to become deceived by that which is good. Now concluding the preface, let us get involved in the Subject Scriptures.

Romans 7:8 – Subject Scripture
But sin, taking occasion by the Commandment, wrought in me all manner of concupiscence. For without the Law sin was dead.

Romans 7:8 – Portion I
"But sin, taking occasion by the Commandment…,"

"But sin" is referring to the sin nature. By the Apostle Paul using the term *"taking occasion"* in this portion of Scripture, he is revealing that the sin nature had a permissible entrance to revive *(Rom. 7:9)*. Paul's choice to take back up what the Lord put away through His death at the time were the precise instruments that the sin nature used to revive *(Rom. 8:7; I Cor. 15:56)*. We can view it like this:

The Law revealed sin, but without coercion. The Law did not force Paul – the Law revealed *(Rom. 7:7)*. When the Law revealed, the Commandment then compelled Paul to a place of decision; thus, the time gap. The characteristic of the Commandment, as we know, has a spiritual principle in that it was ordained to life. This compelled Paul unto Righteousness *(Matt. 22:36-40; Gen. 2:16-17; Rom. 7:10, 12)*. However, because of the Fall of Adam, there was nothing in Paul (that is, in his flesh) to perform the good he wanted to do *(Rom. 7:18)*. Paul's body was rendered useless in its capacity to deal with the sin nature *(Rom. 8:10 – NT: 266 – full sin, "the sin")*. This literally means that he had nothing within his physical makeup to handle spiritual matters of warfare *(II Cor. 10:4)*. Therefore, when he motioned (literally moved) in his own strength and abilities to overcome, the sin nature revived *(Rom. 7:9, 23)*. Regardless of how this may be looked at, Paul tried to live by the Law and, in doing so, the sin nature revived because the strength of the sin nature is the Law *(I Cor. 15:56)*. Once again, this is simply motions of sins in the flesh, which are always by the Law *(Rom. 7:5)*.

Today, many Christians find themselves in this struggle because each one of us lives in a physical body which seems to be the right instrument of use in order to grow in personal Sanctification. Yet this seemingly good way of Sanctification is due to the carnal mind *(Rom. 7:14)* which has innate propensities to "do" rather than maintain Faith. This as well may sound odd because all the while we are doing something good in the flesh; in our effort to overcome, we believe in God. However, we will come to learn that Faith was in the self-effort, and this way of thinking always comes from the carnal mind. For that reason, we must learn through the Mind of Christ *(I Cor. 2:16)* the way that God has made for us, and then walk within this way because the carnal mind is contrary to the ways of God *(Rom. 8:7)*. Yes, it may seem as though we have to do something; however, God does not work in our life based on how we perform in our flesh *(Gal., Chptr 3)*. He works in our life based upon where our Faith is placed *(Rom. 6:3-5; Col. 2:12)*, so we cannot do what we want *(Gal. 5:17)*. We have to do it God's way if we are to experience growing triumph and freedom in the Sanctification process *(Rom. 8:13; I Pet. 1:16)*.

During Paul's struggle, he had not yet learned this. Therefore, the core origin of Paul's dilemma was the principle of the Commandment compelling him unto Righteousness *(Rom. 7:8-11)*. Both the Law revealing and the Commandment compelling were at work within him for his position in Christ *(Rom. 7:12, 22)*. However, it was imperative that Paul understood the significant part they played in his Christian life. Once he came to understand these principles, he would then understand that his will needed to follow his proper decision, wherein the proper decision would resonate into determination and thus maintain his Faith in the Cross when the compelling of the Commandment came. Furthermore, and without any doubt, Paul learned by the Revelation of Jesus Christ that Faith was to remain in the Cross for not only triumph and holiness, but all manner of life and living for his daily Christian walk *(Rom. 6:12-13; 8:13)*. In learning this, the Apostle Paul would be the first human in history with the knowledge of this Revelation, and it would become the foundation of his Gospel Preached to the Churches *(Rom. 1:1; 16:25; Gal. 1:11-12; Eph. 3:3-12)*. The Apostle Paul's Gospel is the Message of the Cross *(I Cor. 1:17-18)*, and this Message is the simplicity that is in Christ *(II Cor. 11:3)*.

As Christians, we must come to understand that God has made our walk with Him to be a simple walk, one in which we can simply rest Faith in His finished work wherein we can experience His love and power at work within us *(Rom. 7:25; 8:2, 11-17)*. It does not get any simpler than this, but our Faith must remain in Jesus Christ, and Him Crucified, in order to continue in an ongoing experience of His love and power at work within us. This is our manner of walking after the Spirit *(Rom. 8:1, 4, 13)*.

The principles we are learning about, and the minutia of detail in which I am drafting them out is to bring understanding to these dynamics going on within and around us. However, if nothing else but the Message of the Cross becomes known and embraced, everything else will fall into place. The Message of the Cross is everything; it is God's established way of victory for us *(Gal. 6:14)*. The intention of this draft is to look into the extraordinary things that have happened in us, and why they are happening. The ongoing dynamics of this are truly amazing to look into and understand. So, let us look further into the Commandment because the Commandment was the catalyst that initiated Paul's decision to engage the ways of his old man, even though at that time Paul did not yet realize it revived the sin nature *(Rom. 7:8-11)*. Meaning, Paul thought he could overcome by physically imposing the Law, yet he did not realize this method of living for God revived the sin nature. This created a cycle of ongoing turmoil until he came to understand the way out.

As we look into the Commandment, through the Truth of Scripture, we find that the beginning of the Commandment is a compelling unto Righteousness *(Matt. 22:36-40; Rom. 7:9-10; I John 3:22-24)*, the end of the Commandment is love *(I Tim. 1:5)*, and Faith works by Love *(Gal. 5:6)*. We have love, God does not – He is Love *(I John 4:16)*, and though we cannot come close to fully comprehending this, in Love, He Gave Himself openly and humbly for all mankind in and through His Atoning and triumphant Sacrifice on the Cross *(John 3:16; Col. 2:12-15; I John 4:8-10)*. Now, Christ is the end of the Law for Righteousness to everyone who believes *(Rom. 10:4)*. Therefore, to keep His Commandments, the Commandment has a beginning, which is to look to Jesus Christ *(Matt. 22:36-40; I John 3:22-24)*, and an end, which is to look to Him Crucified *(John 3:14; Rom. 7:25; I John 3:22-24)*. Thus, the beginning of the Commandment directs us to God, and the end of the Commandment directs us to God. Therein, the Commandment (which was ordained to life) always directs us to God without fail, and this was the very principle Paul was coming to learn.

As the Commandment directed Paul to God, he experienced a compelling to do something. In no uncertain terms, he had to make a decision; this decision was in the arena of his mind, wherein he was to direct his thoughts, desire, Faith, and will. His desire was to overcome *(Rom. 7:22)*, but it was his thoughts, Faith, and will that needed to be properly placed, and his mind was the headquarters for that decision *(Rom. 7:25)*. That is, even though Paul had a desperate desire to overcome, he had to direct his thoughts, Faith, and will away from his body because his will applied to his body was woefully insufficient to deal with the sin nature. Flat out, his will applied to his body resulted in willpower, and his willpower and physical body were an illegal combination in regards to dealing with spiritual matters of warfare *(Rom. 7:5, 18; 8:10; I Cor. 15:56)*.

Therefore, as the Commandment directed Paul to God, he entered the place of decision: the "time gap," wherein he needed the help of God. It was here that his dilemma originated. In other words, temptation had come, the Law had revealed sin, and the Commandment was directing and compelling Paul unto Righteousness. This place, in no uncertain terms, was the place wherein Paul had to make a decision, thus, the time gap. If Paul, by the compelling of the Commandment, applied his will to his body in order to overcome, the result would be motions of sins in the flesh by the Law, which would give occasion for the sin nature within his body to revive through these illegal actions. Nonetheless, now in the time gap, a decision had to be made, yet because Paul did not know where to place his Faith, he made the decision to engage the illegal combination of will and body. Thus, the sin nature revived and apprehended his body to manifest its evil desire *(Rom. 7:15, 23)*.

So then for us; it is when the Law reveals and the Commandment compels that we will enter the "time gap" as well. This is the place of decision where we must, against all odds, decide to move thoughts away from every carnal way we think is good, and place them into the Cross whereby Faith can be properly placed and determination resonates. Herein, our will becomes subservient to our decision and never has a chance to default into our body. This action of deciding where to place thought, desire, will, and Faith are all we can offer God, and we can rest in assurance that He will pick it up from there because He is ever aware of every thought and intention we have *(Psalms 139:23; Heb. 4:10-13)*.

The sin nature can only take occasion by the Commandment when we do not know what to do when we are in the time gap. Therein, our natural course of action will be to do something by combining our will and our body. Our walk will be either by Faith or by works – it cannot be both *(Rom. 7:2-3; Gal. 5:4)*. If it is by Faith, it will be by Faith placed in the Cross exclusively *(I Cor. 2:2)*. If it is by works, it will be through our carnal mind that does not know what to do with the compelling of the Commandment *(Rom. 8:7)*.

This is not directed to create judgment as long as the Cross is not foolishness *(I Cor. 1:17-18; 2:14; Phil. 3:18)*. The Message of the Cross, as it regards Sanctification after Salvation, was not known of by any man before the Apostle Paul was taught by the Revelation of Jesus Christ *(Rom. 1:1; 16:25; Gal. 1:11-12)*. Once Paul came to understand where his Faith was to be placed (that is, the Cross), he disclosed his struggle so that we can not only find comfort knowing our struggle is not uncommon, but also come to understand the same principles going on within and around each of us who are Saved. For this reason, the Apostle Paul begins the disclosure of his struggle in *Romans 7:8 – "But sin, taking occasion by the Commandment" –* unveiling that it is *"by the Commandment"* that sin is given the opportunity to revive if Faith does not remain in the Cross when compelled by the Commandment.

Romans 7:8 – Subject Scripture
But sin, taking occasion by the Commandment, **wrought in me all manner of concupiscence.** For without the Law sin was dead.

Romans 7:8 – Portion II
"…wrought in me all manner of concupiscence."

This portion of *Romans 7:8* deals with three words: wrought, manner, and concupiscence. The word *"wrought"* literally means "to work," the word *"manner"* is defined as "method," and *"concupiscence"* is defined as "evil desires." It may seem incomprehensible that the Commandment would play a part in causing this; nonetheless, this was the case for Paul until he came to understand how to manage the reality of what was actually going on within and around him. Until then, the sin nature took occasion by the Commandment and literally worked all methods to act out its evil desires, using Paul's physical members as the facilitator *(Rom. 7:15, 20)*.

Romans 7:8 – Subject Scripture
But sin, taking occasion by the Commandment, wrought in me all manner of concupiscence. **For without the Law sin was dead.**

Romans 7:8 – Portion III
"…For without the Law sin was dead."

Now, in the balance of *Romans 7:8*, it is important to understand what the Apostle Paul is disclosing. By Paul writing *"For without the Law sin was dead,"* the implication is not that the Law agitates the sin nature. We see qualification for this in *Roman 7:7 – "…I had not known sin but by the Law...*" – revealing that the function of the Law is to reveal, it does not coerce nor force us. It is the Commandment that can cause us to react, wherein the sin nature will revive, which is qualified in *Romans 7:9* – *"For I was alive without the Law once: but when the Commandment came, sin revived, and I died."*

One might argue this and say, "If Paul had not engaged the Law, the sin nature would not have revived; therefore, the Law agitated the sin nature." This statement would be incorrect on the mere biblical fact that the Law does not go away just because we received Salvation *(Rom. 7:25; I Cor. 9:21; Heb. 8:10-13; 10:16-17)*. By Paul writing *"For without the Law sin was dead,"* he is not implying that the Law was removed – it was not. The Law and the Commandment had now been forever changed through Jesus Christ, and Him Crucified *(Heb., Chptr 7)*. Therefore, now that Paul was born again, the ultimate problem was carnal thinking, it was how Paul chose to react to the compelling principle in the Commandment that caused sin to revive. This is, once again, qualified in *Romans 7:9* – *"For I was alive without the Law once: but when the Commandment came, sin revived, and I died."*

Before our Salvation, the Law worked wrath (that is, death) because we had no other resource than that of our carnal mind, willpower, and body. Therefore, because our conscience bore witness to the moral standard written in our heart, our efforts to live by it were manifested in our body, thereby creating wrath. Still, we continued trying harder. Nonetheless, ineffective in our efforts, we made laws unto ourselves, thereby creating more wrath for ourselves. This is qualified within *Chapters 2 through 4 of Romans*, and we can see that this is the plight of all unsaved Man due to the Fall of Adam.

This type of condition is not so for us who are Saved. Our old man is Crucified with Him, our husband of bondage is dead, and the body of sin incapacitated. Our sins have become Washed Away, and our heart has been circumcised with a circumcision made without hands. Because of this remarkable work, we now have the opportunity to live exclusively by Faith *(Rom. 7:25; Gal. 2:19-20; Heb. 10:38)*.

Therefore, the Apostle is saying that, if we do not take back up what the Lord has taken out of the way through His Cross, the sin nature will remain dead. Meaning, once again, for us who are Saved, the Law did not go away; however, the Law is no longer our schoolmaster, it is light. Still, if we try to touch it as to live by it, the sin nature will revive. If we do not touch the Law with our body, we will remain free, which is qualified by *"For without the Law sin was dead."* For this reason, the Apostle Paul writes – *"Wherefore, my Brethren, you also are become dead to the Law by the body of Christ; that you should be married to another, even to Him who is raised from the dead, that we should bring forth fruit unto God" (Rom. 7:4).* Thus, he who remains dead to the Law remains free from the dire effects of reviving the sin nature as a result of trying to live by the Law through means of the flesh. This is why Paul writes – *"for he that is dead is free from sin" (Rom. 6:7).*

When Paul tried to overcome by touching the Law with his body (that is, trying to live by the Law by means of his flesh) the sin nature revived. When the sin nature revived, he exhausted every way he knew to overcome this nature of evil, and he, even though he was Saved, found no means of overcoming through his flesh *(Rom. 7:18).* This was quite a dilemma for a man of God who knew so much about the Law and all that was in it. Nonetheless, not knowing of God's established way of victory when he first engaged this struggle, his only recourse was an ongoing physical reliance on the Law.

Although we may have an idea of what living by the Law looks like, the ways of engaging the Law through our flesh are most often not as obvious as we may think. Nevertheless, the associated consequences of the sin nature manifesting are countless when an individual tries to live by the Law. The manifestation of the sin nature can be as subtle as looming guilt, or as significant as alcohol abuse, sexual abuse, or any numbers of combinations that seem as if they are normal dysfunctions in society today. Though I have used the term "normal dysfunctions," I have done so due to the fact that society thinks that these types of manifestations can be dealt with through psychology and prescription drugs. This is not to say that there are not applications for prescription drugs; this is to say that, most often, the manifestation is a spiritual battle going on in the mind, whereby evil is dominating the human body. Therefore, in no uncertain terms, the only answer is the Cross.

It is exceptionally easy to engage the ways of our old man, that is, carnal thinking through the compelling of the Commandment. Once again, the carnal mind of our old man is intrinsically bound in the desire to live by the Law or any law. For this reason, now knowing the way of victory, the Apostle Paul warns us by writing – *"Beware lest any man spoil you through philosophy and vain deceit, after the tradition of men, after the rudiments of the world, and not after Christ" (Col. 2:8).*

As it was in the beginning, it is today. Satan can be subtle *(II Cor. 11:3)*, and the carnal mind can be deceptive; therefore, living by the Law can come in many ways and many forms. However, regardless of the form it appears in, the Law cannot be lived by through means of willpower and the physical body without reviving the sin nature. Remember, anytime our will supersedes a proper decision for our Faith, our will naturally defaults into our body, which evidences our will and not the Will of the Father.

Romans 7:9 – Subject Scripture

For I was alive without the Law once: but when the Commandment came, sin revived, and I died.

Romans 7:9 – Portion I
"For I was alive without the Law once…:"

This beginning statement reveals the horrible situation Paul found himself in due to not understanding the principle of the Commandment. This situation was altogether much different than the freedom and abundant joy he once experienced at Salvation, until he tried to overcome through his will. Many Christians today have revived the sin nature and do not know how to regain their freedom. I believe the greatest anguish for the Christian is the hopelessness that comes because of failure in his or her desperate efforts to secure victory. However, the Believer can take heart because it was the Will of the Father that Paul's experience was written out so they might understand what is actually going on within them as the way to freedom becomes known.

Romans 7:9 – Subject Scripture
For I was alive without the Law once: **but when the Commandment came,** sin revived, and I died.

Romans 7:9 – Portion II
"…but when the Commandment came…,"

This portion of *Romans 7:9*, *"but when"* reveals that it was not an option. It was a given that, when the Law revealed, *"the Commandment came,"* and with it a compelling unto Righteousness. Therefore, as it was with the Apostle Paul, it will be for us: when the Law reveals, the Commandment will come, and it is during this compelling of the Commandment that a decision will be made. This place is the time-gap wherein the decision that is made will either allow life, resulting in victory and freedom, or produce defeat, resulting in bondage and death *(Rom. 7:15, 23; Gal. 5:19-21).*

In regards to Paul, we do not know what Paul was struggling with, but because he did not know where to place his Faith (therein the time gap), he made the decision for his own will (i.e., his own strength). Although willpower working through the body seemed right, it was not. During this struggle, Paul had yet to understand that his body was dead in its capacity to deal with spiritual matters, and, therefore, by making the decision for his own strength, his Faith was in himself even though he believed in God.

Romans 7:9 – Subject Scripture
For I was alive without the Law once: but when the Commandment came, **sin revived,** and I died.

Romans 7:9 – Portion III
"...sin revived...,"

Here, *"sin"* is written in a literal translation as "the sin," thus speaking of the sin nature. Therefore, the phrase *"sin revived"* leaves no room for us to question whether or not this is a reality. Coming to understand this reality is a good thing, yet it does not mean that the sin nature is our focus – it is not to be. It means if we find we are struggling with sin, we can then come to understand that it is this evil nature making us do things we would never otherwise do *(Rom. 7:15, 20)*. Therein (and most importantly), it is hoped that the reality of this knowledge will bring us to understand that our will working in combination with our body cannot provide the power to overcome this nature of sin. This understanding will then lead us into a proper decision for the Cross wherein Faith will follow and determination will resonate in order to maintain this decision. All of this stays in the subjective position (i.e., intangible position). Here, in this place, the power of God will quicken our body *(Rom. 8:2, 11)*, our strength will not part of the equation, and God receives all the Glory *(Gal. 6:14)*.

Though the Christian may desire to place Faith in Jesus' Resurrection for victory, the Redemption of Man and the toppling of all principalities and powers took place on the Cross, through Jesus' death. The Resurrection was a result of this Victory *(I Pet. 1:18-20; Rev. 5:12; 7:14; 12:11; 13:8; 22:3-4, these verses are no way exhaustive)*. The Resurrection was never in doubt, and His Resurrection and Exaltation are highly significant indeed! Yet, once again, these were accomplished as a result of His triumphant and Atoning Sacrifice on the Cross through His death *(Col. 2:14-15; Heb., Chptrs 8-10; I John 3:8)*.

John 1:1 tells us Whom Christ Jesus is – *"In the beginning was the Word, and the Word was with God, and the Word was God." John 1:14* tells us how He came – *"And the Word was made flesh, and dwelt among us...." John 1:29* tells us why He came – *"The next day John sees Jesus coming unto him, and said, Behold the Lamb of God, which takes away the sin of the world." Colossians 2:14-15* tells us how He accomplished the purpose for which He came – *"[14]Blotting out the handwriting of Ordinances that was against us, which was contrary to us, and took it out of the way, nailing it to His Cross [15]And having spoiled principalities and powers, he made a shew of them openly, triumphing over them in it." John 19:30* tells us it was upon the Cross, through His death, the plan that had been foreordained in Eternity past was now finished – *"When Jesus therefore had received the vinegar, He said, It is finished: and he bowed his head, and gave up the ghost."*

Though these *verses* are an outline of significant Truths, these Truths cannot be separated. They begin with the Cross, and they end with the Cross – these Truths are the foundation of the Cross.

Therefore, our ongoing true growth in personal Sanctification hangs in the balance of understanding them as the anchor of our Faith.

The Devil will do all he can in order to cause us to place our Faith in anything other than the Cross *(Gal. 1:6-9; II Cor. 11:3-4)* because his ultimate goal is to destroy our life. However, if he cannot immediately destroy our life, his main push (as it has been from the beginning) is to cause us to believe a lie, whereby we misplace our Faith. If we do not break free from his lie, he knows we will become infective in our walk, wherein, given enough time, it is possible to shipwreck our Faith *(Gal. 5:4; Phil. 3:18; I Tim. 1:19)*. Though talking about sin, the nature of sin, and how to deal with sin is a difficult subject to face, it cannot be avoided because coming to understand the principles behind the struggle will bring clarity to the struggle. Without this clarity, we are left with a plethora of erroneous ideas as to what on earth is going on, and this is a truly exhaustive walk.

As I have previously stated, the Resurrection of Jesus Christ was able to take place as a result of the Sinless Offering of Himself, encompassing the Shedding of His Blood, His Vicarious Atonement, and triumphant death on the Cross. Therefore, though it may seem unusually odd to place our Faith in Jesus Christ, and Him Crucified, it is only through Faith in His Cross that we can remain dead to the dynamics of the sin nature, and alive in the likeness of His Resurrection *(Rom. 6:3-7)*. There is no other way for our Christian walk *(I Cor. 1:17-18; Gal. 5:17; 6:14)*. For this reason, the extraordinary disclosures by the Apostle Paul give us the opportunity to understand that the Cross is the only answer for our struggle – the only answer for sin. When we come to understand this, the substance of hope comes wherein Faith is renewed and, to us who believe, a life of victory, freedom and joy become the ongoing experience.

Paul's struggle began by looking back through the carnal mind of his old man and making the decision to live the way he used to live for God, which was by the Law *(Phil. 3:6)*. Therein, every motion in his flesh was by the Law and the sin nature revived. The sin nature revived because it had the legal right *(I Cor. 15:56; II Cor. 3:6; Gal. 3:10)*; the term "legal right" is proper because sin works through a Law depicted by the Apostle Paul as *"the Law of Sin and Death"* *(Rom. 7:23)*. Thus, *"sin revived,"* due to Paul breaching into the Law, shows us the guidelines that the sin nature works through.

Let us deal with the phrase "motions of sins" that will help us understand what it means to breach into the guidelines of the Law of Sin. The Apostle Paul writes – *"For when we were in the flesh, the motions of sins, which were by the Law, did work in our members to bring forth fruit unto death" (Rom. 7:5)*. Within *Romans 7:5* we can see that *"when we were in the flesh"* the *"motions of sins"* were *"by the Law,"* and the result was *"fruit unto death."* Although, by Paul writing *"For when we were in the flesh,"* we may think of our condition prior to Salvation. This is not the case. Functioning in the flesh is easy to do after we become Saved; it is simply done through carnal thinking *(Rom. 7:8-11)*. Meaning, anytime will and the physical body are combined as the means to deal with spiritual matters, the intention to make the combination is always by carnal thinking. This type of thinking always desires to live by the Law. When the application is followed through, the sin nature revives because the strength of it is the Law *(I Cor. 15:56)*.

The Apostle Paul is simply describing human willpower working in conjunction with the physical body, in regards to Sanctification, as functioning *"in the flesh."* However, when the power of the Cross becomes known and embraced by the Believer that is struggling with sin, he or she now understands the past tense – *"For when we were in the flesh."* The phrase *"motions of sins"* is an intriguing choice of words in regards to living by the Law because the nature of sin is like an enemy that is crouching, waiting for illegal motions – not much, just enough in the flesh that evidences the illegal application of will and body *(Psalms 10:9-10; Rom. 7:18, 21; 8:10)*. The result of this illegal application is *"motions of sins"* which evidences our efforts are by the Law, therein breaching the guidelines of the Law of Sin whereby *"sin revived."*

Romans 7:9 – Subject Scripture

For I was alive without the Law once: but when the Commandment came, sin revived, **and I died.**

Romans 7:9 – Portion IV
"…and I died."

Now in the balance of *Romans 7:9*, Paul's statement *"and I died,"* reveals the reality of the sin nature taking him captive after he had become born again. Paul did not die physically; he experienced the wages of sin, the sting of death *(I Cor. 15:56; II Cor. 3:6)*. This horrific experience simply took place because of his decision to engage the Law unlawfully, that is, to use his flesh due to the compelling of the Commandment *(Rom. 7:8)*. All of this may sound dramatic, but it is an understatement to those in bondage.

A dear friend of mine began to struggle with sin. However, the harder he tried to break free from it, the worse sin became and, after a while in this struggle, he became overwhelmed with condemnation. During this time, he was attending a church that taught if an individual had a problem it meant they were not working hard enough in their efforts to overcome. One afternoon sitting in a parking lot, my friend put a gun against his head and ended his life. For many, once the sin nature revives, the vile and heinous evil is indescribable and can seem unbearable. Today, there are men and women throughout the world in desperate need of freedom and the only answer to make them free is the simplicity that is in Christ. Who will bring this Message to them?

Romans 7:10 – Subject Scripture
And the Commandment, which was ordained to life, I found to be unto death.

Romans 7:10 – Portion I
"And the Commandment, which was ordained to life…,"

The Apostle Paul is finding that the Commandment is playing a part in how he deals with the sin nature. By stating *"And the Commandment, which was ordained to life,"* he is discerning that the Commandment compels unto Righteousness because it was ordained to life, yet this Righteousness is found only in God *(Rom. 10:4)*. Therefore, this expressed action (that is, compelling) directs to God exclusively. This is a much different ordination that is initiated by Man.

After the Lord God formed the man, Adam, and breathed into his nostrils the breath of life, He then put him in the Garden of Eden wherein he gave him liberty and freedom with the exception of just one command – *"16And the Lord God commanded the man, saying, Of every tree of the Garden you may freely eat: 17But of the Tree of the Knowledge of Good and Evil, you shall not eat of it: for in the day that you eat thereof you shall surely die" (Gen. 2:16-17)*.

This original command was ordained to life; it was ordained to keep Adam dependent on the Lord God for any need that he may have had in the face of temptation. Keep in mind, when God speaks, it is altogether different from when Man speaks. In other words, it is up to God as to the dispensation of time an event should last *(Genesis – Revelation)*. When He put this command forth, there was something very significant within it due to His overall love and plan for Man. This being the case, we should not underestimate the significant principle about the Commandment today, nor until we are changed from this mortality and put on immortality.

So then, by the Apostle Paul writing *"which was ordained to life,"* he is revealing just that – originating from God, the Commandment was ordained to life. Due to the Fall of Adam, the Law was written by God to reveal our condition, the Commandment was ordained by God to compel us unto Righteousness wherein we can get out of our condition. However, God does not force any direction upon us; that is, when the Law reveals and the Commandment compels, the choice is ours as to how we get out of or move on from our condition. Upon the compelling, if our Faith is placed in our efforts, the result will be failure, bondage and condemnation *(Rom. 7:5, 9, 15)*. If our Faith is placed in the Cross, self-efforts will not become part of the equation, and the result will be triumph, freedom, and joy due to the presence of the Holy Spirit *(Rom. 8:2, 11-17)*.

Now then, back to Adam. In Adam's temptation, he had the choice to turn to the Lord God for help or, through unbelief, doubt what the Lord God had said. When the command was given to Adam, Eve was not yet made. However, after God made Eve, the Devil used the faculties of the Serpent to deceive Eve, wherein she facilitated Adam's decision to eat from the Tree of the Knowledge of Good and Evil. Though Eve became deceived, Adam chose to Sin through unbelief *(I Tim. 2:13-14)*, and mankind deals with the consequences of his Sin each and every day.

For we who are born again, we now have a type of Adam's walk prior to his Fall. Yes, an altogether different kind of walk due to the consequences of the Fall, but nonetheless a type of walk as Adam had due to the magnificent events that took place within us upon our Salvation. Thus, we now have liberty and freedom in a way as Adam had before his Fall. Though this experience is limited in the sense that we know there is so much more, nonetheless, even in this limited degree, this is the experience. Now, through the events of the Cross *(Col. 2:14-15; Heb. 7:18)* we have the Commandment *"which was ordained to life"* directing and compelling us to the Lord God for any help we may need. Therefore, if we will refrain from believing a lie when temptation comes and, instead, place our Faith in Whom Jesus Christ Is, and all that He has done to Redeem us from the consequences of Adam's Sin, God will help us overcome the world, the flesh, and the Devil.

The enticements of the Devil present themselves in a seemingly tantalizing array of colors, yet all of them are embedded in his original design: to bring a fall in your life and mine. There are those that appear good for knowledge, those that appear pleasurable to look at, and those that appeal to the appetite. Yet, when eaten, regardless of the duration of time, the result is death. Although the child of God is aware of most of them, the Devil has made dealing with sin seem so complicated when it is not. Knowing this, the Apostle Paul wrote – *"But I fear, lest by any means as the serpent beguiled Eve through his subtilty, so your minds should be corrupted from the simplicity that is in Christ" (II Cor. 11:3).*

The simplicity that is in Christ is the Cross: there are no complexities or performances, simply sincere Faith from a believing heart placed in the Cross gives the Spirit of Life the liberty to help us effectually overcome and grow in holiness. So when the Law reveals, and the Commandment *"which was ordained to life"* compels, will it be a decision of performance resulting in motions of sins in the flesh, which are by the Law, or a decision to place Faith in the Cross, believing the Lord God is able to effectually help?

Romans 7:10 – Subject Scripture

And the Commandment, which was ordained to life, **I found to be unto death.**

Romans 7:10 – Portion II
"...I found to be unto death."

The Word of God is so remarkable. How can that which God has ordained to life cause death? Whenever the things of God are mismanaged, it is the result of the carnal mind. Thank God for His endless mercy and love while we learn to discern.

The Apostle Paul's statement *"I found to be unto death"* is the paradox of flesh trying to manage spiritual matters, and the Commandment most certainly has a spiritual component. The Commandment is not bad; it was how Paul chose to respond to the compelling principle of the Commandment. Paul wanted to do good, and he wanted to overcome, but he had not yet known the way of Sanctification when he first engaged this struggle. As a result, he was unable to discern what to do when the Commandment came. Without this discernment, his only resource was his own abilities that brought only death.

Romans 7:11 – Subject Scripture

For sin, taking occasion by the Commandment, deceived me, and by it slew me.

Romans 7:11 – Portion I
"For sin, taking occasion by the Commandment...,"

In a literal translation, *"For sin"* is written "For the sin." Once again, this is speaking of the nature of sin, that which we were conceived in and born with upon natural childbirth *(Psalms 51:5;*

Rom. 5:12). When the Apostle Paul came to realize that it was this nature of sin *"taking occasion by the Commandment,"* he must have been astonished. Moreover, the way in which the Apostle has repetitively displayed the principle of the Commandment within *verses 8-11*, emphasizes the importance of coming to understand the dynamics of sin finding its way by the Commandment. For this reason, our decision to overcome sin must be embraced, and this should go without saying. However, our will must be subservient (i.e., come in second place) to a decision to set Faith in the Cross.

When our will takes second place, determination resonates, whereby all of our power remains in the subjective position (i.e., intangible realm), thus circumventing the use of our body. This is why determination is meant for Faith; our determination is the subjective tool that (when used properly) keeps Faith away from our body and, by doing so, maintains it in the Cross *(I Cor. 2:2; I Tim. 6:12)*. If we apply our will to our body and motion to perform in any effort to overcome in any capacity, the sin nature – *"taking occasion by the Commandment"* – will literally apprehend us.

Though we describe willpower as if it were an isolated attribute with a handle, it is not. As a matter of fact, it may seem rather ambiguous in many ways; it is affected by the decisions we make and, of course, the headquarters for decisions is in our mind *(Rom. 7:25)*. None of this is a vast mystery; very simply, it is up to each of us to embrace the Truth of the Cross. When the Truth is embraced, it is done by making the decision. Maintaining the continued embracement is an ongoing and mindful choice that simply turns into determination due to the many obstacles that want to detour us.

Make the mindful decision about the Cross wherein Faith will follow; then, as the Law reveals and the Commandment comes, will is not applied to the body. If this decision is made, determination keeps the decision and does not manifest as willpower in the body.

Thus, will takes second position behind determination for the proper decision. Only a decision for the Cross can do this. If the proper decision is not made, will defaults into the body as willpower, and, in no uncertain terms, the sin nature will be *"taking occasion by the Commandment."*

R**omans** 7:11 – Subject Scripture
For sin, taking occasion by the Commandment, **deceived me,** and by it slew me.

R**omans** 7:11 – Portion II
"…deceived me…,"

This portion of *verse 11* is quite staggering to think about for two reasons. First, the Apostle Paul is revealing the nature of sin. Second, he is revealing that this nature works through his efforts of "good." We will come to see this as we make our way through his struggle. For now, as it regards this portion of *verse 11*, in Paul's journey to know the truth, he desperately desired to overcome every obstacle. He knew the good that he thought he could do, but he could not find anything within his flesh that gave him the ability *(Rom. 7:18; 8:10)*. This was most likely extraordinarily difficult for the Apostle to understand at first because he wanted to do good, but he could not do what he wanted in what he thought was the right way *(Gal. 5:17)* – he had to do it God's Way *(Rom. 6:7; 7:25; Gal. 2:19-20)*.

In the initial beginnings of Paul's struggle with the sin nature, he had not yet received nor been taught by the Revelation of Jesus Christ. Therefore, Paul was without the knowledge for growing in Sanctification. Due to this position he found himself in, he was without the discerning capacity to manage the compelling principle of the Commandment, and thus without the knowledge that the sin nature revived when he used his body for spiritual matters. Furthermore, and more than likely, Paul did not yet understand that the Commandment was compelling him, accentuating his desire to do good. Nevertheless, now compelled by the Commandment, he was deceived in thinking he could resist temptation and restrain the sin nature by his own power *(Rom. 8:7)*; so, the sin nature revived. For this reason, he writes – *"For sin, taking occasion by the Commandment, deceived me."*

Romans 7:11 – Subject Scripture
For sin, taking occasion by the Commandment, deceived me, **and by it slew me.**

Romans 7:11 – Portion III
"...and by it slew me."

In the balance of *verse 11*, this portion of Paul's statement reveals once again that it was by the Commandment that the sin nature revived and, whereupon reviving, he died *(Rom. 7:9)*. This is an unusual thing to wrap our thinking around, but, as Christians, we must understand that the Commandment originated from God, and therefore has a life ordained purpose, as does the Law. However, the unsaved are not spiritually discerned, and cannot understand this because their carnal mind sees both the Law and the Commandment as one set of rigid rules, yet, as we are coming to see, they are not. For all of us who are Saved, the Law is a spiritual light that reproofs and instructs the way of life *(Prov. 6:23)*, and the Commandment, originating from God, was ordained to life *(Rom. 7:10)* and therein compels us unto Righteousness *(Matt. 22:36-40; I Tim. 1:5)*. For this reason, we must understand all of this is unseen, intangible, and we cannot use the tangible to utilize them. Although each of us has

Faith, desire, and will, if the Cross is not maintained, regardless of the circumstances, as the object of our Faith, the physical body will become the default instrument of use. Therein, every effort for triumph and freedom will be motions of sins in our flesh, which will be by the Law *(Rom. 7:5)*.

Romans 7:12 – Subject Scripture
Wherefore the Law is Holy, and the Commandment Holy, and just, and good.

Romans 7:12 – Portion I
"Wherefore the Law is Holy…,"

As we begin *verse 12*, the Apostle Paul makes it clear that the Law originated from God, and therefore *"the Law is Holy."* For some, the Law tends to their upbringing, and God designed it this way for this reason, for the unsaved. The Law is a schoolmaster that brings them to Christ that they might be justified by Faith *(Gal. 3:24-25)*. For we who are Saved, it is a spiritual navigation component: a spiritual light that reproofs and instructs the way of life *(Prov. 6:23)*. As stated, the Law reveals the intangible because the Law is the truth *(Psalms 119:142)*, revealing every way of sin on the outside and within us *(Psalms 119:101, 104, 110, 115, 126)*.

The Law reveals everything, including thoughts that are contrary to the Word of God and the Ways of God. This is so that we do not fall prey to the deceitfulness of sin or the nature of it. However, the Law is without coercion; the profound and intended purpose of the Law for us who are Saved is to reveal sin and instruct the way of life. It does not force us to overcome, it reveals. The quality of the Law is Holy *(Rom. 7:12)*, the principles and function of the Law are spiritual *(Rom. 7:14)* and are at work every moment of every day to instruct the way of life, and also reveal sin and the nature of it. This shows the Holiness of the Law *(Rom. 7:7)*.

Romans 7:12 – Subject Scripture
Wherefore the Law is Holy, **and the Commandment Holy, and just, and good.**

Romans 7:12 – Portion II
"...and the Commandment Holy, and just, and good."

The Apostle is revealing to us that just as the Law originated from God, the Commandment also originated from God *"and the Commandment is Holy, and just, and good."* The Commandment is *"Holy"* because it was ordained *to* life by God and holds the Law just as a lamp holds light *(Prov. 6:23; Rom. 7:10)* and, as Christians, we are holding both of them within our heart and mind *(Rom. 7:25; Heb. 8:10-13; 10:16-17)*.

The Commandment is *"just"* because it directs us to God. This function of the Commandment is an asset to us because it compels us unto Righteousness, yet, once again, this Righteousness is provided in Christ alone *(Rom. 10:4)*. The beginning of the Commandment compels unto Righteousness *(Matt. 22:36-40)*, and the end of the Commandment is love *(I Tim. 1:5)*, and Faith works by love *(Gal. 5:6)*. We have love, God does not – He is Love *(I John 4:16)*. It was in His Love that He openly and Vicariously Gave Himself for all mankind, and because Jesus Christ kept all of the Commandments, our Faith must find rest in Him and what He has done on the Cross so that the Righteousness of the Law remains fulfilled in us *(Rom. 7:25; 8:4; I Cor. 2:2)*.

Thus, the Commandment has a beginning – to look to Christ – and an end – to look to Him Crucified. For this reason, Christ is the end of the Law for Righteousness to everyone who believes *(Rom. 10:4)*. The Commandment is *"good,"* but not the "good" from the Tree of the Knowledge of Good and Evil. Good and evil from the Tree is a common dichotomy resulting in either full blown evil or full blown good without the need for God. No man, woman, boy, or girl can do good without God. Therefore, the *"good"* of the Commandment is from God.

Romans 7:13 – Subject Scripture

Was then that which is good made death unto me? God forbid. But sin, that it might appear sin, working death in me by that which is good; that sin by the Commandment might become exceeding sinful.

Romans 7:13 – Portion I
"Was then that which is good made death unto me? God forbid...."

The Apostle Paul begins *verse 13* by presenting a rhetorical question that he quickly follows up by answering, *"God forbid."* Paul is revealing an amazing aspect here. Prior to coming to know the way of victory, he was unable to place his Faith properly *(Rom. 7:8)*. Moreover, not knowing the principle of the Commandment, his only resource was that of his will working within his mortal body, resulting in death *(Rom. 7:5, 9, 15, 23)*. Not so as he wrote this. What was once unknown, and thus unmanageable (the compelling of the Commandment), is now a known, manageable asset, an essential principle compelling him unto Righteousness *(Rom. 10:4)*. Therefore, *"God forbid"* that what has been ordained for life should now be unto death.

Romans 7:13 – Subject Scripture
Was then that which is good made death unto me? God forbid. **But
sin, that it might appear sin, working death in me by that which
is good;** that sin by the Commandment might become exceeding
sinful.

Romans 7:13 – Portion II
**"…But sin, that it might appear sin,
working death in me by that which is good…;"**

"But sin, that it might appear sin" is written in a literal translation
as "But the sin, that it might appear the sin." Once again, this is
speaking of the sin nature. The Apostle Paul is presenting a truth:
when he desperately desired to overcome sin, he found he had
aroused the nature of sin due to his efforts of good. Therefore, the
Apostle Paul saw the sin nature for what it was and understood the
diabolical nature of it, and writes, *"working death in me by that which
is good."* This is absolutely paramount for us to understand. Even
though Paul knew how to live by the Law because of his upbringing
(Phil. 3:4-6), when he applied what he knew about the Law, the way he
was formally accustomed, the sin revived and brought death *(Rom.
7:9; II Cor. 3:6)*. That is, although his intentions were good, when he
thought of the good to do and moved to accomplish it, death worked
in him through his good efforts.

The Tree of the Knowledge of Good and Evil in the midst of the
Garden was never to be eaten from. Though we know we were not
meant to have the knowledge of evil, we were never meant to have
the knowledge of good from the Tree – we were created to know God.
It is with the knowledge of good that we continue to think we can
"do it" when we cannot *(Rom. 7:18)*. When we get hold of this, we
will see that Man simply thinks he can fix it, whatever "it" may be.

Man will always try to "do it" without God, believing his efforts are good. This is so deeply embedded within the human race because it is the sin nature trying to deceive through good from the Tree so it can revive and bring death *(Rom. 7:21 – NKJV)*.

This does not negate our responsibility toward good works. Yes, we are to do good works, but it must be through sound Doctrine *(Titus 2:7)*. Meaning, when one functions within that form of Doctrine, good works through the Spirit always follow. Therefore, because it is vital for us to understand what that form of Doctrine is, we will be getting involved in this further in the book.

This statement *"working death in me by that which is good"* clearly reveals that there is literally nothing in us (that is, in our flesh) to perform the good we want to do in trying to resist or restrain the sin nature and thus live for God. When we engage any method to live for God apart from Faith in the Cross, we are literally reaching back through the carnal mind of our old man and engaging the Law in some unlawful way to live by it.

We are to remain dead to the ways of our old man because, though our old man is Crucified, his ways are remembered through our carnal mind *(Rom. 7:5, 9, 14)*. His ways always desire to use our physical body in a quick ditch effort to resist sin, restrain it, or attain some idea of holiness. Although these means and methods have the appearance of godliness, all of them deny the power of the Holy Spirit *(II Tim. 3:5)*.

The Apostle Paul had become freed from the body of sin at Salvation. However, sometime in his walk, his efforts (in his desire to overcome and grow) were by the Law; therein, the sin nature revived, yet Paul did not give up on God. He knew something was amiss. In seeking God, God taught him the way of Sanctification *(Gal. 1:11-12)*, which is found through Jesus Christ *(Rom. 7:25)*.

As Paul, we are born again; we are in the Spirit *(Rom. 8:9)*. All things have become new *(II Cor. 5:17)*. Though the ways of our old man are still known, we are to be renewed in the spirit of our mind by putting on the new man *(I Cor. 2:2, 16; Phil. 2:5)* who, after God, is created in Righteousness and true holiness *(Eph. 4:23-24)*. Yet, as Christians, we must come to understand that the new man's way of thinking comes from the Mind of Christ that we now have, and the Mind of Christ always had the Cross before it *(Matt. 26:39; Phil. 2:5-8)*.

Romans 7:13 – Subject Scripture
Was then that which is good made death unto me? God forbid. But sin, that it might appear sin, working death in me by that which is good; **that sin by the Commandment might become exceeding sinful.**

Romans 7:13 – Portion III
"...that sin by the Commandment might become exceeding sinful."

Once again, *"that sin"* is speaking directly of the sin nature. The phrase *"by the Commandment"* clearly reveals *"that sin"* had taken occasion *"by the Commandment."* The word *"by"* actually reveals the expressed action of the Commandment, that which compelled Paul unto Righteousness, and therein placing him in the time gap. Once in the time gap, sin was able to take occasion *"by"* the Commandment because, through the compelling, Paul made the decision to overcome by combining his will and his body.

The phrase *"might become exceeding sinful"* is speaking of the heinous evil residing in our members, revealed by that which is good (that is, the Commandment), which was ordained to life. Only that which originates from God can reveal the scope of implications made here.

The Law reveals, but the Law reveals without coercion – it does not force us *(Prov. 6:23; Rom. 3:20; 7:7)*. Unlike the Law, the Commandment compels us unto Righteousness. It is during this compelling, if we are not careful, that we will try to live for God by doing good in our self-efforts. However, regardless of the good effort (and there are endless arrangements), the efforts were by the Law, whereby the sin nature will revive, revealing that it found its way through that which is good, showing us – *"that sin by the Commandment might become exceeding sinful."*

For example, as Christians, we have the high moral standard within us in which God desires us to live by, and the Commandment compels us towards it *(Matt. 22:37; I John 3:22-24)*. Still, we cannot live for God by our human strength or even superior intellect *(Rom. 7:18; 8:10)*, but because we so deeply desire to overcome and live for God, we try and try in our human strength and intellect and fail again and again. Why?

It is most difficult for us to refrain from trying to overcome in our power and literally depend on God when the Commandment compels us unto Righteousness. Nevertheless, full dependency on God must be learned because, most often, the good we may think we can do will be the sin nature trying to find a way through the guise of good. This shows us *"that sin by the Commandment might become exceeding sinful."* These implications are a literal reality that will be much easier to see as we approach *Romans 7:21*.

Romans 7:14 – Subject Scripture

For we know that the Law is spiritual: but I am carnal, sold under sin.

Romans 7:14 – Portion I
"For we know that the Law is spiritual...:"

The Apostle Paul begins *verse 14* by allowing us to understand *"that the Law is spiritual"* because it originated from God *(Ex. 24:12)*. In addition, the Law is Holy *(Rom. 7:12)*; therefore, unlike any law that Man has created or will create, this Law has Holy principles of the intangible. For the unsaved it is their schoolmaster, but for us who are Saved it is light unto our path, instructing the way of life.

Romans 7:14 – Subject Scripture
For we know that the Law is spiritual: **but I am carnal,** sold under sin.

Romans 7:14 – Portion II
"...but I am carnal...,"

By the Apostle Paul writing this, he does not relieve himself of the responsibility to properly discern and come to understand the spiritual principles of the Law, nor any other spiritual principle going on within or around him. The Apostle uses the conjunction *"but"* because he had, as we all do, a propensity toward the carnal mind, *but* the carnal mind cannot discern spiritual principles, nor is it subject to them *(Rom. 8:7)*.

The Apostle is letting us know that, although he is mortal with propensities toward carnal thinking, Faith has come *(Gal. 3:24-25)* and he must choose to put off the old man by putting on the new man, wherein he will take on the Mind of Christ *(I Cor. 2:16; Eph. 4:24; Phil. 2:5)*. This frame of mind is vastly different from that of carnal thinking. The great Apostle Paul is not only letting us know of his humanity, but he is also letting us know not to excuse nor allow carnal propensities to get in the way of coming to understand spiritual principles.

Romans 7:14 – Subject Scripture
For we know that the Law is spiritual: but I am carnal, **sold under sin.**

Romans 7:14 – Portion III
"...sold under sin."

Now in the balance of *verse 14*, by the Apostle Paul writing *"sold under sin,"* he makes it clear that every human born, with the exception of Jesus, was sold under sin, is sold under sin, and will be sold under sin when born *(Psalms 51:5; Rom. 5:12)*. Here as well, a literal translation writes "sold under the sin," which directly references the sin nature. Only upon our Salvation into Christ does this nature of sin within our members become incapacitated and we become freed from its grip *(Rom. 6:6-7)*.

The Apostle Paul is unveiling to each of us that there is a propensity to lean on the carnal mind, which can cause a detrimental reliance on the Law even though we are born again. This type of propensity literally gives occasion for the sin nature to revive *(Rom. 7:8)*. Once the sin nature is revived, it captivates the mind and causes us to act out its evil desires regardless of our willpower, as we will come to see in the following Scriptures. It must be noted that, though our willpower is woefully insufficient in combination with our body in regards to dealing with the sin nature, our determination is more than sufficient to move our Faith into the Cross *(I Cor. 2:2)*, wherein we will be made free from the sin nature. This is the Law of the Spirit of Life in Christ Jesus making us free from the Law of Sin and Death as the Cross becomes the anchor of our Faith *(Rom. 7:25; 8:2; I Cor. 2:2)*.

Romans 7:15 – Subject Scripture
For that which I do I allow not: for what I would, that do I not; but what I hate, that do I.

Romans 7:15 – Portion I
"For that which I do I allow not…:"

In the previous *verse (Rom. 7:14)*, Paul introduced the reality of carnal propensities even though we are born again, wherein our carnal mind has the potential of viewing the Mosaic Law as a set of rules. If this view is walked within, it leaves no other resources to live by other than that of our will applied to our body, resulting in the sin nature taking occasion by the Commandment *(Rom. 7:8-11)*.

This beginning portion of *verse 15* gives us an open view into the results of functioning in carnal propensities in regards to spiritual matters. Very simply, this type of propensity is "self" trying to live by the Law and, remember, this can be ever so subtle and have the appearance of good, as if overcoming and living for God would seem to be the result of the method. Although unusual language is used in this portion of *verse 15*, it is better understood in the New King James Translation, which writes, "For what I am doing, I do not understand." The Apostle Paul is saying that he is doing the very thing he does not want to do and does not understand why he is doing it. Thus, he is making it clear that he is now under the direct influence and dominion of the sin nature, and he does not understand why.

Before Salvation, we gave little care about such discernment. However, this changes upon receiving Salvation; everything becomes new, and our desire to grow in holiness comes from a pure heart and a cleansed conscience. After Salvation, we do not want to sin and, when we do, we do not understand why. Yet this goes much deeper because, in order to sin, sin has to be seen and then the decision has to be made to engage it. Once engaged, whatever the sin was and regardless of the time frame until the sting of death comes, upon the sting of death we do not understand why we engaged sin in the first place, and this place can cause great turmoil because we love the Lord.

Can it be said that we actually wanted to sin? The Apostle Paul explains this paradox in *verse 21* wherein he indeed gives us a truly remarkable answer as we will come to see. Nonetheless, as it regards the action of sin, there is not one of us who has done something we wish so badly we did not do. For this reason, the Apostle Paul is not only disclosing his personal struggle, but also the principles regarding what was actually happening to him as a Christian when he went through this struggle.

As stated, this disclosure is not only to let us know that our struggle is not uncommon, but Paul is also unveiling that the overall dynamics of this struggle cannot be dealt with through our carnal mind. Why? Our carnal mind desires to rely on resources of our will working through the resources of our physical body. However, the Apostle does not leave us here; though we may vaguely see these principles now, they precede his magnificent and remarkable victory *(Rom. 7:25; 8:1-2)*.

Therefore, likewise for us, when we come to embrace the way of victory, the principles of good and evil are much easier to discern because of the presence and teaching of the Holy Spirit due to our Faith being properly placed *(Heb. 5:14; I John 2:27)*. So do not give up, continue to press forward!

Romans 7:15 – Subject Scripture
For that which I do I allow not: **for what I would, that do I not;** but
what I hate, that do I.

Romans 7:15 – Portion II
"…for what I would, that do I not…;"

We are again viewing unusual language. Nevertheless, by Paul
stating *"for what I would"* he is saying that he wants to overcome.
The New King James Translation writes "for what I will to do,"
revealing a better view of Paul's will. Paul's desire was right *(Rom.
7:22)*; however, while Paul was in this struggle with the sin nature
he did not know that his will was to be subservient to his proper
decision for Faith's resting place, wherein determination would
have resonated and backed up his proper decision. Until he came to
understand this fundamental truth, he placed his will in his body,
and this was an illegal combination, qualified by *Romans 8:10 – "And
if Christ be in you, the body is dead because of sin…."*

Our body is not to be used to deal with spiritual matters of
Sanctification. If one thinks about it, how can it be? Why would we
try to overcome spiritual darkness with our physical body? Yet we
try and try and fail and fail.

As we move on in this portion of the *Romans 7:15*, by Paul stating
"that I do not" he is revealing that he sees what he wants to do, but it
is continually out of his reach and capacity to do it. The New King
James Translation writes "that I do not practice." Each one of us
wants to overcome as well, but inevitably we find that we cannot in
our own power.

151

Romans 7:15 – Subject Scripture

For that which I do I allow not: for what I would, that do I not; **but what I hate, that do I.**

Romans 7:15 – Portion III
"...but what I hate, that do I."

Here, in the balance of *Romans 7:15*, by Paul making this statement, we need no further language explanation. It is quite clear that he is doing the very thing that he did not want to do, and we can assess that, by Paul using the descriptive word *"hate,"* he was dealing with condemnation in his failing to secure victory and freedom. For this reason, once he came to understand the way of victory, the first description of his victory deals with condemnation – *"THERE is therefore now no condemnation to them which are in Christ Jesus, who walk not after the flesh, but after the Spirit" (Rom. 8:1).* If this is the case, in regards to Paul dealing with condemnation, he knows that condemnation closes the prison door because it causes the carnal mind to flourish in exponential efforts by the Law, thus closing off the view to the ways of God *(Rom. 8:7).*

Though there are many dangerous facets to the carnal mind, one of them is that the carnal mind, in regard to condemnation, can be all-consuming if we do not know the way of victory. The first danger of this type of consumption is that condemnation can cause us to find other methods to come out from under its oppression. Thus, our search for other methods can be all consuming and lifelong. The second danger of consumption is that condemnation can become a deep and crippling handicap by stopping us, locking us in a prison, consuming our hope. Once the carnal mind can flourish as it does with condemnation, it can (to a greater degree) cause us to give up hope, whereby we can lose our way in Christ. Although it is most often in desperation that we find the truth (which was most likely Paul's experience), we must never give up in our journey to know the truth, wherein we will find true and lasting freedom.

When we are under condemnation, it is a horrible place for us to be. This condemnation is due to evaluating the failure against the Law and not assessing the failure with forgiveness by looking unto Jesus Christ, and what He has done by fulfilling the Law and Satisfying its Penalty in our place on the Cross *(Rom. 7:4-6; 8:3-4; Col. 2:13-15)*. Therefore, condemnation is always the result of making this subtle unlawful assessment. Our assessment should always be an examination to see if we are in the Faith *(II Cor. 13:5)*.

Our examination may look like this: As I have taken the time to look at my walk, I realize that I was Saved and delivered from the Law by the body of Christ – He has done it All. Therefore, I was made free, but as I look back I can see that the problems began when I tried to make myself better; I tried to live by the Law because I certainly did not feel like this when I received Salvation. I can see that, when I tried, everything changed and the detrimental effects began to happen. Now I can see that the harder I tried, the worse things became, and condemnation most definitely seemed to increase. So then, if condemnation reveals that I am living by the Law in some way, then I must be living by the Law in one degree or the other regardless of how subtle my engagement.

Although I feel as though these effects are unbearable, I believe the Bible is True and freedom will come as I move my thoughts into the Cross and away from my failures. I realize this is a difficult decision, but I now know it is the only decision that will bring me true, lasting freedom. I now realize that I will always fail in my own self-efforts when imposed within spiritual matters, and sometimes I may fail miserably beyond what I think God can redeem. Yet I will take heart! I know for sure that my justification was not partially done, it was accomplished on the basis of Faith alone apart from anything I did except believe, repent, and confess. Therefore, I know the only requirement for my Sanctification is to believe in Jesus Christ, and Him Crucified. Right now, I have determined that this is going to be my manner of walking with God, and I will not be moved until the Spirit of Life in Christ Jesus has made me free and brought me victory, peace, and joy.

So far within portion three of *Romans 7:15*, we have expounded upon *"but what I hate,"* so let us now look into the balance of this portion – *"that I do."* By the Apostle Paul writing *"that I do,"* he is disclosing that he is doing the very thing that he hates. However, by Paul making this disclosure, he is revealing that the sin nature can once again have dominion over our mind and body *(Rom. 7:9, 20, 23)*. Although the statements dealing with the sin nature have been brought to light and stated much, this reality can be easily overlooked. We can find ourselves perhaps distantly looking at the horrors we see on the news as people do things so horrific to themselves or others every moment of every day that defies human comprehension, yet we have the same evil residing within our physical members (regarding the sin nature). As we peer upon their actions produced by this evil nature (some unsaved by demonic possession), we believe we would never do such. However, when the discovery of God's established way of victory is made, there is then discernment, understanding, and clarity as to why Jesus said – *"Father, forgive them; for they know not what they do..." (Luke 23:34).*

Romans 7:16 – Subject Scripture undivided
If then I do that which I would not, I consent unto the Law that it is good.

Once again, the language is unusual. Nonetheless, by the Apostle Paul stating *"If then I do that which I would not,"* he is saying, "If he does what he does not want to do." Therein, this reveals that, whatever it was that he was doing, it was greater than his willpower to resist. By the Apostle writing *"I consent unto the Law that it is good,"* he is simply stating that he agrees that the Law is good by revealing the nature of sin behind the action of sin.

Romans 7:17 – Subject Scripture undivided
Now then it is no more I that do it, but sin that dwells in me.

Romans 7:17 is a profound and staggering *verse*. The revelation that caused Paul to write *"Now then it is no longer I that do it, but sin that dwells in me"* must have been epic on so many levels. However, this revelation can only be seen by the spiritual mind of the mature *(I Cor., Chptrs 2-3)*. Otherwise, those functioning in no other resource than that of their carnal mind would run with this as an excuse. It may be difficult to grasp that the sin nature is within the physical members of our mortal body *(Rom. 7:23)*, yet if the world could understand this fundamental fact, the unanswered complexities of pain, sin, death, wars, divisions, and hate in the world could be reduced to one single culprit – the Devil – who is awaiting the ultimate enforcement of his defeat and eternal doom *(Rev. 20:14-15)*.

The Christian should never use this *verse* as an excuse, which is why it is so very important to hate even the stain of sin. It will only be the truly mature Christians who will so desperately desire to live for God in holiness that will be able to discern between the principles of good and the principles of evil *(Heb. 5:14)*. It is because they have moved forward in their desire to overcome that they have engaged this same struggle as the Apostle Paul did. Yet because of their desire to overcome, God will teach them His established way of victory just as He taught Paul *(I John 2:27)*.

Romans 7:18 – Subject Scripture
For I know that in me (that is, in my flesh,) dwells no good thing:
for to will is present with me; but how to perform that which is good
I find not.

<h3 align="center">**R**omans 7:18 – Portion I
**"For I know that in me (that is, in my
flesh,) dwells no good thing…:"**</h3>

The Apostle Paul begins *verse 18* by unveiling an irrefutable fact,
one that we should ponder. In our pondering, we as well can come
to this conclusion and begin our journey in how the Sanctification
process is truly walked out. Once the Apostle Paul came to understand
how to walk it out, he gives us great insight in *Romans 8:10 – "And if
Christ be in you, the body is dead because of sin; but the Spirit is life
because of Righteousness."* A literal translation writes: "the body is
dead because of the sin," which, once again, directly addresses the
sin nature.

The reason our body is now dead is because the strength of
the sin nature is the Law *(I Cor. 15:56)*. Upon Salvation, our body
was rendered supernaturally useless so that it would not be used
in spiritual matters, thus not giving occasion to the sin nature.
Conversely, when we use our body in spiritual matters (any form of
Sanctification), it not only evidences the unlawful engagement of the
Law, but also revives the sin nature. Therefore, our body is rendered
dead upon Salvation. This is a paradox, yet we can view this reality
by looking into the conditions of pre- and post- Salvation.

Prior to Salvation, the sin nature was kept alive by our old man
and his carnal mind that were intrinsically bound in efforts of
trying to keep the Law through means of our intangible willpower
in combination with our physical body. Though we were unable to

discern these principles, this was in fact the way it was, and willpower was our only resource to live a good life. However, (in one way or the other) we were unable to live up to the demands of a good life, and so we created other Laws to avoid the moral standard of the Law. More than likely, we created very subtle laws, yet, they were laws nonetheless *(Rom. 2:14-15)*. With no other way to live free from this condition, we remained under the overwhelming reign of the sin nature because the strength of the sin nature is the Law.

Upon Salvation, our old man is Crucified, the sin nature incapacitated, and our body rendered dead so that it does not give occasion to the sin nature. Thus, we are no longer to use our willpower and body as the resource to live for God. Instead, our determination maintains Faith in the Cross which gives the Holy Spirit the latitude to effectually quicken our mortal body to live for God *(Rom. 8:2, 11, 13-14)*. Maintaining the proper decision through determination becomes a vital aspect in the good fight of Faith *(I Cor. 2:2; I Tim. 6:12; II Tim. 4:7)*.

There is literally nothing in our flesh that can be used as a viable resource in our desire to grow in Sanctification and thereby live for God. Why? The scope of Man's current condition came through the Fall of Adam. Therefore, the scope of walking through this condition before Eternity is entered into is one in which we must learn dependency upon God.

This is a paradox. We are born again. We are in the spirit and yet we, for the time being, live in a mortal body we cannot utilize to live for God. Nonetheless, for this reason, God has given us His Cross through which the Holy Spirit has the latitude to work within our lives as Jesus Christ, and Him Crucified, becomes the object of our Faith *(Rom. 7:25; Gal. 2:19-20; 6:14)*.

As it was for Salvation, it is for Sanctification. You see, when we were in sin and unable to come to God *(Rom. 3:10)*, we simply responded to His Love, and on the foundation of simply believing in Him, and what He has done on the Cross, we repented, confessed, and He Saved us. We did nothing to receive Salvation except repent, believe, and confess *(Rom. 10:9-10)*, yet after Salvation we come to think we can handle matters in our own strength without realizing what we are doing *(Rom. 7:8-18)*. This is because of the knowledge of "good" that we attained due to Adam's decision to partake of the Tree of the Knowledge of Good and Evil.

Yes, we are born again, and we speak in other tongues due to the indwelling of the Holy Spirit. Still, this has never changed our complete inability to restrain the sin nature and attain holiness in our human power. We simply do not have (nor will we ever have) the ability we think we have while we are in this temporal mortal body. Even when we take on immortality we still, though wonderfully made, did not coexist with God, we had a beginning – God does not. The only reason we can look around and perhaps see some semblance of controlled sanity in the world is because of God's Grace, without which unimaginable destruction would cave in upon all mankind.

We should not be fooled; the magnitude of Adam's Fall has left us in a position of moral bankruptcy beyond our current comprehension *(Rom. 3:9-20)* because it is the "good" that the world is running on and, for the time being, Satan is the god of this world *(Gen. 3:5-7; II Cor. 4:4)*. Though we are born again, we do not have what it takes to live for God in human power. For this reason, the Apostle Paul writes – *"For I know that in me (that is, in my flesh,) dwells no good thing."*

Romans 7:18 – Subject Scripture

For I know that in me (that is, in my flesh,) dwells no good thing: **for to will is present with me; but how to perform that which is good I find not.**

Romans 7:18 – Portion II
"...for to will is present with me;
but how to perform that which is good I find not."

By the Apostle Paul stating *"for to will is present with me,"* he has made a clear discernment, which should not be taken lightly. That is, he has the desire to live for God, yet he has assessed his willpower, which only results in catastrophic consequences when applied in the Sanctification process. Thus, he states, *"but how to perform that which is good I find not."*

In order for us to make this type of assessment, we must stop and evaluate *who* we are in Christ and *what* we are in Christ. Our position is indeed in Christ *(Rom. 6:3-5)*; however, our condition is in need of His Strength *(Rom. 7:18; 8:10-17)*. We must learn to live through His Spirit; there is no other way *(I Cor. 1:17-18)*. In such an evaluation, we not only realize our inability to satisfy the demands of the Law, but also realize our inability to overcome any obstacle that would get in the way of such an endeavor. Thus, we learn to depend on Him. To come to such a place begins with the fear of the Lord, quite a different step of assessment than that of self-righteousness.

One day we will hear the remarkable story of the Apostle Paul's journey that brought him to this place. For now, we see that he has engaged this assessment, and after thoroughly examining every possibility for triumph, he found nothing within his physical and spiritual makeup in a combined effort with his will to restrain the sin nature and attain freedom. Likewise, we simply do not have what it takes to do good without God.

Romans 7:19 – Subject Scripture
For the good that I would I do not: but the evil which I would not,
that I do.

Romans 7:19 – Portion I
"For the good that I would I do not…:"

Beginning with *"For the good that I would,"* we once again see
unusual language. Nonetheless, the Apostle Paul is saying, "For the
good that I want to do." By Paul stating *"I do not,"* he is saying that
the good he wants to do is continually out of his reach. Though most
difficult to understand, this portion of *verse 19* is not possible to
circumvent for anyone prior to receiving the Revelation of the Cross.

Inwardly, we know what to do, yet without the knowledge of the
Cross for Sanctification, we cannot do it. Unable to perform that
which is good, the efforts will be to engage any type of good method
in order to satisfy the condemnation. Such is the plight of many in
today's modern Christianity and, as the author of this book, this
was my personal plight before I came to understand the remarkable
Message of the Cross.

Romans 7:19 – Subject Scripture
For the good that I would I do not: **but the evil which I would not,
that I do.**

Romans 7:19 – Portion II
"…but the evil which I would not, that I do."

By the Apostle Paul stating *"but the evil which I would not,"* we
again see unusual language. Nonetheless, whatever the evil may have
been, Paul did not want to do it. This clearly reveals his will, in a
combined effort with his body, was no match against the sin nature.

By Paul writing *"that I do,"* no further language explanation needs to be given. He makes it clear that whatever the evil may have been, he ended up doing it.

Although difficult to acknowledge, this is the catastrophic circumstance plaguing so much of today's modern Christianity. In this type of condition, the Christian will seek out any method to stop what he or she is doing simply because of his or her love for the Lord. For this reason, the carnal mind of many men has devised tens of thousands, if not millions, of their own answers, and thus erroneous gospels, in an attempt to fix their perspective view of the problem *(Gal. 1:6-9; II Cor. 11:4)*. However, all of these devised answers are apart from the one answer that God has established through Jesus Christ for our Sanctification. These devised answers leave both Saved and unsaved overcome by that which they are trying to overcome. There is but one Answer – Jesus Christ, and Him Crucified.

Romans 7:20 – Subject Scripture undivided
Now if I do that I would not, it is no more I that do it, but sin that dwells in me.

The Apostle begins *verse 20* with more unusual language, but nonetheless, by writing *"Now if I do that I would not,"* he is bringing to light that when he does the evil he does not want to do, he knows what he is doing. However, he is without the power within his flesh to stop doing it. Likewise, the Christian knows when he or she is sinning, all the while knowing it is wrong; the moral Law reveals this *(Rom. 7:7)*. This is a most terrible place for the Christian to be, and this place is a breeding ground for condemnation unless the way of victory is seen and embraced.

The language is clear in the balance of *verse 20* – *"it is no more I that do it, but sin that dwells in me."* Again, *"sin"* is written in a literal translation as "the sin," making it clear that the sin nature in

Paul's physical members is making him do the evil he does not want to do. When this is understood, each of us, when peering into the private library of our mind, would find that all of the actions of sins committed come from the same source: the unrestrained sin nature.

The Apostle Paul first brought this to light in *Romans 7:16-17* – *"¹⁶If then I do that which I would not, I consent unto the Law that it is good. ¹⁷Now then it is no more I that do it, but sin that dwells in me."* The Apostle simply unveils the plain truth of the matter: when the Christian does what he or she does not want to do it is not he or she that is sinning – it is the nature of sin within his or her members.

As stated, it must have been epic when the Apostle Paul discovered *"it is no more I that do it, but sin that dwells in me."* It must be understood that the scope of this revelation can only be seen by the spiritual mind of the mature; otherwise, the unsaved functioning in no other resource than that of the carnal mind would run with this as an excuse. Although it may be difficult for us to grasp that the sin nature is within our physical members. It is a fact that we, as Christians, must come to understand. This fact is not to be our focal point; however, when the magnitude of this is understood, the necessity of the Cross can then be embraced, whereby a true Resurrection life begins.

Though the world will never understand this, if it did, the unanswered complexities of pain, sin, death, wars, divisions, and hate could be reduced to one single culprit – the Devil – who is awaiting the ultimate enforcement of his defeat and eternal doom. As stated, the Christian should never use *"it is no more I that do it, but sin that dwells in me"* as an excuse, which is why it is so very important to hate even the stain of sin. Therefore, it will only be the truly mature Christians, who will so desperately desire to live for God in holiness, who will be able to discern between the principles of good and the principles of evil *(Heb. 5:14).* It is because they desired to overcome that they engaged this same struggle as the Apostle Paul did and, because of their desire to overcome, God will teach them His established way of victory, just as He taught Paul.

Romans 7:21 – Subject Scripture: New King James Version
I find then a Law, that evil is present with me, the one who wills to do good.

Romans 7:21 – Portion I
"I find then a Law...,"

The statement *"I find"* has come about through the Apostle Paul's decision to discern, and therein gain insight as to what is actually going on within him that is causing him to do the things that he does not want to do. The Apostle did not gain this discernment through his own intellect; he was taught it by the Revelation of Jesus Christ *(Gal. 1:11-12)*. Yet the posture Paul must have taken in order to properly discern began with the fear of the Lord, which is the beginning of wisdom *(Psalms 111:10)*. This is a posture of understanding that there is another way other than a way of his own, or that of others – posture that sees the human inability, yet sees God's ability and forgiveness. Although we do not know just how this may have looked in the heart and mind of the great Apostle Paul, nonetheless, at some point he made the decision that in God alone is the answer, He alone is the Teacher, and He alone will teach him if he seeks. Therein, in seeking, God reveals and Paul discerns, stating *"I find then a Law."* However, this Law is the Law of evil, and it is present with Paul, as we will come to see.

We can liken this Law to the Law of Gravity. Once again, the gravitational forces at work within the Law of gravity function within fixed guidelines resulting in the title or term "Law of Gravity."

Gravity is not the Law, the fixed guidelines that the gravitational forces work within are the Law. Likewise, Paul finds that the forces at work against him are working within a fixed guideline. Therefore, the Apostle Paul writes *"I find then a Law,"* and we are about to find out what these forces are and what guidelines they work within.

Romans 7:21 – Subject Scripture: New King James Version
I find then a Law, **that evil is present with me, the one who wills to do good.**

Romans 7:21 – Portion II
"…that evil is present with me, the one who will to do good."

By the Apostle Paul stating *"that evil is present with me,"* he is revealing an irrefutable fact. With the exception of Jesus, every human being that has been born, is alive today, or will be born, is born with this evil. This is the consequence of Adam's Sin and the condition of Man as a direct result of Adam's decision to partake of the Tree of the Knowledge of Good and Evil.

In the balance of *Romans 7:21*, the Apostle Paul brings another significant fact to light. However, this may be the most significant fact of evil dynamics discovered within his struggle. By Paul stating *"the one who wills to do good,"* he has discerned that the evil in his members is the one willing him to do good. This is difficult to wrap our mind around because it is as if evil understands what is going on. Nonetheless, this is what is being disclosed.

It must be noted that the Apostle Paul does not use the title "sin" (the sin nature) as he did when he started the beginning of his disclosure in *verses 8 through 11*. Instead, the Apostle uses the title *"evil."* In order to understand why the Holy Spirit had Paul write it out this way, we need to bring the components of the old man and the husband into this picture *(Rom. 6:6; 7:2-3)*. Remember, the old man is a way of thinking *(Rom. 7:8-11, 14)*, and the husband is the enforcer of this way of thinking *(Rom. 7:3, 6; 8:7)*. Therefore, in order to expound on *verse 21* accurately, we must stay within the scope of Scripture context regarding the principles at hand and their applicability to Paul's struggle *(Rom., Chptrs 6 & 7)*.

Though Paul's old man was Crucified *(Rom. 6:6)* and the husband was dead *(Rom. 7:2)*, in Paul's true and holy desire to live for God, he intently looked through the carnal mind of his old man. By doing so, the husband came to life and began to enforce that carnal way of thinking. Once this way of thinking conceived an idea through which it could perform, Paul then applied his subjective will to his objective body. That is, Paul used that which was to remain in the intangible position and used his physical body in order to bring his intangible desire into the tangible realm. From there, every motion Paul made, due to his will being manifested, he did in the flesh. The entire process can be compressed into one definition – "living by the Law" *(Rom. 7:5)*. Now that his will was energizing his flesh, willpower became the resonating result, all of which could only come about with the unlawful intention to live by the Law. Therein, the body of sin (that is, the sin nature), which was incapacitated when Paul received Salvation, revived and took dominion once again *(Rom. 7:9)*.

Although the events of Paul's struggle were dramatic, Paul's habitual recourse in the beginning was his carnal mind. Yes, his old man was Crucified; the problem was that the old man's ways of carnal thinking were still known *(Rom. 7:14)*. Therefore, the deeper his desire to live for God, all the more intent was put into his carnal mind. All the while, this way of thinking was ever more strengthened by the husband, the principle of enforcement *(Rom. 7:2-3)*.

We must remember that Paul's true and holy desire was to live for God, but without the knowledge as to where his Faith was to remain placed, the desire was easily mistaken for the carnal desire to do good (perform in his flesh). Moreover, we must keep in mind that all of this originated as the Law revealed sin and the Commandment came and compelled. Therein, Paul made the decision to place his Faith in his flesh (self-efforts), which resonated willpower that simply backed his intentions, thereby giving the sin nature occasion to revive *(Rom. 7:8-11)*. Not knowing how to circumvent this carnal way of thinking, Paul applied more willpower. However, unbeknownst to him was the sin nature being strengthened by his efforts. These are the culminating dynamics of the old man, the husband, and the sin nature that fall under the title *"evil"* in this *verse 21*.

Similar to Paul, our true and holy desire is to live for God. However, as it was with Paul when he first engaged this struggle, it most certainly will be with us. Thus, as it was with Paul, this desire can be easily mistaken for the carnal desire to do good through our flesh. This carnal desire comes as a result of Adam partaking of the Tree of the Knowledge of Good and Evil *(Gen. 3:7)*. Therefore, we must be careful what we do with our desire to overcome, and this is the discernment that must be made *(Heb. 5:14)*.

When we apply our will to our physical body in any capacity for our Sanctification, it equates to living by the Law and is entirely contrary to the ways of God *(Luke 9:23; Phil. 2:5; Rom. 7:25; 8:2, 7)*. Our will must take second place to the proper decision, and must become subservient to our proper decision for Faith. This keeps our will from defaulting into our physical body. For this reason, determination is meant for Faith because determination remains in the intangible position and does not demand the use of the physical body. After discovering this truth, Paul then writes out the dynamics, which is seen in the clear contrast between *"will"*- *Romans 7:18* and *"determination"* – *1 Corinthians 2:2*.

Romans 7:18 – "For I know that in me (that is, in my flesh,) dwells no good thing: for to will is present with me; but how to perform that which is good I find not."

I Corinthians 2:2 – "For I determined not to know any thing among you, save Jesus Christ, and Him Crucified."

Though this book deals with multiple spiritual dynamics that are actually going on within our lives as Believers, the goal and most important aspect is to unveil the answer for overcoming when sin presents itself. Therefore, understanding what is actually happening at temptation will become a significant help in understanding the vital need for properly placing Faith. For this reason, the Apostle Paul unveils these staggering dynamic principles and it is why I have expounded on them the way that I have.

Ultimately, the Apostle Paul is unveiling that, once we become born again, we can no longer try to live for God by the Law without reaping the associated consequences. Even today, as easy as this may sound, we might think that each of us would come to learn how not to live by the Law. However, as in Paul's day, the carnal mind will create laws on how not to live by the Law for at least three reasons. First, the carnal mind wants to do something good through the flesh. Second, the way of victory may not be known. Third, without the knowledge of the way of victory, it is not possible to discern what on earth is going on. Therefore, the Apostle Paul unveils what is going on by starting with the difference between the Law and the Commandment. Through this, we might come to understand their principles.

The conclusion for *Romans 7:21* is that, due to the Fall of Adam and the way in which Satan caused Adam to Fall *(Gen. 3:1-7)*, evil took eminent domain within the human members *(Rom. 6:6; 7:23)* and the sin nature was, from then on, passed onto to all mankind *(Rom. 5:12)*. We can only imagine what or how the spirit, soul, and body of the human were like before the Fall. For now, we simply do not know. However, we do know that when we received Salvation, our body became dead because of this evil *(Rom. 8:10)*, and one Day our vile body will be changed and shall be fashioned like unto our Lord's glorious body *(Phil. 3:21)*. This simply means that we cannot take detours because every detour needs a gate through which to enter.

Remember, each once of us is dealing with the spiritual, and the gate is the body. In order to step into the detour one must use the gate. Though the main road is narrow and the obstacles appear large, as if there is no way around, we must stay the course and trust God to remove them. Why? Because the very notion that any other way seems the good way to take reveals that it is the carnal mind of our old man we are making our assessment through, which is completely contrary to the Ways of God. If the proper assessment is not made, we will use our gate and enter into the detour, and we do not have the strength to keep out the diabolical forces trying to apprehend us.

Romans 7:22 – Subject Scripture
For I delight in the Law of God after the inward man:

Romans 7:22 – Portion I
"For I delight in the Law of God…"

After we receive Salvation, most often we are taught to avoid the Law because we have been delivered from it *(Rom. 7:6)*. This type of teaching comes from a remiss interpretation of Scripture. For example, *Romans 6:14 – "For sin shall not have dominion over you: for you are not under the Law, but under Grace."*

Without the knowledge of the Cross for Sanctification after we become Saved, it is most difficult, if not impossible, to understand our relationship with the Law. Therefore, we are left thinking that *Romans 6:14* is telling us to avoid the Law. However, in doing so, we end up living by the Law without realizing what we are doing. Thus, the many misconceptions and deceptions begin. Paul was in this debacle after he received Salvation. Though we would like to think that he came out of the gate flawlessly walking with God, this was not the case *(Rom. 7:8-23)*.

By staying within Scripture passages that directly and specifically disclose Paul's struggle *(Rom. 7:7-25)*, we can qualify that his struggle began when the ordained to life principle of the Commandment came as the Law revealed sin *(Rom. 7:7-11)*. The Law was not the problem nor was the Commandment – the problem was that Paul did not understand the principles within them now that he was born again. Therefore, he could not manage them until he understood them. As a result, he found what was ordained to life to be unto death *(Rom. 7:10, 13)*.

This was quite a debacle. Nonetheless, and more than likely, this was when Paul began to see that living by the Law strengthened sin. We may also get an idea as to what living by the Law looks like, perhaps as blatant as traditional ceremonies, or what the Mormon, Jehovah Witness, and the other Law-driven religions function under by having no understanding of Whom Jesus Christ truly Is. However, the idea we may get is most often not the case. Living by the Law can be as subtle as simply forcing ourselves to do something godly so that we will feel better. Even by using the word "force" we can get the idea of aggression, yet even this is not the case.

The point is that living by the Law can be incredibly subtle, and this was the debacle that Paul found himself within after he received Salvation. Though he may have aggressively pursued the Law through his flesh at first, he most definitely found that functioning in any kind of law through the flesh was simply rooted in "the Law," and therefore strengthened sin, regardless *(Rom. 7:5; I Cor. 15:56)*. For this reason, we can conclude that, without the knowledge of the principles (at least for the Law and the Commandment), Paul mismanaged them, whereby the sin nature revived, and he found himself doing the things he did not want to do *(Rom. 7:15)*.

Though we read and study the astonishing passages surrounding Paul's struggle, we can only imagine from our personal experience that Paul was distraught many times. On the one hand, Paul knows the Law perhaps like no other man, yet on the other hand, he sees his inability to live up to the moral code he knows so well. His heart's cry must have been one of anguish because he loved God and desired to live by the Law, knowing the Law came from God. Though we do not know the deeper, more personal emotions other than what has been disclosed, it is easy to see that Paul became desperate to understand how the Law and the Commandment were to be part of his life without living by them through the means of his flesh.

Yet how would the Apostle Paul know that the Law did not go away upon receiving Salvation? The answer to this question is found within the Salvation experience. When Paul received Salvation, his old man was Crucified, and the body of the sin nature incapacitated *(Rom. 6:6)*. The husband died *(Rom. 7:2)*, and his sins were Washed away by the Vicarious, Atoning Blood of Jesus Christ *(Eph. 1:7; Col. 2:12-13)*. In addition, Paul's heart was circumcised with a circumcision made without hands *(Col. 2:11)* and, upon these remarkable events, the Laws of God were put into Paul's heart and written in his mind *(Heb. 8:10-13; 10:16-17)*. Now, the moral standard established by God within the Law shined its light in a way Paul had had not known. Therefore, the Law became a much more significant part of his life.

Though just these few magnificent events took place upon Paul's Salvation, these events became known of once he was taught by the Revelation of Jesus Christ. Wherein and whereby this remarkable Revelation, Paul would find that the Law did not go away but went from schoolmaster to light, revealing and instructing the way of life. Once coming to understand all that he received and was taught by the Revelation of Jesus Christ, he would then write it out in detail for us.

We do not know whether or not Paul Authored Hebrews; if written by Paul, then he Authored over half the New Testament. Therefore, his statement *"For I delight in the Law of God"* was made from within this debacle as he came to discern what he had received; though he did not understand at first, he knew that his view and approach to the Law was to be all together much different than he had known before, as we will come to see.

Romans 7:22 – Subject Scripture
For I delight in the Law of God **after the inward man:**

Romans 7:22 – Portion II
"...after the inward man....:"

The Apostle Paul is speaking of the intangibles, such as who he really is – he is a spirit with a living soul, made in the image, after the likeness of God. Yet his spirit and soul are housed within a mortal body – he is a triune being *(Gen. 1:26-27; 2:6-7).*

Romans 7:23 – Subject Scripture
But I see another Law in my members, warring against the Law of my mind, and bringing me into captivity to the Law of sin which is in my members.

Romans 7:23 – Portion I
"But I see another Law in my members, warring against the Law of my mind...,"

The Apostle Paul unveils three more irrefutable facts in this portion of *verse 23*. The first fact is found in his statement – *"But I see another Law in my members."* Paul is identifying the location of this other Law; it resides in his physical members. The second fact is the specific intent of this Law, that is, it is *"warring against"* him. Yet, the Apostle states that this other Law is specifically warring against *"the Law of my mind,"* which is the third fact. By Paul stating *"the Law of my mind,"* he is revealing a Law we may not have known.

"The Law of the Mind" (the Law of the Christian Mind) is that which desires to live for God due to the Laws of God now residing in our heart and mind *(Heb. 8:10-13; 10:16-17)*. In addition, we have the Mind of Christ *(I Cor. 2:16)*, and now we can direct our thoughts, desire, Faith, and thereby, our will with much greater clarity *(Matt. 22:37; Rom. 7:25; I Cor. 2:2; Phil. 2:5)*.

As we look at the overall of portion I, *verse 23*, by the Apostle Paul stating, *"But I see another Law in my members, warring against the Law of my mind,"* he is speaking of the Law of Sin and Death, and the dynamics of the sin nature (that is, evil *[Rom. 7:21]*), willing him to use his physical body in order to take occasion and revive *(Rom. 7:8-11)*. This is the war.

Paul's carnal mind desires to live by the Law, yet he is dimly discerning that there is another way, a way in which he can stand in Faith, a way in which, as he stands in Faith and does not move, somehow God will help him. Therein, he is warring with the desire to engage his physical body to overcome versus standing in Faith to overcome without the use of his physical body. However, without the Revelation or knowledge of where exactly to place his Faith for the effectual working of the Holy Spirit, his only recourse is his physical body.

What remarkable discernment this must have been as he was being taught! The magnitude of this struggle most likely became accentuated due to the culmination of events wherein the Apostle Paul began to discern *(Rom. 7:21; Heb. 5:14)*. The Apostle Paul knew that he was born again; he knew that he believed in Jesus Christ, he knew that he had Faith, and he knew that he had the will, yet nothing was working. Therein, he knew something was amiss.

Paul's body was neutral, as ours is – it was neither holy nor unholy, neither good nor bad. It was a tent that Paul lived in during his humanity. It was used naturally every day; however, it could not be used to grow in Sanctification without breaching into the Law of Sin and Death. This would have been the normal "good fight of Faith." Yet, this war going on in the mind of the Apostle was heavily accentuated due to the nature of sin reviving by already breaching into this diabolical Law *(Rom. 7:8-15)*. The Law of Paul's mind was saying, "I want to overcome," yet his carnal mind was saying, "Use your physical body." All the while, the Mind of Christ was saying, "Do not do anything, Paul. Simply place your Faith in My Cross and wait."

We can personalize this war for ourselves in two ways. The first way is before sin: when temptation comes, we quickly motion to do something to resist the temptation before we fall into its grasp. The second way is after sin: when condemnation comes, we quickly motion to do something to come out from under the looming oppression of guilt in order to get back to where we thought we were before we fell. In either of these two positions, the decision was made to apply our will to our body, wherein resonating willpower backed up the decision, which resulted in motioning the physical body to overcome the temptation, or get out from underneath condemnation.

The motion may have been to call a friend, go to church, read the Bible, pray, fast, and so on. All of these are vital parts for sure, as well as blessings to our Christian walk. However, when the intent to engage them is to resist temptation or come out from underneath condemnation, the intent will always be found embedded in trying to live by the Law or by-product laws of the Law. Therein, the very thing we tried to resist or come out from underneath, continues to overcome us.

The way we innately think we are to depend on God in order to overcome, versus the way that God is teaching us to depend on Him, is vastly different. This is simply because our intentions are right. Thus, it is so natural to use our body for methods of law to resist temptation, restrain sin, or come out from underneath condemnation. Nonetheless, whether it is before sin or after sin, whether in temptation or under condemnation, we can never motion in the body to do something without God.

There is only one way for Salvation. After Salvation, there is only one way for Sanctification because there is nothing in us (that is, in our flesh) to perform the good that we want to do. Our body is dead, and therefore our will cannot be applied to our body. Our will has to come in second place to our decision to place Faith properly. Once Faith is properly placed, determination is the ongoing rampart for this proper decision. For this reason, determination is meant for Faith because, unlike our will, determination remains in the intangible position.

Once again, determination is meant for moving our thoughts and Faith away from self-imposed efforts where they can be placed into Jesus Christ, and Him Crucified. As stated, *I Corinthians 2:2* gives us great insight into the cornerstone for our Faith – *"For I determined not to know any thing among you, save Jesus Christ, and Him Crucified."*

Within *I Corinthians 2:2*, the Apostle Paul takes specific use of the word *"determined"* in describing the subjective position, as opposed to *Romans 7:18* wherein we find Paul taking specific use of will and flesh – *"For I know that in me (that is, in my flesh,) dwells no good thing: for to will is present with me; but how to perform that which is good I find not."*

The Apostle Paul found that, when his will took first place, it naturally defaulted into his body as willpower, thereby giving the sin nature occasion to revive. The combination of will and body simply produced motions of sins in the flesh, which are by the Law. Therefore, where a decision starts in the subjective, it never leaves the intangible realm when it resonates into determination. This is of great significance when making and maintaining the proper decision for Faith, because Faith is intangible. This is not so with our will. Our will starts in the subjective realm, yet, when it takes first place, seeing any type of method for Sanctification other than the Cross, our will naturally defaults into the objective position. Once again, for this reason, our body is dead as the tool for growing in triumph and holiness. Therefore, until the Trump of God sounds, we must refrain from using our body. This is the war going on in our mind; however, this is the good fight of Faith *(I Cor. 2:2; I Tim. 6:12; II Tim. 4:7)*.

If there is a struggle with sin now, there is for sure a whirlwind of darkness drumming up more darkness; nevertheless, the core fight going on within the mind is one about Faith and where Faith is to be placed. Faith is the substance of things hoped for, and the evidence of things not seen *(Heb. 11:1)*. Faith is to be placed in the Cross with a determination that it shall not be moved to any other thing. In this intangible fight, there will be great hope and absolute assurance of the Spirit of God calming the storm.

It is the most remarkable opportunity for us to ever ponder that Jesus Satisfied the Law and upon the Cross He Vicariously Shed His

Blood for us. He condemned sin in the flesh, Atoned for the Sin of the world, and thus Paid the Penalty of the Law. Not only was all this done to Redeem us from the Penalty of our sins, but also to keep the Righteousness of the Law fulfilled within us who believe due to our ongoing inability to live up to the moral standard of God's Law and those things which were contrary to us in the Law and Ordinances.

Furthermore, and just as significant in many other ways, it was through His death that He destroyed him who had the power of death, that is, the Devil *(Heb. 2:14-15)*. Therefore, by the magnificent and established events of the Cross, our decision must be to know Jesus Christ, and Him Crucified, and no other thing for our Sanctification *(I Cor. 2:2; Gal. 6:14; Rev. 12:11)*. Walking within this Revelation are peace, joy, and rest. Peace because, as we maintain Faith in the Cross, our body will not be motioned by our will, but quickened unto the Will of the Father by His Spirit. Joy, because, by this decision, the Spirit of God bears witness with our spirit that we are the Children of God, and there is rest for our soul because there is no condemnation in this environment *(Rom. 8:1-17)*.

Without this magnificent Revelation of the Cross, the war going on in the mind can be overwhelming. Christians in this condition know they love Jesus. They know they have Faith, willpower, and the desire to live a life of overcoming. Yet without knowing where to place their Faith, turmoil, heartache, and unrest are the experience because the Law of Sin in their members is warring against the Law of their mind.

Romans 7:23 – Subject Scripture
But I see another Law in my members, warring against the Law of my mind, **and bringing me into captivity to the Law of sin which is in my members.**

Romans 7:23 – Portion II
"...and bringing me into captivity to the Law of sin which is in my members."

The balance of *verse 23* reveals the reality of the sin nature literally taking the Apostle Paul captive even after his Salvation. By writing *"the Law of sin,"* he reveals that the nature of sin works through a Law. The guideline or permissible parameter for *"the Law of sin"* is self-imposed efforts in any attempt to deal with spiritual matters of Sanctification. Such attempts (regardless how they appear) are motions of sins in the flesh, which are by the Law *(Rom. 7:5)*. Yet it can be any law or any other thing that would cause us to combine our will with our body in order to carry out any form of Sanctification. All of these "other things" are apart from the way that God has established through Jesus Christ, and Him Crucified.

The many methods of self-imposed efforts, regardless of their appearance, are always efforts of trying to live by the Law, which are the carnal mind and ways of the old man *(Rom. 2:14-15)*. The carnal mind is not subject to the ways of God *(Rom. 8:7)*. Therefore, it does not understand what to do with the compelling of the Commandment, so the carnal mind relies on trying to live by the Law. Living in this manner is known as "serving the in the oldness of the letter." Nonetheless, this type of lifestyle revives the sin nature and brings death *(Rom. 7:9; II Cor. 3:6)*.

As within *Romans 7:21 NKJV* – *"I find then a Law, that evil is present with me, the one who wills to do good"*– Paul has brought us here to *Romans 7:23*, where once again he identifies the sin nature. Yet unlike *Romans 7:21* wherein Paul encompassed the dynamics of the old man, the husband, and the sin nature by addressing them under one title "evil," here in *Romans 7:23* he gives us the title through which the dynamics of the sin nature function. Hence, *"the*

Law of sin." As we will come to see, Paul is under the dominion of the sin nature because he did not understand the guidelines – Law through which sin functions. Therein, not knowing, he tried to overcome by applying his will to his body, which of course was by the Law *(Rom. 7:5)*.

Regardless of how this is expounded upon, whether exhaustively, concisely, or through entirely different diction, it is not possible to avoid the fundamental fact that the sin nature resides within our members and it functions through a Law of its own. A conservative estimate today would conclude that there are millions who love the Lord, yet have found themselves overcome by the very thing they are trying to overcome, simply because they are trying to live by the Law in their desire to live for God. The result of this is chaos and anytime there is chaos, it always leads those in it to think that there is more to what is going on when there is not.

One of the main goals of the Devil and his associates is to create chaos, and he can do this by causing the Believer to live by the Law because the result is a life of turmoil, and thereby, distraction. However, we as Christians have the simplicity that is in Christ *(II Cor. 11:3)*, and this simplicity is far different from the mindset and devised religious methods that have been, and will continue to be, created by man and fallen Angels. This simplicity is the Cross *(I Cor. 1:17-18)*.

Anytime another method is devised or created to replace what God has already established through Jesus Christ, and Him Crucified, the devised method produces another Jesus with another gospel *(II Cor. 11:4)*. This erroneous Jesus and gospel of heresy becomes another seedbed that brings about a delusion that promises victory and freedom through living by the Law. Living by the Law can come in many forms and a variety of different ways, some of which, as I have stated, are incredibly subtle. Nonetheless, all of them are completely against the walk of Faith, which does not require the physical body to live for God *(Rom. 7:25; 8:1-17)*.

Much of today's teachings have become twisted through the carnal mind of a man. Many Christians are left to believe that they had fallen from Grace when they sinned. However, this is completely contrary to the Word of God – *"...But where sin abounded, Grace did much more abound..." (Rom. 5:20)*. Does this mean that we should go on sinning? No! And for this reason, Grace is needed for when we fall, and so God's Grace is present within our life. As a result, we can get up and carry on as we seek the True Source (Jesus Christ) and True Means (Him Crucified) for Sanctification.

The way in which we fall from Grace is by engaging the Law in some way as to live by it through our human strength and methods. However, there are those who flat out refuse to believe that there is any other way other than living by the Law. For those who choose to live in this way, the Apostle Paul writes – *"Christ is become of no effect unto you, whosoever of you are justified by the Law; you are fallen from Grace" (Gal. 5:4)*. If an individual goes far enough in any method apart from God's established way, he or she can become an enemy of the Cross of Christ – *"For many walk, of whom I have told you often, and now tell you even weeping, that they are the enemies of the Cross of Christ..." (Phil. 3:18)*.

Although many methods will be seen when we are in a struggle, we must come to realize that it is because of our love for the Lord and our desire to overcome that we have found ourselves in desperation seeking freedom, because no other way has worked. Our very efforts reveal this. Therefore, we must never give up! Yes, it is easy for us to fall into the perception that the struggle was engaged because we may have sinned. However, the struggle began because our desire was not to sin, nor continue in sin. Therefore, regardless of the circumstances, there is not a sin that His Blood will not cover, past, present, or future. For this reason, we are never to give up! Our walk is by Faith and as we seek Him, He will show us the way. We will come to see this with Paul's experience.

Romans 7:24 – Subject Scripture
O wretched man that I am! Who shall deliver me from the body of this death?

Romans 7:24 – Portion I
"O wretched man that I am!..."

The Apostle Paul writes no further of his struggle and concludes by writing *"O wretched man that I am!"* Though, at first glance, we may come to a conclusion about this statement, there is much more going on here than we may think. The word *"wretched"* is defined within the biblical Greek word *talaiporos* (ταλαίπωρος, NT: 5005, tal-ah'-ee-po-ros). It means miserable, to bear, enduring trial, as supporting weights, lead, reach, and uphold.

The Apostle opens the conclusion of his struggle with this statement because he now knows the answer. He has phrased it in this humble manner because, in bearing the heavy burden of this struggle, he has endured. Though miserable indeed, he never gave up believing God to reveal His ways and, in seeking, the Lord Revealed *(Gal. 1:11-12)*. Now knowing the answer, he can uphold that which he has been called for, whereby he would lead by example *(Phil. 3:17; Heb. 6:12)*.

Romans 7:24 – Subject Scripture
O wretched man that I am! **Who shall deliver me from the body of this death?**

Romans 7:24 – Portion II
"…Who shall deliver me from the body of this death?"

The great Apostle Paul concludes *Romans 7:24* with a "rhetorical question," (more specifically, a "known question") in order to set the stage for the intended Message he brings forth in *Romans 7:25*. For Paul knows Who will deliver him, and through what Means, as we will come to see in Chapter 9 – Part III.

PART III

God's Established Way of Victory

The Law of God

ROMANS 7:25

PREFACE

T hroughout the years, scholars have referred to the Epistle of
Romans as the Mount Everest of the Bible due to the many
spiritual principles disclosed within *Chapters 6 & 7*. Once these
principles are discerned, all else within the great Epistle can be seen
and understood. Without this discernment *Romans 7:24 – "...Who
shall deliver me from the body of this death?"* – will not be understood
as a "known question," thereby setting the carnal stage wherein the
magnificence of *Romans 7:25* will be overlooked. Conversely, with
discernment, *Romans 7:24* is revealed in its "rhetorical question"
position, thus concluding Paul's struggle and setting the stage for
*Romans 7:25 – "I thank God through Jesus Christ our Lord. So then
with the mind I myself serve the Law of God; but with the flesh the
Law of sin."*

It is easy to pass over *Romans 7:25* at first glance; however, *Romans 7:25* is chronologically seated between Paul's rhetorical question in *Romans 7:24* and his first descriptive evidence of victory in *Romans 8:1*. Therefore, not only does *Romans 7:25* hold the answer to his victory, but also secures *Romans 7:25* as one of the most significant Scriptures in the Word of God. Thus, as we peer into this remarkable Scripture, we can see seven principles to Biblical Christianity:

One: the Christian and God
Two: the Christian's posture and attitude
Three: the Christian's only answer for victory and leading of the Holy Spirit
Four: the use and purpose of the Christian's mind
Five: the Christian's spirit and soul
Six: the Christian's relationship with the Law of God
Seven: the Christian and the flesh

Romans 7:25 – Subject Scripture

I thank God through Jesus Christ our Lord. So then with the mind I myself serve the Law of God; but with the flesh the Law of sin.

Romans 7:25 – Portion I: Principle One
"I..."

It may seem unusual to divide the Scripture here and bring up *"I,"* but many thousands who love the Lord God depend on so many others for their help. Although this is a wonderful thing, our full dependency must be exercised in God through Jesus Christ, as we will come to see.

Romans 7:25 – Subject Scripture
I **thank God** through Jesus Christ our Lord. So then with the mind
I myself serve the Law of God; but with the flesh the Law of sin.

Romans 7:25 – Portion II: Principle Two
"...thank God..."

This remarkable expression can be taken for granted; nonetheless,
it fits into the Scripture context perfectly. It is an expression of
gratitude in a continual offering of thankfulness, acknowledging
all that Jesus Christ has done on the Cross for us through His death.
This attitude goes beyond the tangible appearance of things and
trusts in God's Sovereignty regardless of the circumstances *(Job
13:15; Heb. 11:1; 12:2).*

Romans 7:25, in its entirety, holds seven truths, two of which, the
Apostle Paul comes to understand that his will applied to his physical
body will not deliver him from the power of the sin nature. The Holy
Spirit has Revealed to and taught Paul *(Gal. 1:11-12)* that deliverance
comes as Faith remains in Jesus Christ, and Him Crucified *(Gal.
6:14).* This offering of thanksgiving comes through the Apostle's
acknowledgement of this great truth.

Likewise, as Christians, our thoughts and actions become
renewed and shaped around this truth *(Phil. 3:7-11).* It is the
embraced and exercised knowledge of this truth that always results
in a continual thanksgiving as we believe from the heart that Jesus
Christ is the Source, and the Cross is the means for all of our victory
and manner of walking after the Spirit *(Rom. 8:1, 4, 13-14; Phil.
4:13).* For this reason, giving thanks is the Will of God *(I Thess. 5:18)*
because thanksgiving comes from the knowledge that we triumph
over only through His Vicarious Blood Shed and triumphant death
on the Cross *(I Cor. 15:57).*

As we mature in Christ, we come to know of the constant spoken and unspoken need for God's love and power, and our attitude of gratefulness becomes our seat of true worship toward God *(John 4:23-24; II Cor. 9:11)*. Martin Luther referred to gratitude as "the basic Christian attitude"; thus, when the Power of God working through Faith in the Cross becomes understood, thanksgiving becomes the ongoing attitude of gratitude. In addition, with an attitude of gratefulness, the Cross will not be made into a laboring effort; instead, gratitude will help mold and shape our life *(II Cor. 4:7-18)* wherein, we too will *"thank God."*

Romans 7:25 – Subject Scripture

I thank God **through Jesus Christ our Lord.** So then with the mind I myself serve the Law of God; but with the flesh the Law of sin.

Romans 7:25 – Portion III: Principle Three
"...through Jesus Christ our Lord...."

This magnificent portion of *verse 25* gives all Believers the answer for Sanctification and intimacy with God. Prior to Paul being taught the answer, his struggle was profound; it had failure, frustration, confusion, and condemnation regardless of how he tried to overcome. Although Paul had Faith, the desire to live for God, and will, what was once put down had revived, so he remained overcome *(Rom. 7:23)*. Apprehended by sin, Paul found himself pressing against a giant he was unable to go through. What did Paul discover that changed everything?

Having Faith, desire and will, yet failing to press through, Paul knew that something was amiss. Never giving up on God *(Rom. 7:24)*, he sought Him, wherein He taught him to stand fast *(Rom. 9:11; I Cor. 16:13)*. In standing fast, God taught Paul a new way, a living way, a way in which he could pass through by placing his Faith in the One

Who has already passed through death by death through the offering of His Own body on the Cross *(Col. 1:21-22)*.

Realizing he could experience intimacy, holiness, and the power of God only *"through Jesus Christ,"* Paul placed his Faith in Jesus Christ, and Him Crucified, and passed through. On the other side, he writes – *"¹⁹For I through the Law am dead to the Law, that I might live unto God. ²⁰I am Crucified with Christ: nevertheless I live; yet not I, but Christ lives in me: and the life which I now live in the flesh I live by the Faith of the Son of God, who loved me, and gave Himself for me" (Gal. 2:19-20)*. Now walking with God in triumph and ongoing freedom, he writes – *"But God forbid that I should glory, save in the Cross of our Lord Jesus Christ, by Whom the world is Crucified unto me, and I unto the world" (Gal. 6:14)*.

From cover to cover, the Word of God points the Believer to the Cross. The Old Testament sacrifices were "types and shadows" pointing to Christ, and what was to take place on the Cross. They looked forward, and we now have the opportunity to look back. Though we cannot go back in time to the event, God has established through Jesus Christ, and Him Crucified, that we remain supernaturally planted in the likeness of His death and the likeness of His Resurrection as the Cross becomes the object of our Faith. Thus is the meaning of *"through Jesus Christ our Lord."*

Romans 7:25 – Subject Scripture
I thank God through Jesus Christ our Lord. **So then with the mind** I myself serve the Law of God; but with the flesh the Law of sin.

Romans 7:25 – Portion IV: Principle Four
"...So then with the mind..."

"So then" is drawing a resolution, which is one of the most (if not *the* most) important resolution in the Apostle Paul's walk in Christ.

Without this resolution, he would have remained in his struggle with sin, and if he remained in this struggle, the New Testament would not look as it does today. God does not violate the will of Man in regards to whether or not he or she wants to seek God for the answer *(before the Cross – Gen. 3:3-13; after the Cross – I Cor. 1:17-18)*.

With that said, *"So then"* is drawing a resolution that begins with Paul revealing he is no longer serving objectively (i.e., serving with his body) – he is serving subjectively (i.e., serving with his mind). Hence, *"So then with the mind."* This verbiage is what the Apostle Paul is saying, and therefore significant indeed, but Paul is not implying that our walk in Christ is a mental assent without godly works. Paul only begins his resolution by pointing us to the foundation of how he is to serve, which is with his mind – not his body. Therein, properly serving, the Holy Spirit will quicken him unto the Will of the Father, as we will come to see. Until then, let us look into our mind now that we are born again.

In the context of *Romans Chapter 7*, our mind views, perceives, divides, reasons and proves the principles of our new nature in contrast to the sin nature, the nature of evil that dominates the mind of all unsaved Man due to their unregenerate condition. Due to this, their physical body is under complete subjection to evil because their mind is continually dominated by the nature of evil, regardless how "good" their life may appear. This is not so for we who are Saved; our mind is the arena for directing our thoughts, desire, Faith, and will. When these are properly placed, our decision resonates into determination and becomes a rampart of defense *(I Cor. 2:2; I Tim. 6:12; II Tim. 4:7)*.

Although we have just only touched on the general difference between our mind as Christians and the mind of unsaved Man, delving beyond this surface scope (though fascinating) serves no purpose in regards to our walk in Christ, which is simply by Faith.

Therefore, investigating beyond the Word of God is not my intent, yet we must understand that our mind is the headquarters as to how we run our life; thus, our life is not just happenstance. Our life is drastically changed by the decisions we make, and our mind is the headquarters for these decisions. However, the most important decisions are the ones that deal with Faith – "deal" in the sense that our Faith will be placed in one of two places, and the decision to choose will come from within the headquarters of our mind.

The first place – the proper place – for our Faith is the Cross. When the decision is made to make the Cross the focal point and view for all manner of life and living, the ongoing decision turns into determination, whereby the result will be beyond what is possible to express due to the presence of God, joy, and rest.

The second place for Faith is the body. If the body is chosen, the ongoing decision will resonate willpower and, regardless of our desire to live for God, our willpower is woefully insufficient in overcoming the sin nature once it revives *(Rom. 7:15, 18, & 23)*. Once the sin is revived, our mind will be filled with chaos, unrest, and an uncontrolled live-streaming of evil, like a whirlwind of darkness arousing more darkness. Why?

The decision to apply our will to our body (regardless of the method), is simply motions of sins in the flesh and, because they are always by the Law *(Rom. 7:5)*, the sin nature will revive *(Rom. 7:8-11)*. If the ongoing decision for this combination of will and flesh is undeterred, the sin nature is evermore strengthened *(Rom. 7:23; I Cor. 15:56)*. For this reason, the Apostle Paul foreran this struggle, dealing with these issues until he received and was taught by the Revelation of Jesus Christ *(Gal. 1:11-12)*. Therefore Paul, understanding the consequences of choosing the physical body to deal with spiritual matters is so dire, begins his resolution by directing us to the foundation from where he serves – *"So then with the mind."* Unless we seek God for this Revelation, we will naturally follow the patterns of living by the Law and reap the associated consequences that cannot be avoided.

Those of us who have had time in our walk with Christ know what it is like to fail over and over, and we may have spent a lot of time trying to figure it out to no avail. However, a fact remains seen when we fail: though we believe in God, have Faith and the desire to overcome, we can still find ourselves failing. It is not that God is failing us – it is us not knowing or embracing the way of Sanctification (that is, victory that He has established for us through Jesus Christ). His way for our Sanctification begins with the Revelation of His way; then the decision if left up to us as to whether or not it will be embraced as the means of walking with God. This will be a daily decision, and it will be with our mind that each of us will decide.

Now then, the mind is the seat upon where we direct thoughts, desire, Faith, and will *(Rom. 7:25; Phil. 2:5; I Tim. 6:12).* Our desire can be right *(Rom. 7:22),* but our thoughts, Faith, and will can be misplaced. If our thoughts are misplaced, our Faith and our will follow *(Rom. 7:8-11).*

Our desire should always be that of overcoming sin and growing in holiness, but if we do not make the decision to bring our thoughts captive to the security of the Cross, Faith will find its place in the obscurity of other ways *(Rom. 8:7; II Cor. 11:4, 14; Gal. 1:6-9),* and our mind will be taken captive to the sin nature, regardless of our desire and willpower *(Rom. 7:15, 19, 23).* Though our will applied to our body creates willpower, once again, it is woefully insufficient to overcome the nature of sin – not so with our determination. Our determination is more than sufficient in backing up the decision to move our Faith into the Cross and keep it there *(Rom. 7:25; I Cor. 2:2).*

As our thoughts are brought to the security of the Cross, the same Spirit that raised Jesus from the dead, now having the latitude through which to effectually work in us, quickens our mortal body unto the Resurrection life that God desires for us *(Rom. 8:2, 11-17; Gal. 2:19-20)*. This type of experience is the longing of each of us who are Saved, but it cannot be attained by combining our will and our body, regardless of the method *(Rom. 7:18; 8:10)*. The wonderful opportunity we have to walk with God in triumph and ongoing freedom is simply experienced as Faith becomes anchored in Jesus Christ, and Him Crucified *(Gal. 6:14)*. Once this becomes embraced, the rest will fall into place!

How can we do nothing, yet expect to experience our body quickened by the Spirit of God? We can always do something; however, without God's energizing power at work within us, we cannot secure lasting victory, peace or joy within ourselves.

In regards to experiencing the power of God by not utilizing our body, let us say, regardless of the circumstances, we do nothing but stand. Yet in our stand, we make the decision and become determined to set our mind on knowing nothing else except Jesus Christ, and Him Crucified *(I Cor. 2:2)*. In addition to this decision, we believe that God knows the thoughts and intents of our heart in this matter *(Heb. 4:10-13)*. By this act of Faith, first and foremost, we have pleased God *(Heb. 11:6)*, but also, on the basis of this act of Faith, we have entered into the Law of the Spirit – we have entered into the guidelines that the Spirit of Life functions within *(Rom. 8:2)*. Furthermore, by properly placing our Faith, we are now functioning in that form of Doctrine. Nevertheless, by this act of Faith, the hour will come wherein the Spirit of Life will quicken our mortal body unto the Will of the Father, all by His power, and this will be an undeniable and life-changing experience.

To press this a little further, let us look at the example of our will. We know that our will is intangible, but when applied to what we want to do, it is manifested in our physical body, thus turning into willpower. However, if our will and our physical body are an illegal combination in regard to spiritual matters of living for God the way He desires, then what are we to do with willpower? Nothing because it requires our body! Though we may will to do good, there is nothing in us (that is, in our flesh) to perform the good we want to do *(Rom. 7:18).*

Since this is the reality of our current position as human beings, and God is aware of our thoughts, He knows when we make the decision to place our Faith in His Son, and what His Son has done for us through His Sacrifice and death. Thus, we can be assured that God knows, and is ready to help us when we make the proper decision. Once again, for this reason, the Apostle Paul he writes – *"For I determined not to know any thing among you, save Jesus Christ, and Him Crucified" (I Cor. 2:2).* This is the good fight of Faith *(I Tim. 6:12; II Tim. 4:7).*

We must remember that our victory comes through Faith in Whom He Is, and what He has done on the Cross Vicariously through His Atoning Shed Blood and triumphant death *(Col. 2:12-15; I John 3:8);* His Resurrection qualifies this. Therefore, the decision to place Faith in Jesus Christ, and Him Crucified, is truly everything we can bring, and thus give to God *(Matt. 22:37; John 19:30; Heb. 4:10-13).*

As Christians, we should be careful not to underestimate the value of this decision toward the Cross, because the Cross made it possible for the Lord God to circumcise our heart so that we can now love Him with all our heart, soul and mind – all of which are the intangibles of unseen things. Laying down everything and literally depending on the Spirit of Life to come to our aid by placing Faith in Jesus Christ, and Him Crucified, is one of the single most difficult endeavors we can undertake. Yet it can be accomplished with a mind that determines to serve the Law of God, as we will come to see.

Romans 7:25 – Subject Scripture
I thank God through Jesus Christ our Lord. So then with the mind **I myself serve** the Law of God; but with the flesh the Law of sin.

Romans 7:25 – Portion V: Principle Five
"...I myself serve..."

This portion is referring to the intangibles of what Paul truly is – a spirit with a soul – and though both live in his physical body, he is not using his body to serve; he is using the intangible faculty of his mind, whereby his spirit and soul follow.

As stated previously, Paul found that when he made the decision to apply his will and his body in regard to spiritual matters, it always resulted in him unlawfully engaging the Mosaic Law in one way or the other. Paul wanted to live up to the moral standard of the Law, and he tried as a result of being compelled by the Commandment when the Law revealed sin *(Rom. 7:7-11)*. The problem with trying to live for God through will and body was that this combination revived the sin nature. Accentuating the problem, the harder Paul tried, the stronger the sin nature became *(I Cor. 15:56)*. Once Paul came to understand these principles, he writes *"I myself serve."* Paul is serving with the intangibles of which he really is *"I"* (his spirit), and *"myself"* (his soul); he is serving with the faculty of his intangible mind. Thus, the meaning of *Romans 7:25* so far – *"So then with my mind I myself serve."*

Paul finds a significant truth about serving with his mind, rather than his body and, once he comes to fully understand, he writes – *"And if Christ be in you, the body is dead because of sin; but the Spirit is life because of Righteousness" (Rom. 8:10)*. The Apostle Paul came to understand why his body was made dead upon Salvation. He also came to understand the carnal mind of the old man wants to use

195

the physical body for spiritual matters. Paul's conclusion was his will must take second place to his decision toward and for the Cross.

Yes, we live in the world – we are mortal. However, everything we truly are is intangible for the time being. What we will be when we put on immortality is yet to be known. Therefore, each of us is a spirit with a soul, a mind, desires, thoughts, and belief. This is why our walk with God is by our intangible decisions and Faith. Therefore, in order to experience God's effectual power, our intangible decision is intended to resonate in our desire to live for God, and thus back up, reinforce, and maintain where our intangible thoughts, Faith, and will are to remain.

The testimony of truth within this portion of *Romans 7:25* is to unveil that the magnificent way of victory is walked out with unseen things. God does not operate based on what we do; He operates in our life based on where we place our Faith. This is not a Faith that makes a mental ascension to God without works. However, we must understand that works follow properly placed Faith *(Titus 2:7)*; works do not qualify one as a Christian. Therefore, let us look into Faith and works.

Many tensions have arisen as some have imagined a contradiction between Paul and James regarding Faith and works for Justification, Salvation, and Sanctification, yet there is no such contradiction for Justification and Salvation, and there is no such contradiction after Salvation for Sanctification.

Paul says a man becomes justified by Faith without the deeds of the Law *(Rom. 3:23-28)*. James says a man should be a doer of the Word *(Jam. 1:23)*. Paul says freedom from the sin nature comes by Faith alone *(Rom. 6:17-18; 7:25; 8:1-2)*. James says a man should be a doer of the work *(Jam. 1:25)*. Paul says if a man justifies himself by the Law, he has fallen from Grace *(Gal. 5:4)*. James says a man becomes justified by his works *(Jam. 2:21)*.

In conclusion, the sinner becomes born again through Faith alone, plus or minus nothing *(John 3:16)*. Now born again, he or she overcomes as a Christian through Faith in the Cross, plus or minus nothing *(I Cor. 1:17-18)*. Yet Faith is not alone without works. Good works will not justify a man before God, but a justified man, woman, boy, or girl who is free from the sin nature will do good works acceptable unto God in this life and the life to come.

Works are never to be the object of our Faith; if they are, they are of the flesh and always by the Law *(Rom. 7:5)*. Conversely, when our Faith is properly placed, the Spirit of God will quicken our body, wherein good works supernaturally follow. Therefore, as we once again view *Romans 7:25* so far – *"So then with the mind I myself serve"* – we see that Paul is serving with the intangibles: mind, spirit, and soul, so that the Spirit of God can move the tangible body to produce good works acceptable unto God *(Rom. 8:1-4)*.

Before moving on, I previously stated that Paul is drawing us to an intended resolution by writing *"So then."* This seemingly simple statement is one of the most (if not *the* most) important intended resolutions in the Apostle Paul's walk in Christ. This resolution is the turning point. Paul has discovered that the Law is no longer a schoolmaster to him *(Gal. 3:24-25)*; the Law is now light, revealing God's moral standard for him and instructing the way of life. Therefore, he now knows that the Law plays a tremendous and significant role in his life. In this discernment, Paul concludes that he can no longer use his body to live by the Law; by stating *"So then,"* he has resolved that instead of serving with his body, he is serving with his spirit and soul by way of the faculty of his mind. Yet what on earth is the Apostle Paul serving? As unusual as it may be, with his mind he is serving *"the Law of God,"* as we will come to see.

Romans 7:25 – Subject Scripture

I thank God through Jesus Christ our Lord. So then with the mind I myself serve **the Law of God;** but with the flesh the Law of sin.

Romans 7:25 – Portion VI: Principle Six
"...the Law of God...;"

The Apostle Paul is serving *"the Law of God"* with his mind; this remarkable example is one the great Apostle desires each of us to follow *(Phil. 3:17; Heb. 6:12).* Before we get involved with why the Apostle sets this example, let us recap the first five fundamental principles for Biblical Christianity so far.

One: *"I...."* Learning to walk in triumph and freedom is a personal choice, one in which full dependency upon God is sought after and learned through the Doctrinal Truth of His Word. Our victory does not come through the carnal mind or methods of man. Therefore, as we seek God, He will teach us greater depths of depending upon Him.

Two: *"thank God...."* Once the way of victory is seen and embraced, thanksgiving will simply become the ongoing attitude of gratefulness.

Three: *"through Jesus Christ our Lord...."* The Apostle Paul unveils the magnificent answer that he was in search of during his struggle with the sin nature. The answer is Faith resting in Jesus Christ, and Him Crucified. Thus is the meaning of *"through Jesus Christ."* It is by anchoring Faith in the Cross that we experience the leading of the Holy Spirit, deliverance, lasting freedom, joy, rest, holiness, intimacy with God, and everything else encompassing an abundant life.

Four: *"So then with the mind...."* We now understand the remarkable difference between the mind of the Christian and the mind of unsaved man, and we are now beginning to understand the purpose of our mind.

Five: *"I myself serve...."* Paul brings clarity to us who are Saved. Serving is with the intangibles – the mind, spirit, soul; therein are our thoughts, desire (heart), belief, Faith. When we properly *"serve,"* our will follows.

Now that we have recapped the first five fundamental principles of Biblical Christianity, let us get involved in the example the Apostle Paul sets for us to follow – *"I thank God through Jesus Christ our Lord. So then with the mind I myself serve the Law of God...,"* and why, he would serve the Law of God with his mind. As we begin to discover why the Apostle Paul sets the example, we must understand our current position. First, we must know that the Mosaic Law functions within our life in a way that it could not have now that we are in Christ. Second, it is important to keep in mind that, during the events of our Salvation, our heart was circumcised with a circumcision made without hands, thus revealing the greater spiritual scope of the Law.

Prior to Salvation, the Law was our schoolmaster; the Law played such a significant role in our life, it brought us to Christ that we might be justified by Faith. However, after Salvation, though we are no longer under the principle schoolmaster, this does not mean that the Law no longer plays a role in our life – it does indeed *(Rom. 7:7, 25; I Cor. 9:21).*

For this reason, *"the Law of God"* is an incredibly unique Law. So unique, it is penned just three times within the New Testament, and each location falls within the context of Paul's struggle: *Romans 7:22, Romans 7:25,* and *Romans 8:7.* Although *Romans 8:7* seems to fall outside of his struggle due to the fact that it follows his victory, it is seated in perfect chronology and application to Paul's struggle. *Romans 7:22* is during his struggle, *Romans 7:25* is during his victory, and *Romans 8:7* is after his victory. Therefore, let us look into each of these three remarkable Scriptures.

Romans 7:22 – *"For I delight in the Law of God after the inward man…."* Though Paul delights in the Law of God, he unveils that he is still held captive to the Law of Sin *(Rom. 7:23)*. Why? Although Paul takes use of the title *"the Law of God"* during His struggle, he had not yet understood the scope of the finished work of the Cross which now fully ensconced the Mosaic Law being Satisfied through Jesus Christ' Vicarious Shed Blood and death. Furthermore, through His death he had destroyed the works of the Devil; this also meant rectifying the manifold dynamics of the consequences of Adam's Sin, and the effects that evil had on the human being. Thus, Paul did not yet understand the impact that the Law had on the sin nature now that it had been incapacitated upon his Salvation. Therefore, not fully understanding the scope of what had been accomplished through the Cross, he continued touching the Law with his body, and thereby continued to be overcome by that which he was trying to overcome.

Romans 7:25 – *"So then with the mind I myself serve the Law of God…."* Paul, still delighting in the Law of God, is now free. Why? Paul, now understanding the scope of the finished work of the Cross, is no longer serving the Law with his body, he is now serving the Law of God with his mind, spirit, and soul, wherein his Faith and will followed *(Rom. 8:1-4)*.

Romans 8:7 – *"Because the carnal mind is enmity against God: for it is not subject to the Law of God, neither indeed can be."* Paul directly addresses the carnal mind. Why? Though repetitious, the carnal mind desires to use the body. If the body becomes thought of as the choice instrument, the husband will reinforce this type of carnal thinking. Convinced this is the right road and the good way to go, every motion will be by the Law, and the sin nature will revive. All of this was due to carnal thinking, which *"is not subject to the Law of God."* By the Apostle Paul using the phrase *"not subject"* within *Romans 8:7*, it means that the carnal mind has literally made up its mind. This is due to the husband, the Principle of Enforcement *(Rom. 7:2-3).*

WHAT IS THE LAW OF GOD, AND WHY DOES THE APOSTLE PAUL GIVE US THIS REMARKABLE EXAMPLE?

The Law of God is an amazing Law in which many dynamic principles take place. Its totality is complete in the Cross and, because of this, the Apostle Paul instructs us, through his example, to serve the Law of God with our mind. In order for us to understand Paul's example, let us first look into why the Law of God is complete in the Cross.

We know Jesus Christ kept the Law perfect in every way, yet He Suffered its just due Penalty Vicariously for all mankind on the Cross through death. For this very reason, from the finished work of the Cross on, Christ is now the end of the Law for Righteousness to everyone who believes *(Rom. 10:4).*

Now, let us look into an application that may help better reveal the Apostle's example. I have taken use, once again, of *Galatians 2:19* due to the impact that the Law can have on our life if we do not understand how to go through the Law. The Apostle Paul writes – *"For I through the Law am dead to the Law that I might live unto God."* In order to understand *Galatians 2:19*, we must acknowledge that no man, woman, boy, or girl can live by the Law; one simply cannot do it without experiencing guilt and the assorted bondages associated by trying. Therefore, since we cannot live by the Law, we have to go *"through the Law."* However, in order to accomplish this, it will have to be by Faith – Faith exclusively placed in the Cross.

We are able to go through the Law by placing Faith in the Cross due to Jesus Christ Satisfying the Law and Vicariously Paying the Penalty through His Shed Blood and death on the Cross. Christ is now the end of the Law for Righteousness to everyone who believes *(Rom. 10:4)*. Therefore, for we who believe, as we exercise Faith through Jesus Christ, and Him Crucified, the Righteousness of the Law remains fulfilled with us, and we are able to go *"through the Law."* This is the meaning of *Romans 7:25* so far – *"I thank God through Jesus Christ our Lord. So then with the mind I myself serve the Law of God."*

There is another remarkable dynamic happening as well when we serve *the Law of God* with our mind. As we exercise Faith in Jesus Christ, and Him Crucified, we not only pass through the Law, but are simultaneously and supernaturally planted in the likeness of Jesus' death *(Rom. 6:7; Gal. 2:20)*, wherein the Spirit of Life in Christ Jesus can, upon our death while we live, raise us in the likeness of His Resurrection *(Rom. 8:2, 11, 14)*.

Prior to our Salvation, we did not know, nor could we have ever come to know this. So, we lived by the Law instead of going through it because the Bible tells us that our carnal mind was at enmity or hostility against God, and was not subject to the Law of God *(Rom. 8:7)*. Furthermore, the amazing dynamics of the Law of God reveal His ways *(Heb., Chptrs 8-10)*. This means that we now have the Mind of Christ *(I Cor. 2:16)*, which can acknowledge the way in which God desires to help us live for Him – through Christ.

Another way this can be viewed is, because the Law of God is now ensconced in the finished work of the Cross, when we look to the Cross, we are serving the Law of God with our mind. Vice versa, when we serve the Law of God with our mind, we are looking to the Cross where the scope of the Law was Satisfied and the Penalty Paid. Therefore, the inseparable proper view for *the Law of God* is the

Cross, whereupon, the Penalty was Paid in Full through Jesus Christ, and Him Crucified. Thus, the Apostle Paul leaves us a magnificent example by writing – *"I thank God through Jesus Christ our Lord. So then with the mind I myself serve the Law of God."*

Romans 7:25 – Subject Scripture
I thank God through Jesus Christ our Lord. So then with the mind I myself serve the Law of God; **but with the flesh the Law of sin.**

Romans 7:25 – Portion VII: Principle seven
"…but with the flesh the Law of sin."

Here, in the balance of *verse 25*, the Apostle Paul unveils an unavoidable fact. By the Apostle Paul writing this portion, he is not implying that we are to serve the Law of sin with our flesh. The Apostle is simply saying that the Law of Sin will remain in our flesh until the Trump of God sounds, upon which we will put on immortality *(I Cor. 15:52-54; I Thess. 4:13-18)*.

For now, due to the Fall of Adam, our spirit cannot effectively work with our mind, soul, and body as originally designed *(I Pet. 2:11; Gal. 5:17)*, even though our spirit knows the things of God and our soul feels. For this reason, the Apostle Paul wrote – *"12For now we see through a glass, darkly; but then face to face: now I know in part; but then shall I know even as also I am known. 13And now abides Faith, Hope, Love, these three; but the greatest of these is Love" (I Cor. 13:12-13)*.

Now born again, we are walking out a remarkable miracle; we are living within the greatest love story ever known. Today, we have the opportunity to enter in not only rest, but abundant life and a much more intimate relationship with our Lord as our Faith finds rest in Whom He is, and what He has done by Giving Himself on the Cross for us.

CHAPTER 10

Walking After the Spirit

ROMANS 8:1

PREFACE

In the United States, one suicide takes place every 16 minutes and, according to the World Health Organization, depression is one of the leading causes of mental disability, with approximately 121 million people worldwide suffering from it. Today, the average age of suicide is 16 years old, and the National Institute of Mental Health states that approximately 18 million people suffer from depression in America alone.

Although we do not find the word "depression" in Scripture, we do find the root for the symptom. Depression is the result of condemnation and, if we do not know what it means to walk after the Spirit, we will experience condemnation *(Rom. 8:1, 4).*

The word "depression" comes from the Latin word *deprimere,* meaning to press down or depress. The word "condemnation" is defined within the biblical Greek word *katakrima* (κατάκριμα, NT:

2631, kat-ak'-ree-mah), which means adverse sentence (the verdict). The English definition for "the verdict" is defined as a single decision made concluding all issues presented in the matter.

In the case of mankind, the matter is Adam's Sin; all issues have been presented in this Case. The conclusive evidence presented deemed the verdict to be death and eternal separation from God. Regardless of what is believed and how complex the world may seem, the bottom line is that every person is born under the verdict of Adam's Original Sin *(Psalms 51:5; Rom. 5:12)*. Without receiving a full Pardon *(John 3:16)*, the sentence is eternal separation from God, and death *(Rev. 20:11-15)*.

How can a loving God send a person to Hell? I remember hearing this question one afternoon while several of us were on the streets sharing the Gospel. As a young Christian, I was thinking to myself the same question. The pastor we were with provided an answer that I have not forgotten today. He said, "Your Penalty has already been Paid through God's Son. The decision to accept Him, and what He has done is up to you."

Those of us who have accepted the Atoning work of God's Son have received a full Pardon. We are washed through Faith in His Shed Blood, and our eternal life rests on Whom Jesus Christ Is, and what He has done on the Cross. Even after receiving Salvation, condemnation can be experienced unless we come to understand what it means to walk after the Spirit, and walk therein.

Walking after the Spirit sounds easy enough, yet this walk is vastly different from what we may think. Let us look at *Romans 8:1* – *"THERE is therefore now no condemnation to them which are in Christ Jesus, who walk not after the flesh, but after the Spirit."* With vivid clarity, we can see that the Apostle Paul reveals a qualification for not experiencing condemnation; our walk must be after the Spirit. If our walk is not after the Spirit, it will be after the flesh by default *(Rom. 8:1-4)*, because it is not possible to walk after the Spirit and the flesh at the same time – it is either one, or it will be the other *(Gal. 5:4)*. The Apostle is not saying that we have lost our Salvation if condemnation is experienced. God's Grace is sufficient where sin abounds, yet this does not mean that we can remain in sin that Grace may abound *(Rom. 6:1-2)*.

Romans 8:1 is part of the context passages of Paul's struggle with the sin nature, and therefore the Apostle Paul has concluded that he cannot walk with God in growing Sanctification by use of self-efforts. When he tried, it not only gave the sin nature occasion to revive, it placed him outside the Righteousness of the Law fulfilled in Christ. This resulted in the Righteousness of the Law not remaining fulfilled in him due to his inability to satisfy the demands of the Law in his attempts for triumph. Thus, the experience was condemnation.

Within *Romans 8:1*, the phrase *"who walk"* is defined in biblical Greek within the word *tapeinophron* (ταπεινόφρων, NT: 5012a, tap-i-no'-frohn), and it means to be humble (i.e., humble-minded). The same phrase *"who walk"* is used again in *Romans 8:4*; however, in the context of *Romans 8:4*, it is defined in biblical Greek within the word *peripateo* (περιπατέω, NT: 4043, per-ee-pat-eh'-o), which means to walk about, to be occupied with, to live, deport oneself, or follow (as a companion or votary).

Within the Greek definition, we find the term "deport oneself." This term means to agree with, harmonize with, or conduct oneself in a specific manner. Within the same Greek definition, we find the word "votary," which comes from the Latin word *votus* and means "devote."

As we correlate *Romans 8:1* and *Romans 8:4*, the application means to be of a humble mind and occupy ourselves in a devotion to the way the Spirit desires to lead so that our walk can be after His leading. These two *verses* use the same phrase *"who walk,"* yet the defined difference is due to the dynamic benefits of truly walking after the Spirit. In the context of Paul's struggle with the sin nature, he came to understand that he could no longer condemn himself for his inabilities. This is a big deal and, as stated, it does not mean that Paul continued in sin by overlooking sin, and thus should be our position.

The Apostle Paul is revealing to us that when we see our inabilities, a humbleness of mind that recognizes the fact that Jesus Christ Satisfied the full demands of the Law causes us to grow in thankfulness for what He has done. This mindset grows evermore as we come to understand more and more of our current condition. When we condemn ourselves, we are ultimately negating the tremendous Sacrifice of the Cross, and think that we have the means within ourselves for Sanctification. Although we may not ever act out this latter mindset, it can literally create a prison of darkness. We can see the results of this with acute depression; thus is *Romans 8:1*.

When this mindset is acted upon, it results in a lifestyle of self-efforts as opposed to occupying oneself in a devotion to the way the Spirit desires to lead. This type of lifestyle disallows the Righteousness of the Law remaining fulfilled within his or her life; thus is *Romans 8:4*.

The act of trying to live by the Law can be very subtle, yet it originates condemnation. When we see our failure(s) and then pass judgment on ourselves, this act is a method of imposing the Law. Over time, if this type of thinking is not stopped, it leaves us thinking that we have not done enough, or we need to do something. This results in attempts to live by the Law in order to overcome the looming sense of guilt. In regards to this, the Apostle Paul writes – *"³But with me it is a very small thing that I should be judged of you, or of man's judgment: yes, I judge not mine own self. ⁴For I know nothing by myself; yet am I not hereby justified: but He Who judges me is the*

Lord. *⁵Therefore judge nothing before the time, until the Lord come, Who both will bring to light the hidden things of darkness, and will make manifest the counsels of the hearts: and then shall every man have praise of God" (I Cor. 4:3-5).*

When we try to overcome a condemning thought by trying to do good, even with the best of intentions, the very nature of what is being done is by the Law *(Rom. 7:5)*, and is at the core of carnal thinking. However, if the Christian is without the knowledge of the Cross for triumph and freedom, this type of carnal thinking is his or her only resource *(Rom. 7:8-11, 14)*.

Walking after the Spirit is to devote oneself to the leading of the Spirit, and each of us would most likely agree on this one point, but do we all agree with the way the Holy Spirit desires to lead? This is the quandary because we can be of a humble mind, devoted to God and occupied with serving the Lord, yet we can still be under condemnation. If condemnation is the experience, then it means that our walk is not after the Spirit but after the flesh. This is not to bring judgment, it simply means that if we are under condemnation, we have not agreed and therein embraced how the Holy Spirit desires to lead. The answer to the quandary is to learn how the Spirit desires to lead so the choice can then be made to walk after His leading.

Coming to understand how the Holy Spirit desires to lead is the single criteria for a magnificent, victorious, and joyful walk with God. However, everything in this world and everything in our flesh is saying no to the way that God has established for the leading of His Spirit. The way in which we think to walk after the Spirit is so contrary to the way that God has established that over 70% of pastors' struggle with depression according to the 2010, May 18th Edition of *The Christian Reporter.* That being the case, what about the laity?

I made the statement, "everything in this world and everything in our flesh is saying no to the ways of God." What I mean is that condemnation is everywhere; society is based on it. For example, dieting commercials are most often joyfully presented by those who are losing or have lost weight. No problem, right? Well, if someone had not mentioned to the individual that they could stand to lose a few pounds, it most likely would not have been a problem whether the individual was overweight or not. However, the seed is now planted, leaving the individual with quite a bit to think about and, most likely, not the best of thoughts. Though this may seem insignificant, for those who see their self as overweight, it can turn into a debilitating life of increased condemnation. Moreover, eating disorders such as anorexia and bulimia are life threatening, and the acute condemnation within the mind of those suffering from it is heart breaking.

We can find the same type of dynamics associated with many mental illnesses, yet if condemnation became non-existent would these so-called "mental illnesses" subside? What about parents that are left dealing with one of their children that have committed suicide? Though they may have done their best as parents, the condemnation that comes due to what they think they could have done may be lifelong. What about the loss of a spouse to a divorce? What about the runaway child? What about the child that has become an outcast because of the way he or she dresses or talks, or doesn't talk?

As I was watching the news recently, a breaking story took front and center of the news headlines. The helicopter cameramen had their view on a man in a small boat just off the shore of a lake. I came to watch this late in the event, but they were saying that he was making desperate attempts to take his own life with what he could find in the boat. Come to find out, the man was caught looking in the bedroom window of a well-known celebrity. Caught in the act, he fled to the lake where he found the boat he was now in, and it was in this boat that he was trying to take his own life with what he could find.

Although the man's attempts were failing, the commentators openly remarked that they hoped he was successful. These remarks stirred more heinous views from the other commentators, and the comments streamed on as they exploited what they could find about the position the man had put himself in, and him deserving death. No one proposed the slightest statement of mercy for the man, nor was there any statement presented to help neutralize the horrendous judgments streaming out of the mouths of the commentators.

As the helicopter camera panned around, there was what looked like a dozen officers on the shore, and four more heading out in a small boat of their own to apprehend him. As they became close enough, one of the officers jumped into the man's boat and, without a struggle, the officer apprehended the man before he could take his own life. Though this is "normal" news, anguish gripped my heart and I was broken for the man in the boat. Yes, what he did was wrong and no, he should not have done what he did, but what was driving his sin? How much condemnation was he under because of his sin? Was he trying to take his life because he hated what he did? The point is, there was no mercy at all, and the world is run on this type of thinking.

There is a story of a girl who was somewhat shy and did not talk much, and was often rejected by her peers. Through a series of events, some of her so-called friends were able retain a picture of her nude. One person sent it to another, and so on, until it spread throughout the school. At lunch, unaware of what was going on and not understanding why everybody was laughing at her more than usual, one of the students walked over and showed her the picture of herself on her phone. Without anyone coming to her aid, she walked out of school alone that afternoon, and that night she took her own life.

If Jesus said, *"Father, forgive them; for they know not what they do..." (Luke 23:34),* our heart as Christians should be that of mercy, free from condemnation. What is the point of all of this? Mankind is incapable of making decisions through the perception of good and evil unless they come to understand and embrace the leading of the Holy Spirit. The result of His leading will be God's view.

The entire world has its own pulpit streaming commercials, news, politics, health issues, medications, and how to have relationships. On any level, one may plead a case and make perfectly good sense. Another will plead the same case bringing a different view and thereby make perfectly good sense, yet people choose sides. Which side is the right one? It is an inevitable reality of self-demise, unless one receives Salvation and then embraces the leading of the Holy Spirit. In this embracement, there is true discernment to breathe the wisdom of God upon both sides in the hope that they too will come to the knowledge of the One Truth. Nonetheless, the world functions, whatever that function may be, and Man moves through this world's pulpit every day. This is due to the base knowledge of good and evil from the Tree.

Adam's decision that produced his action to eat from the Tree of the Knowledge of Good and Evil brought the Fall of mankind. Though we may easily understand this, it may not be as easy to understand that this catastrophic event resulted in receiving the knowledge of good and evil. This knowledge is the carnal base thinking through which each human has his or her function, and each perceives everything he or she does. Simply said, man was not meant to have this knowledge – the human was magnificently created to know God.

More than likely, everyone would agree that the world would be a better place without the knowledge of evil, but what is most difficult to understand is that we should not have the knowledge of good. It is the knowledge of good by which the world has decided they do not need God, and if the knowledge of good is not discerned properly *(Heb. 5:14)*, it is not possible to learn dependency on God the way He desires. Moreover, it is the knowledge of good by which the nature of evil finds its way, which was comprehensively expounded upon earlier in the *Romans 7:21* Subject Scripture.

There are many questions that surround the Tree of the Knowledge of Good and Evil, but one thing is for sure: man was not meant to go against the Command of God and partake of it. The presentation of the Tree and the Command to not partake of it created a setting, yet why would God do this? Though seemingly odd, free will without the option to decide is a controlled environment, and true love does not control. Though we know this in part, it is impossible to comprehend the infinite love of God and His desire to fellowship with the human being. Nevertheless, God, in His infinite love, would create the man, Adam, all the while in His infinite knowledge, understanding the potential for him to fall at the devices of the one who attempted to usurp His Throne in Eternity past. Knowing all things, He also knew and Resolved what it would take in order to Redeem mankind in the event that Adam did fall. Still, in His incomprehensible love, He formed Adam, breathed into his nostrils the breath of life, and then placed him in the Garden of Eden wherein He intimately walked with him.

Over time, as Lucifer plotted to the extent of his wisdom, he would compose himself through the caverns of his darkened mind and cause Adam and Eve to doubt God by introducing the idea that God was withholding knowledge and wisdom from them *(Gen. 3:4-5)*. As they pondered the lie, though Eve became deceived, believing that there was more, Adam hearkened unto her voice, and they took, ate, and gained the knowledge of good and evil *(Gen. 3:6)*. In this self-reliant act, they became separated from their Creator, their eyes were opened, and now, with a conscience of self, the knowledge of good compelled them to overcome the knowledge of evil *(Gen. 3:7)*. This left them and all mankind through Adam's seed in a fallen state, resulting in a cyclic turmoil of failure and condemnation *(Gen. 3:10, 12; Rom. 2:14-15)*. The results of this are seen in a general evaluation of the world around us.

This turmoil exists for us today unless we come to understand how the Holy Spirit desires to lead, whereby the capacity to discern the knowledge of good and evil will be gained *(Heb. 5:14)*. If we neglect His leading, we will experience the penalty of Adam's sin, the effects of which can range from a continuous looming guilt to a debilitating depression. If we do not come out from under condemnation, killing ourselves can become an ever-present mindset. This as well may sound dramatic and dark, but the reality of condemnation and facets of depression, suicide, murder, and all that we know, see, and experience in our mind and in the tangible world around us should clearly show the current condition of fallen man.

The fallen condition of Man is so bad that unless God gave the Mosaic Law to reveal Man's fallen condition, the human being would not even realize the depth of his or her moral depravity. Still, even with this Law brought forth by God, it cannot be lived through the flesh *(Rom. 8:3)*; it is only meant to reveal Man's condition and therein bring us to Christ *(Gal. 3:24-25)*. Nobody apart from Jesus could have ever or can ever live up to the moral standard of this Law.

The Mosaic Law was put into place as a stopgap measure prior to God coming into this world in order to take the Penalty of Adam's Sin upon Himself, in His flesh and in the Place of all mankind *(Gen. 3:15; John 1:29; I Pet. 1:18-20)*. Moreover, He would also, in His Sacrificial, Atoning and triumphant work on the Cross, Blot out the handwriting of Ordinances that was against us, which was contrary to us; taking it out of the way, nailing it to His Cross *(Col. 2:14)*. Now, through the finished work of the Cross, Christ is the end of the Law for Righteousness to everyone who believes *(Rom. 10:4)*. For this reason, walking after the Spirit is on the basis of Faith alone, apart from any self-efforts in the flesh.

Without Salvation, which can only be found in and through Jesus Christ *(John 3:3, 16; Acts 4:10-12; Rom. 10:9-10)*, the human being will reap the full penalty of Adam's sin, wherein eternal Hell and the Lake of Fire are the final destination *(Rom. 5:12; Rev., Chptr 20)*. Eternal Hell is real, and condemnation is the red flag telling the unsaved sinner that something is wrong *(Rom. 2:11-16; 3:19)*. Since the consequences of Adam's sin are so dire, the reality of condemnation is so enveloping. The reality of this has always been prevalent and widespread throughout the entire human race. However, regardless of the effort to fix condemnation, oppression or depression, the condition will remain if the answer is attempted to be found in psychology, philosophy, imprisonment, drugs, religion, or any other thing apart from Faith in Jesus Christ, and Him Crucified.

Now, for us who are Saved, we must come to understand that, though we are delivered from the Law by the body of Christ *(Rom. 7:4-6)*, we are not Lawless *(Rom. 7:7, 25; I Cor. 9:21; Heb. 8:10-13; 10:16-17)*. This means that, because of the Cross, we now have the Law of God. This is our New Covenant Law due to the finished work of Jesus Christ (i.e., Jesus Christ, and Him Crucified). The Law of God is not a set of rules – it is Holy, and it is spiritual *(Rom. 7:12, 14)* – and as I have previously stated, the Apostle Paul, through his magnificent example, has shown us the benefits of serving the Law of God with our mind. The Law of God is not only the Mosaic Law fulfilled in Jesus Christ; it is housed within it the Law of the Spirit *(Rom. 8:2)* and the Law to Christ *(I Cor. 9:21)*, both of which are ensconced within that form of Doctrine *(Rom. 6:17-18)*. Though this seems comprehensive, it is all summed up in the Cross – the simplicity that is in Christ *(II Cor. 11:3)*.

Through his example, as the Apostle Paul shows us to serve the Law of God with our mind, he is helping us understand that we are to look, think about, and grow in the knowledge of where the Law became fulfilled and the Penalty Paid (that is, the Cross *[I Cor. 2:2; Gal. 2:19-20; Heb., Chptrs 2-10]*). By serving the Law of God with our mind, we simply engage the Law of the Spirit and the Law to Christ. Because the Cross is the legal parameter the Spirit of Life works through, we remain dead to the dire effects of the Mosaic Law, and experience the effectual energizing power of God at work within our life *(Gal. 2:19-20)*. This is what it truly means to walk after the Spirit, and it is all accomplished on the basis of Faith resting in Jesus Christ, and Him Crucified – the Cross *(Rom. 7:25; I Cor. 2:2)*.

Many Christians today are experiencing condemnation simply because their Faith is not in the Cross. Condemnation is experienced to one degree or the other because the Righteousness of the Law is not remaining fulfilled within them. This condition is equated to walking after the flesh *(Rom. 8:1-4)*. Yes, they believe in Jesus and they love Him, but the abundant life is missing because the Cross is not part of the equation. In other words, all Christians believe in Jesus, but most move on from "Him Crucified." By simply bringing the Cross back into the equation of their Faith, they have moved into walking after the Spirit, and as their Faith finds its rest in the Cross, the Holy Spirit will continue to lead and teach them *(John 14:26; I John 2:27)*.

Coming to learn about Jesus Christ, and Him Crucified, as the object for Faith is the Will of the Father for life and living *(Luke 9:23; Gal. 5:18; Phil. 2:5; 3:7-11)*. For this reason, as stated, God has given us the simplicity that is in Christ *(II Cor. 11:3)*.

The scope of condemnation is understandable for those who are unsaved, yet when a Christian denies the Doctrine of the Cross or it becomes seen as foolishness *(I Cor. 1:18; 2:14)*, at best they will experience looming guilt and condemnation. At worst, they have become enemies of the Cross *(Phil. 3:18-19)*.

Though the world is filled with chaos, it simply comes down to two choices: we can walk after the flesh, which is of the carnal mind and is not subject to the Law of God *(Rom. 8:7)*, or we walk can walk after the Spirit, which is subject to the Law of God *(Rom. 7:25)*. Being subject to the Law of God is coming to understand, as Paul came to understand, that Faith must remain in the Cross, wherein we go through the Law and not end up living by it *(Gal. 2:19)*. The result of this determining mindset is inexpressible joy and freedom because the Righteousness of the Law remains fulfilled within us *(Rom. 8:4; 10:4)*.

If condemnation is currently your experience, I understand; I have been there myself. If you are reading this, and actually made it this far in the book, then God is teaching you. Though it is as if you are in a threshold now, yet have not come out the other side and it is still dark – do not give up! You are either one or just a few steps from the inexpressible realm of His presence that will not become a faded experience; it will be lasting joy and freedom exceeding what your imagination could have provided. Let us get started in the Subject Scripture.

Romans 8:1 – Subject Scripture undivided
THERE is therefore now no condemnation to them which are in Christ Jesus, who walk not after the flesh, but after the Spirit.

One of the greatest benefits of Salvation is the freedom that comes when condemnation is gone. Yet because it can once again be experienced, I have chosen not to divide *Romans 8:1* due to the misconceptions of condemnation in today's Christianity.

The Apostle Paul was a Christian during his struggle with the sin nature, and he most certainly struggled with condemnation. Yet what is most marvelous is that, once he came to understand the way of Sanctification through Christ, he addressed condemnation in the first description of his victory. Thus we are given *Romans 8:1*.

However, today there many Christians who have become crippled with condemnation, some so severely that despair has replaced hope and thoughts of suicide are pulling them into deeper and darker corridors within their mind. This, once again, does not mean that they have lost their Salvation. This means it is a heartbreaking reality that the Christian does not have to experience.

Yet, without knowing the way of Sanctification, the result can be a prison built out of condemnation with hopeless despair as the only friend. Just because we are born again does not negate the reality of coming under condemnation; condemnation will cease only if the way of victory is found and a walk after the Spirit begins.

However, there is a significant dilemma that we face today; the way of Sanctification – the answer for properly placing Faith – is little taught. Without this answer, it is not possible to walk after the Spirit in the fullness of the Father's Will. Adding to this dilemma are the altered Bible translations, wherein some it is not possible to ascertain the non-negotiable Biblical Doctrine.

A literal biblical translation writes *Romans 8:1* as – *"THERE is therefore now no condemnation to them which are in Christ Jesus, who walk not after the flesh, but after the Spirit."* However, altered Word for thought translation writes *Romans 8:1* as – *"THERE is therefore now no condemnation to them which are in Christ Jesus."* Within the altered version, we can see that ending portions have been removed. This omission causes the reader to believe that condemnation has been eradicated, and therefore when condemnation is experienced, the Christian has no idea how to deal with it, or why in fact it is even part of their experience.

There are many translations and, in general, they can be broken into five groups: literal translations, word for word, word for thought, thought for thought, and paraphrased. It is my opinion that anything beyond literal translations and a proper word for word translation should not be used for Bible study. However, there are many other translations that should not be read at all. Nonetheless, removing portions of Scripture, watering down Scripture, or not talking about the realities of sin does not make sin and condemnation go away.

When there is a battle, one cannot simply avoid it without consequences. Yet a man is not considered brave just because he runs blindly into battle. A brave man understands the battle and the dangers, but still engages the battle with truth, integrity, and open eyes. In the case of our Christianity, we are in a battle that cannot be avoided without consequences. Therefore, we are to engage our daily life with the Truth, walk in our integrity, and be brave in each battle because our Lord Jesus Christ has gone before us. The bottom line is, we cannot avoid being in this present evil world, but we must not be part of it, and we cannot avoid the reality of the Law, so we must learn of our relationship to it, and we cannot avoid the reality of the sin nature, but it does not have to rule us any longer.

If we can come to understand what walking after the Spirit is and therein walk, then walking after the flesh will be clearly seen for what it is. Until then, the one walking after the flesh will not understand. Walking after the flesh is simply equated into living by the Law, regardless of how subtle it may be *(Rom. 7:5)*. This walk in the flesh may be so subtle, have such an appearance of good, and even have some semblance of victory that we do not even realize what we are doing. Nevertheless, God cannot (nor does He) work through the ways of man, regardless of how good and right they may appear *(Gal. 5:17)*. Yes, we will still experience God's Grace and love if we try in our own efforts, but He has established His way for our Sanctification. Unless this way becomes walked within, condemnation will continue to be the experience.

Condemnation is a red flag telling us that something is wrong; it is telling us that we are functioning by the Law, or some other method devised in some way. The result of this is condemnation; though born again, we are simply experiencing the penalty of the Law. As Christians, it is so very important for us to understand Whom Jesus Christ Is, and what He has done on the Cross, never separating the two for our life and living.

Our love for God is not equated in how much we do or how hard we try in any type of method. Our love for God is equated and revealed by where we place our Faith, which reveals the direction of our heart, our soul, and our mind. For this reason, the Apostle Paul writes – *"For I determined not to know any thing among you, save Jesus Christ, and Him Crucified" (I Cor. 2:2).*

Although I have mentioned *1 Corinthians 2:2* quite a bit already, it is a perfect example of properly placed Faith. In Paul's life, the result was coming to know of God's tremendous love for him, and in this he also came to know of God's love for His Son, and the tremendous cost of what His Son has done for him on the Cross.

This deeper, more intimate knowledge was not only a place free from condemnation – it was a place *(the place)* wherein the Apostle Paul experienced the likeness of Jesus' death, and yet the magnificent benefits of the likeness of His Resurrection. In this wonderful experience, he writes – *"I am Crucified with Christ: nevertheless I live; yet not I, but Christ lives in me: and the life which I now live in the flesh I live by the Faith of the Son of God, Who loved me, and gave Himself for me" (Gal. 2:20).*

As it was for Paul, it is also for us. The likeness of Jesus' death ensures the likeness of His Resurrection; this is where our walk after the Spirit begins. It starts with a decision – one to bring our thoughts to the security of God's Son – and what His Son has done on the Cross for us. This decision is all we have, yet it will be the greatest and most beneficial decision we can make, and because our walk will be after the Spirit, there will be no condemnation!

CHAPTER 11

The Law of the Spirit of Life

ROMANS 8:2

PREFACE

T he Devil cannot change the Gospel *(John 19:30)*, so his main aim is to corrupt it *(Gal. 1:6-9; I Tim. 4:1)*. In this, he has introduced to the world and the Church a lot of deceitfully subtle and complicated answers to overcome sin. These supposed answers have the appearance of dying to oneself *(Rev. 12:9)*; most appear as godliness, but all of his ways deny the power of the Holy Spirit *(II Tim. 3:5)*. The Devil's ways are open and seen for what they are: blasphemy. Satan knows that if he can corrupt and complicate the simplicity that is in Christ – the Cross for Sanctification after Salvation *(II Cor. 11:3; Gal. 6:14)* – then he can destroy our walk, our family, and ultimately our life.

There is only one answer to keep us free from sin, the nature of it, and Satan's deceptions. This is the answer for the entire human race; Salvation for the unsaved, and Sanctification for we who are

Saved. If we can come to understand and embrace the way in which God has established for us, then our walk will be one serving Him in newness of Spirit *(Rom. 7:6)*, free from the nature of sin in our members *(Rom. 7:23)* and every other false way will fade away in the presence of Truth.

Romans 8:2 – Subject Scripture
For the Law of the Spirit of Life in Christ Jesus has made me free from the Law of Sin and Death.

Romans 8:2 – Portion I
"For the Law of the Spirit of Life…"

It is quite amazing that the Apostle Paul begins this remarkable *verse* with the preposition *"For"* instead of simply writing *"The Law of the Spirit of Life."* The preposition "for" is so common in sentence structures that it would be hard to imagine the English language without it. An example would be "equipment *for* the army," which clearly allows us to see that the equipment (whatever that may be) is *for* the army. Although this may seem elementary and insignificant, the manner in which the Holy Spirit had the Apostle begin the sentence of *Romans 8:2*, unveils three truths. This first truth is that this guideline, that is, this specific "Law" has been established in Christ *for* the Spirit of Life. Thus, "the Spirit of Life" functions within a specific guideline, "the Law of the Spirit." The second truth is that this specific guideline is the equipment that has been established in Christ *for* the army, all Christians. The final truth is that this guideline is the equipment that has been established *for* the army's freedom.

Let us look into another Scripture that will help us understand more about this remarkable Law – *"Buried with Him in Baptism, wherein also you are risen with Him through the Faith of the operation of God, Who has raised Him from the dead" (Col. 2:12).*

Within *Colossians 2:12*, we find the word "operation." The word "operation" is defined within the biblical Greek word *energeia* (Ινέ ργεια, NT: 1753, en-erg'-i-ah); from NT: 1756; efficiency ("energy"): – operation, strong, (effectual) working.

Thus, *Colossians 2:12* – "*the Faith of the operation of God*" – gives us remarkable insight for understanding "*the Law of the Spirit of Life*" because both "*the operation of God*" and "*the Spirit of Life*" are experienced in the life of a human being through the guidelines of properly placed Faith.

The terminology "*the Faith of the operation of God*" describes to us that God operates through "*the Faith.*" That is, the "*operation of God*" was, upon our Salvation, experienced through the guidelines of properly placed Faith, which is specifically "*the Faith.*" Likewise for "*the Law of the Spirit of Life.*" The title and terminology "*the Law of the Spirit*" describes to us that "*the Spirit of Life*" is experienced in our life through the guidelines of properly placed Faith; hence, "*the Law*" of "*the Spirit.*"

Although both "*the operation of God*" and "*the Spirit of Life*" are experienced through properly placed Faith, there is a significant difference between the experiences. The difference is that of Salvation and that of Sanctification.

We experienced "*the operation of God*" during our Salvation *(Col. 2:6-12)*, and "*the Spirit of Life*" is experienced through Sanctification, growing in triumph and holiness after Salvation *(Rom. 8:9-17)*.

One may ask: "Is the Faith for Salvation the same Faith for Sanctification?" The answer is yes! I will first explain how we experienced "*the operation of God*" during our Salvation, and then I will explain more about "*the Law of the Spirit of Life.*"

While we were sinners, the Mosaic Law was our schoolmaster that brought us to Christ; thereupon, we then believed in our heart that Jesus Christ died on the Cross for our sins and that God raised Him from the dead. We then moved on our belief by confessing with our mouth, whereupon we received Salvation and, immediately, Faith came *(Rom. 10:9-10; Gal. 3:24-25).* Although we knew our sins were Washed away by the Atoning Blood of Jesus Christ, we may not have been taught that Jesus Christ also triumphed over the Devil through His death on the Cross. Nonetheless, we were still made free from the holds of evil upon receiving Salvation *(Rom. 6:6; 7:2-3).* Thus, our experience and the multiple magnificent events that had taken place upon our Salvation came about through *"the operation of God."*

One may ask: "If *'the operation of God'* took place during my Salvation, and *'the Spirit of Life'* is experienced for my Sanctification, why am I not experiencing *'the Spirit of Life'?'"* The answer is found in how we approach and deal with Sanctification after Salvation. Therefore, let us take a look.

Upon our Salvation, *"the operation of God"* was experienced in our life through the guideline of believing that Jesus Christ died on the Cross, and God raised Him from the dead. Yet, by possibly not knowing why or how we were made free, wherein we could continue in freedom, we removed "Jesus Christ died on the Cross" from our Faith, and believed our victory was in Jesus Christ and God raising Him from the dead. However, by removing "Jesus Christ died on the Cross," that is, "Him Crucified" from our Faith, the default recourse was to use our body for growing in Sanctification. Though we believed in Jesus Christ and remained Saved, we were not experiencing *"the Spirit of Life."*

Viewing the scope of what has been said, one may ask several more questions: "Why was the title, *'the Spirit of Life'* given? What is the guideline, that is, Law that '*the Spirit of Life*' effectually works within? And how can I enter into this Law and experience '*the Spirit of Life*' in my own life?" If these questions are asked, they are great and valid questions indeed! Therefore, let us deal with them.

Scripture unveils "*the Spirit of Life*" just twice: once in *Romans 8:2*, and again in *Revelation 11:11*. In both cases, "*the Spirit of Life*" operates upon the death of the Believer. *Revelations 11:11* reveals "*the Spirit of Life*" raising the physical body after physical death, and *Romans 8:2* reveals "*the Spirit of Life*" raising the Believer once the body is made dead while still physically alive. Therefore, death must come first in order for "*the Spirit of Life*" to energize the Believer; regardless of the death – physical death or death while alive – either way, death must come first *(Rom. 6:7)*. This gives us unique full scope insight into the specific title given; hence, "*the Law of the Spirit of Life in Christ Jesus.*"

Although *Revelation 11:11* makes perfect sense that "*the Spirit of Life*" raised the two Believers who were physically dead, how does the living Believer die in order to experience "*the Spirit of Life*" and yet still physically live? The answer to this has been established within the exclusive guideline, the Law of properly placed Faith.

As stated, we experienced "*the operation of God*" upon Salvation. It is done. If we are experiencing bondage and condemnation, it reveals that we have removed "Jesus Christ died on the Cross" from our Faith in some way in regards to Sanctification. By removing "Him Crucified" from our Faith, the default recourse was to use our body for growing in Sanctification. Though we remain Saved *(Rom. 7:8-23)*; in our self-efforts, we no longer remained dead while alive in this present evil world. Thus, we stepped out of the supernatural benefits of the likeness of Jesus' death. As a result, we stepped out of the guidelines of the effectual working of "*the Spirit of Life.*" Furthermore, due to functioning outside of the exclusive guidelines, the sin nature revived and brought the wrong death *(Rom. 7:9)*. Therefore, the exclusive guideline of *"the Spirit of Life"* is properly placed Faith.

God does not require much from us, but He does require that our Faith be anchored in Jesus Christ, and Him Crucified *(I Cor. 2:2)*. God never changes, lies, or violates that which He has foreordained in Eternity past and established in and through His Son, and what His Son has done for us on the Cross *(I Pet. 1:18-20)*. Therefore, so long as our Faith remains anchored in the Cross, we will remain dead while we live, and experience the effectual working of *the Spirit of Life* in our life.

Romans 8:2 – Subject Scripture
For the Law of the Spirit of Life **in Christ Jesus** has made me free from the Law of Sin and Death.

Romans 8:2 – Portion II
"…in Christ Jesus…"

By the Apostle Paul using the phrase *"in Christ Jesus"* or any derivatives such as *"through Christ Jesus,"* he is, without fail, referring to Jesus Christ, and Him Crucified. He and His Cross cannot be separated from within our Faith in order for us to grow in Sanctification *(I Cor. 1:17-18; Rev. 12:11)*. It was for the purpose of the Cross that He came into the world *(John 3:16; I Pet. 1:18-20)*. Now that "It is finished," It is through Jesus Christ, and Him Crucified that *"the Law of the Spirit"* has been established for us.

Romans 8:2 – Subject Scripture
For the Law of the Spirit of Life in Christ Jesus **has made me free from the Law of Sin and Death.**

Romans 8:2 – Portion III
"…has made me free from the Law of Sin and Death."

As with *"the Law of the Spirit of Life,"* it is with *"the Law of Sin and Death."* These two Laws not only deals with the spiritual, but also the physical human body *(Rom. 7:15, 23; 8:11)*. Many believe that the Christian can become possessed. This is not the case. This is said to help us understand that the problem we are facing is a problem we were born with due to the Fall of Adam, and it cannot be dealt with any other way other than Faith resting in Jesus Christ, and Him Crucified.

If this way of living for God is not embraced, we can simply move off the main road into the detour and eventually shipwreck our Faith. Though the unsaved are in a condition and position that allows them to be held within the dominion of the Law of Sin and Death, there are many Christians who love the Lord with all of their heart, yet are still held under the dominion of sin and death.

Therefore, if you are a Christian (regardless of the sin, the bondage, or even the length of time you have been struggling), if you move your Faith into Jesus Christ, *and* Him Crucified, you will have entered into the Law of the Spirit of Life. Therein, not only will your mind be made free from the captive hold, your physical body will be released *from "the Law of Sin and Death,"* and you will be raised in the likeness of Jesus' Resurrection.

Will this happen instantly? It can most certainly happen in an instant! For me personally, it took time, yet when I came to understand that my Faith simply needed to rest in the Cross, something deeply resonated, and this was instant. I knew this was Truth even though I did not understand at first. One thing I will never forget was the presence of the Holy Spirit helping me look to the Cross each time I made the decision to look to the Cross.

When I first began making the decision to place my Faith in the Cross, it was just minutes later that my mind was on something else, and that was when I began to see dynamics of evil in my members that I did not understand at the time. Nonetheless, I realized the Holy Spirit was helping me each time I made the decision to look to the Cross.

One day, as life was falling apart around me, I determined that I was going to keep my Faith in the Cross, and then, though there are no words to describe it, I experienced the presence of God in a way I had never experienced before, and I had been a Christian for twenty years at that time. Since then, His Word has come alive in my life and I have been filled with inexpressible peace, joy, and rest.

Though I have expounded a bit on *"the Law of Sin and Death,"* let us continue on with this fact of existence from a different perspective. The reason being, without understanding the reality of this Law and the evil forces at work within this Law, we can spend our lifetime binding and loosing the Devil, his associates, and demons, thinking these entities of evil are the problem. Yes, they are a problem, but when our Faith is properly placed, *"the Spirit of Life"* makes us free from *"the Law of Sin and Death."* The result is sin and death no longer ruling our life, and the influences of these evil forces are then seen for what they actually are – influences without the power to back up their lies. We then, by the power of God through Christ, can easily cast away these evil forces without effort, concern, or otherwise.

Once again, in this present evil world, the problem is not outside of us – it is within our flesh. For this reason, the Apostle Paul writes – *"But I see another Law in my members, warring against the Law of my mind, and bringing me into captivity to the Law of sin which is in my members" (Rom. 7:23)*. The Law of Sin that Paul unveils in *Romans 7:23* is the same Law addressed here in *Romans 8:2 – "the Law of Sin and Death."* Yet, this is a title for *"the Law"* that *"Sin and Death"* work through. Sin and death cannot do what they want, when they want, unless the confines they are restricted by are engaged.

It was through Jesus Christ, and Him Crucified, that the Law of the Spirit of Life in Christ Jesus has become established for us, and *"the Law of Sin and Death"* was revealed due to Jesus Christ, and Him Crucified. What do I mean?

Due to the Fall of Adam, with the exception of Jesus, all of us as humans are conceived in the nature of sin and born into our humanity with it *(Psalms 51:5; Rom. 5:12)*. Yet it must be understood that this fallen nature is confined to our physical body *(Rom. 7:23)*, more than likely because Adam and Eve used their physical body to engage the Tree of the Knowledge of Good and Evil. Once the act of Original Human Sin was complete, the intangibles of Adam and Eve's mind became catastrophically affected by the knowledge of good and evil from the Tree *(Gen. 3:6-9)*.

Although we do not know how Adam and Eve were fully affected by their Sin because they were created in the image, after the likeness of God (thus being without sin) we do know the impact and consequences their Sin had and continues to have on the human race. Nevertheless, *"the Law of Sin and Death"* could now be revealed because the Atoning and triumphant Sacrifice of Jesus Christ destroyed the works of the Devil.

Another way this can be viewed is this: because Original Human Sin came by use of the physical body, the Atonement for this Sin, and thus the human race, came by use of the physical body of the Man, Jesus *(Rom. 7:4: Heb. 10:10)*. Therefore, after Salvation is received, the physical body cannot be used to live for God.

The bottom line is, the human body cannot be used for growing in Sanctification or anything else associated with spiritual matters *(Rom. 8:10)*. For this reason, the confines for *"the Law"* of *"Sin and Death"* are the use of the physical body in regards to living for God.

Therefore, upon receiving Salvation, our body becomes dead; it is rendered useless because of the Law of Sin and Death. For this reason, we are not to live by the Mosaic Law or any other by-law, devise, or otherwise that would require our body. If the body is used in the Sanctification process, the confines of the Law of Sin and Death will be breached, and sin and death are given occasion to revive.

We must remember, though living by the Mosaic Law, by-laws, devices, methods, etc., sounds as if we would see what we are doing, most often these ways are subtle, but all of them will breach into the Law of Sin and Death. The only way we can avoid breaching into the Law of Sin and Death is to embrace the way that God has established through Jesus Christ, and Him Crucified. When our Faith finds its resting place in the Cross, we have simply entered into the guidelines for "*the Law of the Spirit of Life,*" and therein we are made free from "*the Law of Sin and Death.*"

CHAPTER 12

The Revelation of the Mystery

ROMANS 16:25-27

PREFACE

Once Salvation is received, God's way of Sanctification is
found in the Revelation of the Mystery. However, it can only
be known when we come to realize that living for God cannot be
accomplished by self-efforts, regardless how good any effort may
appear.

The Apostle Paul was born again when he came to realize that
his ways were not working and sought God, wherein seeking, God
Revealed the way of Sanctification to him *(Gal. 1:11-12)*. Once the
Apostle Paul understood the magnificence within the Revelation, he
writes – *"⁶Howbeit we speak wisdom among them that are perfect: yet
not the wisdom of this world, nor of the princes of this world, that come
to nought: ⁷But we speak the Wisdom of God in a mystery, even the
hidden wisdom, which God ordained before the world unto our glory:*

⁸Which none of the princes of this world knew: for had they known it, they would not have Crucified the Lord of Glory (I Cor. 2:6-8).

These three *verses of the second chapter of I Corinthians* give us four remarkable insights. First, the Apostle Paul speaks wisdom among them that are perfect, that is, mature. The second is that the wisdom Paul speaks is not of this world. Third, neither the world nor the princes of this world knew of this wisdom. Finally, had the princes of this world known of this wisdom, they would not have Crucified the Lord of Glory.

The magnitude of these insights reveals the Wisdom of God, and also reveals the simplicity that is in Christ, which continued through the Cross in order to become established for us *(Rom. 6:3-5, 7; 7:25; 8:2, I Cor. 2:2; Gal. 6:14).*

This is the wisdom spoken among the mature; it is not the wisdom of this world, and it is not possible to gain the depth of this Revelation through human capacity. Though the carnal mind is always trying to gain insight into the mystery of holiness, without this Revelation, the fullness of the mystery cannot be understood. This mystery is the Message of life through death.

Romans 16:25 – Subject Scripture
Now to Him that is of power to stablish you according to my Gospel, and the Preaching of Jesus Christ, according to the Revelation of the Mystery, which was kept secret since the world began,

Romans 16:25 – Portion I
"Now to Him Who is of power to stablish you according to my Gospel…,"

"Now to Him Who is of power to stablish you" speaks of Christ Jesus coming from Eternity into time and divesting Himself for the

purpose of the Cross. For He – Christ – conquered the Devil that had the hold of death through death and is of power to establish you. The word *"stablish"* in this beginning portion is simply an archaic variant of "establish." Following the word *"stablish,"* Paul writes *"according to my Gospel,"* making it clear that this Gospel is his Gospel. Quite a profound statement indeed, but we must understand that Paul neither created his Gospel nor took the calling on himself. God set Paul apart to receive the Gospel – *"Paul, a servant of Jesus Christ, called to be an Apostle, separated unto the Gospel of God" (Rom. 1:1).*

The paramount magnificence within the Gospel that God revealed to Paul was something not known by Man, and therefore Man could not teach Paul. The Gospel was taught to Paul by the Revelation of Jesus Christ – *"¹¹But I certify you, Brethren, that the Gospel which was Preached of me is not after man. ¹²For I neither received it of man, neither was I taught it, but by the Revelation of Jesus Christ" (Gal. 1:11-12).*

Although the Author of Hebrews is unknown, most scholars agree that it was Paul. If this is the case, and I believe it was, then the Apostle Paul wrote fourteen of the twenty-seven New Testament Epistles under the inspiration and supervision of the Holy Spirit. The importance of this should not escape us in that the Gospel, unveiled to us by the Apostle Paul, is the Gospel of Jesus Christ, and Him Crucified.

The Gospel Message of Jesus Christ, and Him Crucified, is the Message of the Cross Revealed and taught to Paul by the Revelation of Jesus Christ *(Eph. 3:1-12).* Once Paul received, embraced, and understood this remarkable Mystery, Paul was then given the vast responsibility of it.

This magnificent Gospel revealed to all, that the Gentiles became part of God's Salvation Plan, and that the Wisdom of God was carried through the Cross unto our glory. That is, the power of

God was able to establish any Believer as the Cross became the focal point of his or her life and living, and thereby the exclusive resting place for their Faith *(I Cor. 2:2).*

Romans 16:25 – Subject Scripture
Now to Him that is of power to stablish you according to my Gospel, **and the Preaching of Jesus Christ, according to the Revelation of the Mystery,** which was kept secret since the world began,

Romans 16:25 – Portion II
**"…and the Preaching of Jesus Christ, according
to the Revelation of the Mystery…,"**

The Apostle Paul's Gospel is the Gospel of Jesus Christ *"and the Preaching of Jesus Christ"* was always *"according to the Revelation of the Mystery."* We may easily understand the preaching of Salvation, but Paul's Gospel ensconced the way of becoming established by the power of God, and thus growing in personal Sanctification after Salvation was received *(I Cor. 1:17-18, 23).* Herein, the Revelation of the Mystery, unto our glory, was unveiled *(I Cor. 2:6-8).* This is the wisdom and knowledge within the full Gospel of God *(Rom. 1:1)* wherein we now had the means to resist temptation, mortify the deeds of the flesh, and live for God victoriously through His Spirit *(Rom. 8:1-31).*

This Mystery hidden in the Old Testament was now revealed through the New Testament Epistles for us. The Scriptures written by the Prophets of Old spoke about the Grace to come *(Rom. 1:2);* they looked forward by Faith and, by the Spirit of Christ within them, they testified beforehand the sufferings of Christ and the Glory that would follow, yet what they wrote was not fully known by them *(Eph. 3:5; I Pet. 1:10-12).* Now in the church age, their writings can be perceived and understood as this Mystery becomes unveiled to us who believe. However, this Mystery is wisdom spoken among the mature – it is not the wisdom of this world *(I Cor. 2:6; Gal. 1:11-12)* – the wisdom that speaks of the power of God establishing us after receiving Salvation.

The foundation of *"the Revelation of the Mystery"* is that which was taught to the Apostle Paul by the Revelation of Jesus Christ. It taught that, by keeping Jesus Christ, and Him Crucified, at the center of Faith, we can remain planted in the likeness of Jesus' death in order to live in the likeness of Jesus' Resurrection while we are yet alive in this present evil world. It is this form of Doctrine that we can believe from a sincere heart and become established in this wonderful experience with God – this is the Gospel of God.

Romans 16:25 – Subject Scripture
Now to Him that is of power to stablish you according to my Gospel, and the Preaching of Jesus Christ, according to the Revelation of the Mystery, **which was kept secret since the world began,**

Romans 16:25 – Portion III
"...which was kept secret since the world began...,"

Before the world began, God the Father, God the Son, and God the Holy Spirit foreordained that the plan of Redemption for mankind and the destruction of all principalities and powers would be accomplished through Jesus Christ, and Him Crucified. Thus, this portion of *verse 25* reveals the reason behind the terminology *"the Revelation of the Mystery."*

Though we may easily understand the Gospel of Jesus Christ for Salvation, within the Revelation of the Mystery, the Cross was the means of toppling all principalities and powers. Therefore, the

Revelation of the Mystery was kept secret since the world began but was revealed to the Apostle Paul after Jesus Christ took away the Sin of the world and destroyed the works of the Devil through His Shed Blood and death on the Cross.

God could have eliminated Satan at any time, yet everything about this Revelation in Jesus Christ was because of His incomprehensible love *(I John, Chptr 4)*. God chose Love and allowed it as the means to triumph and spoil all principalities and powers. He used no raised voice, nor retaliation *(Phil. 2:5-8)*; instead, He used the most amazing plan, *"which was kept secret since before the world began"* *(Primary reference, Rom. 16:25, and qualifying references, I Cor. 2:8; I Pet. 1:18-20)*.

This plan of God unveils more of the unsearchable depth of His love *(Eph. 3:8)*. It was a plan that would require Himself to come into His creation, be made in the likeness of sinful man, and be Crucified by the hands of those He created. Yet this plan of Atonement and triumph through Jesus Christ, and Him Crucified, was kept secret, and though the Light of the world walked among them, it was still not understood by the darkness trying to overcome Him *(John 1:5)*. How incomprehensible is the heinous pride of Evil? Nonetheless, because they did not understand, nor did they know, they Crucified the Lord of Glory to their own destruction and forever sealed their eternal defeat and doom *(John 19:30; Rev., Chptr 20)*. Had they known what they were doing before they Crucified the Lord of Glory, they never would have done it *(II Cor. 2:8)*.

Even today, we see darkness has blinded the minds of those who do not believe and those who do not love the Truth *(II Cor. 4:4)*, making the Cross of Christ of no effect to themselves and those who embrace their teachings *(I Cor. 1:18; Phil 3:18)*. On the other hand, there is a remarkable view from Heaven of the millions upon millions of Christians who have come to embrace and walk in the fullness of this Mystery unveiled. That is, though the Devil was defeated over two thousand years ago because of the Cross, God continually rejoices at the triumphant victory for those who exercise their Faith in His Son, and what He has done on the Cross for them through His death in His Love *(Rev. 7:14; 12:11).*

Romans 16:26 – Subject Scripture
But now is made manifest, and by the Scriptures of the Prophets, according to the Commandment of the Everlasting God, made known to all nations for the Obedience of Faith:

Romans 16:26 – Portion I
"But now is made manifest...,"

What a magnificent statement indeed! What were once kept secret – *"But now is made manifest"* – are the finished work of Jesus Christ and the power of God that is able to establish us who believe as our Faith remains in that finished work. By Jesus proclaiming *"It is finished..." (John 19:30),* the Atonement was Paid in Full, the way of Salvation was made, and then, giving up the ghost, He laid His life down. Through His death, He triumphed over and all principalities and powers. This proclaims the way Salvation and Sanctification were both accomplished on the Cross through the Shedding of His Blood and death, and this was *"made manifest"* to the world. Once again, Salvation is easily understood, but the fullness of the Revelation, though manifest, is waiting to be revealed to those who seek *(Rom. 7:24).*

This plan of Atonement and triumph through Jesus Christ, and Him Crucified, was foreordained in Eternity past *(I Pet. 1:18-20).* His coming was exclusively to Redeem man *(John 1:29; 3:16; Heb. 2:9; 10:12),* triumph over and spoil all principalities and powers *(Col.*

239

2:14-15), destroy the works of the Devil *(I John 3:8)*, and condemn sin in the flesh *(Rom. 8:3)*. Now, through His obedience unto death, divesting Himself for the sake of the Cross *(Matt. 26:39)*, even the death of the Cross, It is finished. His work upon the Cross is established and eternal, and the powers of evil cannot change it for all Eternity.

Satan knows he cannot change God's Revelation in Jesus Christ *(John 19:30)*, so the Devil and his Angels continue (more so today) to bring an array of corrupt gospels into the world and the Church *(II Cor. 11:4; I Tim. 4:1; I John 1:1-4)*. These gospels are not Gospels at all, and steer those who believe them from the simplicity that is in Christ *(II Cor. 11:3)*.

The Devil and his Angels will always make continual efforts to veil, complicate, and pervert *(Gal. 1:6-9)* the Power of God working through Faith exercised in the manifested purpose of Jesus Christ, and Him Crucified *(Eph. 3:4-11)*. Yet, regardless of his efforts, Jesus Christ, and Him Crucified, shall always remain the Source and Means for our Faith. As we come to realize this, our Faith will rest in the Cross and the Cross alone *(I Cor. 2:2; Gal. 2:20)*, whereby we will continue in the supernatural likeness of Jesus' Resurrection while in this present evil world *(Rom. 8:14; Phil. 3:7-11)*.

Romans 16:26 – Subject Scripture
But now is made manifest, **and by the Scriptures of the Prophets, according to the Commandment of the Everlasting God,** made known to all nations for the Obedience of Faith:

Romans 16:26 – Portion II
"…and by the Scriptures of the Prophets, according to the Commandment of the Everlasting God…,"

This portion of *verse 26* makes the validity of Scripture known. Before the events of the Cross, the Scriptures of the Old Testament are God's written Revelation to Man by the Holy Spirit *(II Pet. 1:16-21)*. After the events of the Cross, the Scriptures of the Old Testament were clearly validated. The Epistles of the New Testament came by the Divine Revelation and inspiration of God, and thus, as each and every event unfolds, His Word will continue to be validated. Neither the Devil nor Man can change this.

Romans 16:26 – Subject Scripture
But now is made manifest, and by the Scriptures of the Prophets, according to the Commandment of the Everlasting God, **made known to all nations for the Obedience of Faith:**

Romans 16:26 – Portion III
"…made known to all nations for the Obedience of Faith…:"

By the Apostle Paul writing *"made known to all nations,"* he is unveiling that the Revelation of the Mystery is now the Gospel Message for all mankind, all nations. Eternal Life is a Gift and will be given to whosoever will call on the Name of the Lord, and the fullness of the Revelation of the Mystery is also available to whosoever desires to walk in holiness. As we move on in this third portion of *verse 26*, the terminology *"for the Obedience of Faith"* speaks of learning obedience to this disclosed wisdom of God after Salvation, which is attained through Faith in Jesus Christ, and Him Crucified *(I Cor. 2:2; Gal. 6:14)*. For those who desire a walk in holiness, the Obedience of Faith is the good fight of Faith *(I Tim. 6:12)*.

Romans 16:27 – Subject Scripture undivided
To God only wise, be Glory through Jesus Christ forever. Amen.

Romans 16:27 ends the Epistle of *Romans*. Though this magnificent Epistle holds truths and promises for our life and living within it, between the beginning and end, the theme is the unveiling of the Revelation of the Mystery, which is the fullness of the Gospel of God. It is most remarkable the Apostle Paul begins the Epistle of *Romans* by writing *"Paul, a servant of Jesus Christ, called to be an Apostle, separated unto the Gospel of God" (Rom. 1:1)*, then as he concludes, he writes *"Now to Him that is of power to stablish you according to my Gospel, and the Preaching of Jesus Christ, according to the Revelation of the Mystery, which was kept secret since the world began...," (Rom. 16:25)*. By the Apostle beginning the Epistle in this way, he brings us into his personal experience, much of which we see within his disclosed struggle. By Paul ending the Epistle in this way, he helps us understand all that he learned was from God alone. Thus, he writes, *"To God only wise, be Glory through Jesus Christ forever. Amen."*

By the Apostle Paul stating *"To God only wise,"* he is speaking of God's wisdom in choosing Christ as the source and the Cross as the instrument in order to defeat all principalities and powers and Redeem mankind.

The Apostle's statement *"be Glory through Jesus Christ forever"* speaks of the flawless Obedience of Jesus Christ, and the tremendous Price He Paid, which is qualified by His Resurrection. This gives God the Glory through Jesus Christ forever and throughout Eternity. Ending this great Epistle with *"Amen,"* the Apostle Paul is saying what God has revealed to him and thus what he has written is proper, firm, established, and unchangeable.

As the forerunner of this Revelation, Paul's disclosed experiences have given each of us the ability to glean a wealth of insights that, if embraced, will move us from a life of defeat and despair into a life of fellowship with God in triumph and holiness today. These trials and the spiritual principles within them can be found in *Romans Chapters 6, 7 and 8*. Though the entirety of the book of *Romans* reveals a chronology that is nothing short of amazing, the personal chronology of *Chapters 6, 7 and 8* gives us a close-up snapshot uniquely designed for us to become more knowledgeable in the wisdom of God *(Rom. 11:33)*. When embraced, *Chapters 9-16* unveil the many arrays of life applications.

Earlier, I stated that scholars and theologians alike have described the *Epistle of Romans* as "the Mount Everest of the Bible," and I believe this description is an accurate fit. This *Epistle of Romans* holds within it the framework by which we who are Saved can discover a deep and intimate relationship with God as we rest our Faith in the Cross. Within this great Epistle lays the foundation and framework to what the Apostle Paul defined as that form of Doctrine and, coming from the Mind of the Godhead, it is the oldest Doctrine revealed to mankind *(Rom. 6:17-18; I Pet. 1:18-20)*. That form of Doctrine is the foundation by which all true doctrine comes *(John 7:16-17; Titus 1:9; 2:1; II John 9-10)*. Thus, the Apostle Paul concludes by writing – *"To God only wise, be Glory through Jesus Christ forever. Amen."*

As we look into this chronology of the Epistle of *Romans*, we can find comfort in knowing that the Holy Spirit purposed the sequence of events for us. The Apostle, chosen by God, foreran this struggle so that each of us who are Saved might come to understand that our struggle is not uncommon and, through this, come to know and embrace the answer for triumph and holiness.

Paul did not choose this struggle; he engaged this struggle because of his deep desire to live for God. Likewise, because of our love for God, and our desire to live for Him is so great *(Rom. 7:22)*, we too can engage ways that revive the dynamics of the sin nature through our efforts of good without realizing it. Yet if the Apostle

Paul went through this struggle and the Holy Spirit superintended the Apostle's writings of these spiritual principles surrounding it, we can gain comfort knowing that God chose Paul to forerun it for us *(Gal. 1:11-24)*. Therefore, if and when we engage in this struggle, we can now come to understand what is happening within us, but, just as Paul, we can come to understand and embrace God's established way of Sanctification and experience abundant life filled with lasting freedom, joy, love, and peace.

A Brief Chronology of Romans

Chapters 1-3: Prior to Salvation, the Holy Spirit draws us to God; we then realize our condition as a sinner and desperate need of our Saviour.

Chapters 4-5: It is only in our acknowledgment of need that we can respond to God drawing us to Him and receive Jesus Christ as Lord and Saviour by Faith, plus or minus nothing. Upon receiving Salvation, we have become justified by Faith alone, not by works of the Law, but by the Law of Faith.

Chapter 6: We now understand our destination is no longer eternal Hell, but Eternal Life in Christ Jesus. We learn that we are baptized into His Death, and we can now live in the likeness of His Resurrection – we have been made free.

Chapter 7:1-7: We understand the Penalty was Paid and that we are no longer under the Law. Therein, we begin to understand that we are not to live by the Law – we are to live by Faith.

Chapter 7:8-23: Now born again and marveling in the experience of this supernatural wonder, we know we are no longer under the Law. Still, at some point, we sin in either thought or deed, but it is significant enough to stumble us in some way. The emotions are grief (because we sinned) and perplexity (because we do not understand why we sinned or even had thoughts of sin). The sincere response is not to allow it to happen again, yet, without realizing it, we engage the Law in some way and the sin nature revived. This is where the Apostle Paul found himself, and, without exception, this will be the experience of all of who are truly born again. It is a place of struggle and failure to gain victory over sin. The desperate desire to overcome temptation and sin and to live for God is the very reason this place became engaged. However, this place is not a place of judgment; it is a place – "the place" – where we can learn the great way of victory from the Holy Spirit.

Chapter 7:25: This *verse* ends *Chapter 7,* and for a remarkable reason. We find *Romans 7:25* seated between *Romans 7:24* and *Romans 8:1,* revealing that this magnificent verse holds the answer. Though it is veiled to those who do not love the Truth, it will be unveiled to those who love the Truth, and therein choose the Mind of Christ in which he or she will come to discern what it truly means to walk after the Spirit.

Chapter 8:1-4: These Scriptures describe the Apostle Paul's victory and the manner by which his victory came as a result of his placing Faith in Jesus Christ, and Him Crucified.

Chapter 8:5-39: These Scriptures reveal the absolute necessity of resting Faith in Jesus Christ, and Him Crucified.

Chapters 9-16: There is much within these *chapters*, but in a general scope of them (once the Cross becomes seen, known and embraced), the array of life applications within these *chapters* can be rightly understood, divided, applied, and walked in through the Resurrection Power of God.

CHAPTER 13

Christ is The Source
The Cross is The Means

I CORINTHIANS 1:17-18, 23-24

PREFACE

The Cross is a remarkable display of God's wisdom and love accomplished through Jesus Christ, and Him Crucified. If what was to be accomplished at the Cross was known, none of the princes of this world would have Crucified the Lord of Glory *(I Cor. 2:8)*. Now that *"It is finished" (John 19:30)*, the Devil and those following him will do everything within their power to cause our Faith to be placed in anything other than the Cross.

The Devil clearly understands that his defeat and eternal doom came through the Cross *(I John 3:8)*; he also understands that the body of sin becomes incapacitated within the Believer when he or she receives Salvation. However, the Devil very clearly understands how to preach his own gospels that give occasion for the body of sin to once again revive *(II Cor. 11:4, 13-15)*.

247

The Devil cannot change the Will of God, and he cannot change the events that have been established through the work of the Cross. Because of this, his ongoing efforts are to keep us from the knowledge of the Cross for our victory. Without the knowledge of the Cross, we will use our physical body in the effort to try and live for God, and in doing so, the body of sin will revive. Under this dominion of evil, our walk will remain ineffective at the very least; at the most, he will destroy our life *(Phil. 3:18; I Tim. 1:19)*.

Coming to understand the culprit behind the struggle will bring clarity to the struggle. Without this clarity, we are left with an endless stream of erroneous ideas as to what is going on. Triumph over sin and the glorious presence and leading of the Holy Spirit come but one way – the Cross.

Death must first come in order to experience true life in Christ *(Rom. 6:7)*, this is the wisdom of God established through Jesus Christ, and Jesus Christ has set the example for us. For this reason, the Apostle Paul writes – *"⁵Let this mind be in you, which was also in Christ Jesus: ⁶Who, being in the form of God, thought it not robbery to be equal with God: ⁷But made Himself of no reputation, and took upon Him the form of a servant, and was made in the likeness of men: ⁸And being found in fashion as a man, He humbled Himself, and became obedient unto death, even the death of the Cross" (Phil. 2:5-8)*.

Beginning with *Philippians 2:5* – *"Let this mind be in you, which was also in Christ Jesus"* – we see the personal application – *"Let this mind be in you."* In order to make this application for our life, we must come to know the Mind of Christ Jesus.

With certainty, Christ Jesus came to do the Will of His Father Who is in Heaven *(John 4:34)*, and this gives us a major glimpse of understanding the ultimate priority of what Jesus was thinking all the time *(Matt. 26:39).* In order for Jesus to do the Will of His Father, He divested Himself, this was His Mind.

Let us look once again into *Philippians 2:8 – "...and became obedient unto death, even the death of the Cross."* By the Apostle Paul writing the word *"death"* twice, he is allowing us to see into Jesus' walk, and thus, Mindset. The first description of *"death"* in *Philippians 2:8 – "And being found in fashion as a man, He humbled Himself, and became obedient unto death"* – is obedience unto death while He was alive in His humanity. This obedience was a continued divesting of Himself, that is, not His Own Will, nor His Own Power but a divesting of Himself unto the Will of His Father.

Christ Jesus knew Whom He was and why He came, and He was obedient to the entire Scope of every moment of His humanity *(Heb. 4:15).* During this time, His frame of Mind was the Authoring of Faith, meaning God cannot cease to be God Eternal. Therefore, in His humanity, He divested Himself for the sake of the Cross, wherein He was led each and every moment by the Holy Spirit unto the Will of the Father. Jesus learned complete obedience unto this first description of death while alive in His humanity *(Heb. 5:8).*

In regards to the Man, Jesus, Authoring Faith, the word "author" in biblical Greek is defined within the word *archegos* (ἀρχηγός, NT: 747, ar-khay-gos'), which means a chief leader. The Man, Jesus, Authored Faith, becoming the Chief Leader by walking in Faith for us. It is most amazing that the Word God was made flesh for the purpose of the Cross, yet this was the Will of the Father. In order to accomplish the Father's Will in the likeness of men, Christ Jesus Authored Faith, divested Himself, and as the Man, Jesus, chose to walk in this manner, this was the Mind of Christ. Everything associated with Authoring Faith (and therein leading) was wrapped around the Cross *(Heb. 12:2).*

The second description of *"death"* is in the latter portion of *Philippians 2:8* – *"...even the death of the Cross."* This death is that which took place on the Cross *(Matt. 27:46, John 19:28, 30; Luke 23:46)*. All that Christ Jesus learned in the first description of death (divesting Himself) was followed through in a like manner unto His physical death on the Cross.

We do not have to die a physical death to atone for our own sins, nor could we ever. We do, however, have to become obedient unto the first description of death, by learning to divest our own selves while we are in our humanity in order to experience the second description of death, though alive. Yet because He went before us, as it was with Jesus being raised from the dead, we too will experience the likeness of His Resurrection *(Rom. 8:2, 11)*.

When we let the Mind of Christ become our mind, our desire will be to submit ourselves to the Will of the Father Who is in Heaven, and as it was with the Father's Son, the Cross will be before us. With this, our death comes as we place Faith in Whom He is, and what He has done on the Cross through His death. This is what it means to take up our cross daily *(Luke 9:23)* – the Cross is the means, and Christ is the source *(Rev. 12:11)*.

I Corinthians 1:17 – Subject Scripture
For Christ sent me not to baptize, but to Preach the Gospel: not with wisdom of words, lest the Cross of Christ should be made of none effect.

I Corinthians 1:17 – Portion I
"For Christ sent me not to baptize,
but to Preach the Gospel...:"

By the Apostle Paul writing *"For Christ sent me not to baptize,"* he is not implying that baptism has been done away with. He is saying that the ceremonial tradition of water baptism will not, in and of itself, bring about the death necessary to live a Resurrection life.

John the Baptist was the last Old Testament prophet, and the details we are given in regards to Jesus' baptism by John in the river Jordan are remarkable indeed. However, by Jesus stating *"It is finished…,"* baptism is no longer an outward work, but an inward baptism – a cutting away of the old, a circumcision made without hands – a work that cannot be attained through any means of an outward work *(Col. 2:11-12).*

As it regards being baptized into Jesus Christ, the Apostle Paul writes – *"³Know you not, that so many of us as were baptized into Jesus Christ were baptized into His Death? ⁴Therefore we are buried with Him by baptism into death: that like as Christ was raised up from the dead by the Glory of the Father, even so we also should walk in newness of life. ⁵For is we have been planted is the likeness of His Death, we shall be also in the likeness of His Resurrection"* (Rom. 6:3-5).

Our baptism took place upon Salvation through Faith alone apart from any outward work. This is not to say that one cannot receive Salvation while in ceremonial baptism by water. Rather, ceremonial baptism by water does not Save the individual, nor does the water ceremony baptize the individual in Jesus' death. Understanding our condition, we repent, believe in Whom Jesus is, and what He has done through His Shed Blood and death and His Resurrection – this brings about Salvation into Christ.

If death required a ceremonial baptism by water, then additional ceremonies would be required when one sinned, resulting in a life of ongoing ceremonies for cleansing. Thank God that this is not the case *(Heb., Chptr 9).* Baptism into Jesus' death and the raising in the likeness of Jesus' Resurrection is a reality that took place upon our Salvation as a result of Faith, plus or minus nothing. The continuing benefits of this are also through Faith, plus or minus nothing. For this reason, the Apostle Paul writes – *"For Christ sent me not to baptize."*

Paul had a purpose for presenting this statement due to the divisions that were taking place by not understanding Faith and works – things done in the body for Sanctification. This purpose: *"to Preach the Gospel"* which, if properly preached, would result in the power of God unto Sanctification. We must always remember that the Gospel Paul preached was the Gospel of Salvation <u>and</u> Sanctification, both of which can only be obtained through Faith apart from ceremonial works *(Salvation – John 3:16; Sanctification – Rom. 8:13; the Gospel – I Cor. 1:23; the result – Gal. 2:20).*

I **Corinthians 1:17** – Subject Scripture
For Christ sent me not to baptize, but to Preach the Gospel: **not with wisdom of words, lest the Cross of Christ should be made of none effect.**

I **Corinthians 1:17** – Portion II
"…not with wisdom of words, lest the Cross of Christ should be made of none effect."

The preaching of the Gospel is *"not with wisdom of words."* True biblical preaching does not come from the mind of man – it comes by the Revelation of Jesus Christ *(I Cor. 2:4-8).* The verbiage the Apostle Paul uses – *"lest the Cross of Christ should be made of none effect"* – reveals the obvious: the Cross has an effect! Yet, is the effect obvious? Each Christian has an innate knowledge that he or she must die to self, but every other way will be sought out by so many because the Cross, although understood for Salvation, is foolishness for Sanctification.

In our mortal life, the likeness of Jesus' death must come first in order to experience the likeness of His Resurrection, and this death is found as Faith finds its rest in Jesus Christ, and Him Crucified *(Rom. 6:7; I Cor. 2:2)*. The power of God working through Faith in the Cross is God's established way of victory and is mighty for us who are Saved, but the Cross is made of none effect within our life if it becomes rejected *(Phil. 3:18)*, as we will come to see.

I Corinthians 1:18 – Subject Scripture
For the Preaching of the Cross is to them that perish foolishness; but unto us which are Saved it is the Power of God.

I Corinthians 1:18 – Portion I
**"For the Preaching of the Cross is to them
that perish foolishness…;"**

As we begin *verse 18*, we must remind ourselves that the Apostle Paul is speaking to us who are Saved *(I Cor. 1:1-16)*. By Paul writing *"For the Preaching of the Cross,"* he is saying, "For the Preaching of Jesus Christ, and Him Crucified" *(I Cor. 1:23)*. Due to the residue of our carnal mind, we somehow think to move on from the Cross when in fact the Apostle Paul writes the opposite – *"⁶As you have therefore received Christ Jesus the Lord, so walk you in Him: ⁷Rooted and built up in Him, and stablished in the Faith, as you have been taught, abounding therein with thanksgiving" (Col. 2:6-7)*.

Some teach (therefore many believe) that we are to move on from the Cross once we receive Salvation. By believing this ideology, the only road taken in order to move on will be that of ceremonies through devised methods, all of which are done in the flesh and by the Law. This mindset is derived from a remiss interpretation of

God's Word within the passage context of *Hebrews 6:1-6.* Therefore, let us investigate these *verses.*

"¹Therefore leaving the Principles of the Doctrine of Christ, let us go on unto perfection; not laying again the Foundation of Repentance from dead works, and of Faith toward God, ²Of the Doctrine of Baptisms, and of laying on of hands, and of Resurrection of the dead, and of Eternal judgment. ³And this will we do, if God permit. ⁴For it is impossible for those who were once enlightened, and have tasted of the Heavenly Gift, and were made partakers of the Holy Spirit, ⁵And have tasted the good Word of God, and the powers of the world to come, ⁶If they shall fall away, to renew them again unto Repentance; seeing they crucify to themselves the Son of God afresh, and put Him to an open shame" (Heb. 6:1-6).

Hebrews 6:1 sets the cornerstone whereupon *verses 2-6* are built, so let us begin with *verse 1* – *"Therefore leaving the Principles of the Doctrine of Christ, let us go on unto perfection; not laying again the Foundation of Repentance from dead works, and of Faith toward God...."*

The premise for a proper interpretation of *Hebrews 6:1* begins with gaining insight into *"the Principles of the Doctrine of Christ"* so that we understand what we are *"Therefore leaving."* In order for us to gain this insight and understanding, we must first look into our Salvation.

Before we received Salvation, we recognized our condition (our sin); no one needed to tell us what our sins were – our sins were unveiled as we had begun to come to Christ – God's moral Law for us revealed this *(Rom. 2:14-15; Gal. 3:24-25)*. This is not an assumption; it is a reality within every human soul that comes to Christ. Nevertheless, because of the abounding presence of God's Grace when we came to Him, we did not have to go through each and every sin because somehow in our recognition of His Greatness, we knew that He knew. Therefore, upon believing in God and believing that He sent His Son to die on the Cross for our sins, we asked Him to Wash our sins away by the Atoning Shed Blood of His Son. All of this taking place through simply believing, we then expressed our continued belief in that He raised His Son from the dead and He then Saved us. This is Salvation, and herein is the foundational insight into *"the Principles of the Doctrine of Christ."*

Let us now see what we are *"Therefore leaving."* In order for us to accomplish this, it is important for us to understand that before Jesus Christ became the Vicarious Atoning Sacrifice, the sacrifice for sins was through ceremonial "types and shadows." That is to say, before the Cross, the Old Testament saints believed in God, were repentant in their heart, and confessed their sins. Still, before Jesus Christ became the Atoning Sacrifice for Sin, their offering for the remission of sin was through the blood sacrifice of animals. These ceremonies were "types and shadows" of what was to come. Though these "types and shadows" were acceptable to God before the Atoning Sacrifice (His Son), these blood sacrifices did not cleanse their conscience *(Heb. 9:9)*. Not only did it/they/those things not cleanse their conscience, these "types and shadows" for the sacrifice of sins had to be done again and again *(Heb. 9:7)*. Upon the physical death of the saint, he or she was brought into Abraham's Bosom (Paradise) because the way had not yet been made for the believing saints to spend Eternity with God.

The Cross changed all of this. Jesus Christ made the way by the Shedding of His Blood, and by the offering of His body once for all through death on the Cross. Through this Vicarious Atoning and triumphant Sacrifice, those who had descended in Abraham's Bosom were led out of that region by Christ Jesus because the way had been victoriously made *(Eph. 4:8-10; Heb., Chptrs 9 & 10)*. Now, through the finished work of His Cross, the Remission of sins unto Salvation, and ongoing Sanctification are through Faith in Whom Jesus Christ Is, and what He has done. Furthermore, unlike the "types and shadows" of Old Testament sacrifices, New Testament Remission of sins (Salvation) cleanses our conscience from dead works *(Heb. 9:9)*. Therefore, after the Remission of sins unto Salvation, we are to walk exclusively by Faith apart from any "types and shadows" of Old Testament ceremonial sacrifices *(Heb. 10:22)*. For this reason, the Author writes, *"let us go on unto perfection."*

The problem can come after we receive Salvation. Now that we are born again, we can continue in efforts of trying to atone for our own sin by repeatedly repenting and confessing because our conscience may come under condemnation. This cycle reveals four conditions, the fourth of which ends in a catastrophic effect. The first condition is that of condemnation – condemnation evidences bondage to sin due to repeated carnal repentance. The second condition is the evidence of living by the Law - this is evidenced due to the reality of condemnation. The third condition is misplaced Faith. Whenever Faith is misplaced, the result is living by the Law, which produces condemnation. The fourth condition, and most importantly, is that to ourselves, we are crucifying the Lord again due to our unbelief *(Heb. 6:6)* – unbelief in regards to His Atoning Sacrifice and Its Precious ability to cleanse us from our sins through Faith alone, apart from "types and shadows" of ceremonial performances. These are works and methods in the flesh and by the Law.

By the Author of *Hebrews* writing *"¹Therefore leaving the Principles of the Doctrine of Christ...,"* he is not speaking of leaving the way in which we received Salvation, which is the Cross *(Col. 2:6-12)*. He is letting us know that we must leave the fundamental carnal mind of repentance and confession wherein we may think we are gaining Sanctification in this type of ceremony. For this reason, the Author writes – *"¹...not laying again the Foundation of Repentance from dead works, and of Faith toward God, ²Of the Doctrine of Baptisms, and of laying on of hands, and of Resurrection of the dead, and of Eternal judgment. ³And this will we do, if God permit."*

This fundamental carnal thinking is a "type and shadow" of what once was, and there are only two reasons we would be caught in this cycle. Though we may have a sincere heart, we may not know better or we have rejected the completeness of Jesus Christ's Atonement. If we reject what Jesus Christ has done through His Shed Blood and death on the Cross as the way of Atonement and the way of Sanctification, the Author of *Hebrews* writes – *"⁴For it is impossible for those who were once enlightened, and have tasted of the Heavenly Gift, and were made partakers of the Holy Spirit, ⁵And have tasted the good Word of God, and the powers of the world to come, ⁶If they shall fall away, to renew them again unto Repentance; seeing they crucify to themselves the Son of God afresh, and put Him to an open shame" (Heb. 6:1-6).*

My desire is to help each of us who desire to grow in Sanctification understand what is going on so that we, regardless of where we are at, can go on unto perfection. Those who teach any ideology that leads the Believer into thinking that they are to leave the Cross as the means of Sanctification fail to understand *"the Doctrine of Christ"* is the Cross, and *"the principles"* are the "types and shadows" of what once was. The Author of *Hebrews* is letting us know that we are to move on from the "type and shadows" of Old Testament sacrifices that are carnal confession and repentance wherein we think we attain Sanctification each time we perform such ceremonies. We must never leave *"the Doctrine of Christ."*

"⁷For many deceivers are entered into the world, who confess not that Jesus Christ is come in the flesh. This is a deceiver and an Antichrist. ⁸Look to yourselves, that we lose not those things which we have wrought, but that we receive a full reward. ⁹Whosoever

transgresses, and abides not in the Doctrine of Christ, has not God. He that abides in the Doctrine of Christ, he has both the Father and the Son. ¹⁰If there come any unto you, and bring not this Doctrine, receive him not into your house, neither bid him God speed: ¹¹For he who bids him God speed is partaker of his evil deeds (II John 7-11).

The Author of *Hebrews* is not implying that we no longer need to repent in order to move on unto perfection. We must repent. However, true Faith sees the completeness of the Cross and understands what Jesus Christ there did is enough. This results in a continual heart of thankfulness with a humble mind that recognizes our condition yet understands our position. Our condition is a progressive growth in the Sanctification process, which takes place only through His Spirit as we learn how to depend on God for everything. Still, we are fully Sanctified in our position in Christ. In the Eyes of God, we are complete in Him – Christ is now our Righteousness. True Faith understands this and leaves the "types and shadows" of what once was.

If we are without the knowledge of how to go on unto perfection, our only recourse will be to stay in the "type and shadows" of repentance unto dead works even though we believe in God. If we are presented the way to move on and reject it, the Apostle Paul writes – *"For the Preaching of the Cross is to them that perish foolishness."*

I Corinthians 1:18 – Subject Scripture
For the Preaching of the Cross is to them that perish foolishness; **but unto us which are Saved it is the Power of God.**

I Corinthians 1:18 – Portion II
"...but unto us which are Saved it is the Power of God."

Though obvious, Paul's statement *"but unto us which are Saved"* is directed to all of us who are born again. The Apostle is saying *"it"* is the Cross *(I Cor. 1:17 – Portion I)*, thus *"the Power of God"* unto us which are Saved. The Message of the Cross is the simplicity that is in Christ *(II Cor. 11:3)* – simplicity wherein we who believe can simply rest our Faith in the Cross *(I Cor. 2:2)* and become the recipient of the effectual working of the Spirit of Life, quickening our mortal body unto the Will of the Father *(Rom. 8:11, 14)*.

I Corinthians 1:23 – Subject Scripture
But we Preach Christ Crucified, unto the Jews a stumbling block, and unto the Greeks foolishness;

I Corinthians 1:23 – Portion I
"But we Preach Christ Crucified…,"

As we begin *verse 23*, the Apostle Paul brings to light exactly what he preached. Paul received the Revelation of the Mystery and had the vast responsibility in delivering it, but Paul also held a great responsibility in the way he delivered it. This Message is a hard Message. If there is persecution, it will be the result of preaching this Message *(Gal. 5:11; 6:12-14)*. Today in the Western culture, we have become saturated with watered down, seeker sensitive preaching. However, when the focal point of preaching becomes Christ Crucified, the preacher wonders at times if he is in a zero-tolerant country due to the persecution that comes by preaching this Message.

This Message dismantles the theology of the most seasoned Christian who has not yet come to understand it, yet when a new Christian first hears this remarkable Message, they rejoice with open arms because they have not been exposed to the wisdom of man. There were many that had turned from the Faith in Paul's day to preach their own theologies *(II Cor. 11:4; Gal. 1:6-9)* – praise God this did not detour Paul. The knowledge of this magnificent truth strengthened his determination to know Jesus Christ, and Him Crucified, and nothing else for his manner of walking with God in triumph and freedom *(Gal. 6:14)*

I Corinthians 1:23 – Subject Scripture
But we Preach Christ Crucified, **unto the Jews a stumblingblock,** and unto the Greeks foolishness;

I Corinthians 1:23-24 – Portion II
"...unto the Jews a stumbling block...,"

The idea here in this second portion of *verse 23* is that the preaching of Jesus Christ, and Him Crucified, was a stumblingblock to the Jews. The Jews demanded that people live by the Law and, because of their unbelief, they chose to live by their religious methods instead of what could otherwise be Faith placed in what Jesus Christ had fulfilled and Satisfied on the Cross through His death *(Rom. 8:3-4, 10:4)*. The idea that Jesus Christ was now the end of the Law for Righteousness to everyone who believes was a major stumblingblock to the Jews.

Do not be fooled – coming from many pulpits today are teachings embedded in laws, ordinances, and religious methods devised by the carnal mind of man. They may or may not be preached with mal-intent, but preaching of this type is going on in one way or the other. The catastrophic problem with this type of heresy is that it always results in motions of sins in the flesh, which are by the Law *(Rom. 7:5)*. Thus, the very things those in this condition are trying to overcome, instead overcome them again and again *(I Cor. 15:56; II Cor. 3:6)*.

I Corinthians 1:23 – Subject Scripture
But we Preach Christ Crucified, unto the Jews a stumblingblock, **and unto the Greeks foolishness;**

I Corinthians 1:23 – Portion III
"…and unto the Greeks foolishness…;"

The idea here in this third portion of *verse 23* is the pride of intellectual carnal wisdom. If the human being cannot get past pride working through the wisdom of the carnal mind, then the realization that all human efforts are woefully insufficient to live by the Law will never be known. Therein, this great truth we have in the Cross will remain foolish to them, and because they do not love the truth of the full Gospel of God in Jesus Christ, their only choice is to believe a lie. In this, they will rest their Faith in their own wisdom and that of other men *(Col. 2:8, 20-23)*.

The Cross can be rejected on just two levels: those who think their ways and methods are better – *"unto the Jews a stumblingblock"* – and those who would rather rely on the carnal mind of intellectual wisdom – *"unto the Greeks foolishness."* Either way, both of them end in "types and shadows" of ceremonial performances by the Law, regardless how good, significant, or subtle their methods may appear.

I Corinthians 1:24 – Subject Scripture undivided
But unto them which are called, both Jews and Greeks, Christ the Power of God, and the Wisdom of God.

The Apostle Paul brings wonderful News! *"But unto them which are called"* are all those who have accepted the invitation of Salvation and have the desire to live for God in truth according to His written Word, not wavering nor compromising from it. They will know for certain that they have become called. The statement *"both Jews and"*

Greeks" speaks of all mankind. *"Christ the Power of God"* speaks of the Power of God working in us who are Saved as our Faith rests in Jesus Christ, and Him Crucified *(I Cor. 1:17-18; 2:2).* The ending portion – *"the Wisdom of God"* – speaks of all that was foreordained in Eternity past, superintended by the Holy Spirit into time *(Matt. 1:20)* and made manifest in these last days for us *(I Pet. 1:18-20).* This is the Wisdom of God, not Man.

CHAPTER 14

Worship

JOHN 4:23-24

PREFACE

Worship can be incredibly powerful. It was designed by God so His children *(Rom. 8:14-17)* could express just that: "worship." It was designed as a wonderful means of expressing our adoration because of His incomprehensible Love made manifest for us through Jesus Christ, and Him Crucified *(Gal. 2:20)*. When we come to know and understand the Power of God working through Faith in Jesus Christ, and His finished work, we then come to understand the meaning of taking every thought captive unto the obedience of Christ *(II Cor. 10:5; Phil. 2:5)*. This is one of the most important truths that we can come to understand and walk in, due to the need to remain free from the nature of sin in our members.

Though the sin nature is made incapacitated at Salvation, if it is revived, it will heavily influence our spirit and soul once our mind is brought captive to it. In this condition, it will taint and distort our worship toward the Father. It is not so much a problem as long as it remains incapacitated and we remain dead to it *(Rom. 6:7)*, but it calls from the grave through the ways of our old man, which are known by our carnal mind *(Rom. 7:2-3; 8:7; Eph. 4:22; Col. 3:9)*. This is the core reason we need to understand the power of God working through Faith in the Cross after our Salvation.

As previously stated, our spirit is for God and knows the things of God, and our soul is for the body and feels. Yet due to the Fall of Adam, our spirit and our soul cannot effectively work with our mind and body as originally. Once again, our heart is desperately wicked above all measure *(Jer. 17:9)*. Therefore, until we put on immortality, we will constantly need to remain dead to remain free in order to ensure that our soul and spirit are worshipping God the Father as He desires.

Knowing this, Satan has devised many other false ways that can lead us to believe we can die to ourselves through them. All the while, we can become so distracted that we miss the simplicity that is in Christ when trying to attain this death.

There is only one answer through which we who believe can remain planted in the likeness of Jesus' death so that we can remain free in the likeness of His Resurrection and truly worship the Father He desires.

John 4:23 – Subject Scripture undivided
But the hour comes, and now is, when the true worshippers shall worship the Father in spirit and in truth: for the Father seeketh such to worship Him.

"But the hour comes, and now is" unveils God's very presence is among us (Emmanuel – God with us *[Isa. 7:14]*). John's statement – *"when the true worshippers"* – refers to those remaining free by the truth in Jesus Christ, and Him Crucified; hence, *"But the hour comes,*

and now is." These are true worshippers who *"shall worship the Father in spirit and in truth."* John 4:23 speaks of our spirit, by which we are to worship God. This is the importance of understanding spiritual purity in order to be a true worshipper. John's statement *"and in truth"* is directly referring to the pureness of the Word of God.

There are many truths whereby anybody can establish what they consider being truth, yet unless it merges seamlessly into the Word of God, it is a counterfeit. For example, there can be a lot of things going on within praise that may not be pleasing to the Father – meaning, if the Message of the Cross is not embraced, the odds are those not embracing the Message have their soul yoked in an unholy way to the body of the sin. This results in will-worship. This can be the case within an entire Church, regardless of how good the praise and worship are, due to secular music, and this type of music being embraced by the Believer. This does not mean that everything needs to be scrutinized in a religious pursuit by the Law; there is Grace, but we must understand that if it is God the Father we are praising and worshipping, then we are to worship Him free from unholy things.

John 4:23 actually gives us the way we can come to the Father in worship, which is in spirit and truth. Any other way will be in the soul, and the soul is dramatically affected by the sin nature once it is revived. Our soul is the faculty between our spirit and our body; therefore, our body manifests what our soul feels, so even when we are free from the influences of the sin nature in our own life, we must guard against any type of music that would allow our soul to become tainted, and thus affect our spirit. In other words, a true worshipper worships God in spirit and truth, and because our soul has emotions and enjoys music, we must be careful what we listen to and therein engage because it affects our spirit.

Our physical body is neutral, neither holy nor unholy *(II Cor. 5:10).* Though the Apostle Paul speaks of our "vile body" *(Phil. 3:21),*

Daniel E. Armour

he is speaking in the context of corruption within the flesh *(Rom. 7:24)*, which is why our body is now dead because of the sin nature *(Rom. 8:10)* or unable to perform the good we want to do *(Rom. 7:18)*. Our body is an instrument, a tent by which our spirit and our soul live in for now. This is why we so badly need to remain dead to the body of this death presently in our members *(Rom. 7:23)*, for he who is dead is free from *the* sin *nature (Rom. 6:7)*.

The Truth will make the Believer free *(John 8:32)*; however, remaining free literally means remaining in the Truth, so understanding the Truth and remaining in it becomes the qualifier for true worship. Christ Jesus is Truth; everything known to mankind consists in Him *(Col. 1:17)*. He is Life; no man has life outside of Christ *(I John 1:2, 4; I Tim. 1:1)*. He alone is the Way *(John 14:6)*, and His Way is the Cross *(Matt. 26:39; Phil. 2:5-8)*. Ending *verse 23*, by John stating, *"for the Father seeketh such to worship Him,"* he is bringing to light that God the Father is specific in His acceptance of worship. Thus, we must learn to remain in the Way of Jesus Christ.

John 4:24 – Subject Scripture undivided
God is a Spirit: and they that worship Him must worship Him in spirit and in truth.

How remarkable and magnificent a statement – *"God is a Spirit"* – and yet He is revealed through His Son *(Matt. 11:27; John 8:19)*. For this reason, we can only come to the Father through Jesus Christ *(John 14-6)*, and no man comes to Jesus Christ unless the Father draws him *(John 6:44)*. Furthermore, because *"God is a Spirit,"* it is impossible to please Him without Faith, for he who comes to God must believe that He Is *(Heb. 11:6)*.

The balance of *John 4:24* disclose the requirements to worship the Father once again. The Author uses the word *"must,"* which means

266

that the ways in which we worship the Father have requirements – *"they that worship Him must worship Him in spirit and in truth."*

We cannot conjure up the Holy Spirit by our efforts, by our worship or by our anything. The Holy Spirit is exactly Whom He Is – Holy. There will soon come a day when our body will be changed from corruptible to incorruptible, and we put on immortality. Until then, this corruption (though defeated at the Cross) can revive and dominate the Believer. Therefore, worshipping God in spirit and in truth begins in the intangibles of Faith, and not performances in the flesh. Yes, worshipping God is made manifest in the physical; however, the premise is to worship the Father in spirit and in truth because He is a Spirit. When this is properly done, the actions manifesting in the body will be proper. This can only be done if we remain dead to the ways of our old man. The only answer is the Cross.

As the Believer places Faith in the Redemptive work of Jesus Christ *(I Cor. 2:2)*, they become the recipient of the effectual working of the Spirit of Life, working through Grace *(Rom. 8:2)*. It is here that the Apostle Paul could proclaim – *"I am Crucified with Christ: nevertheless I live, yet not I, but Christ lives in me: and the life which I now live in the flesh I live by the Faith of the Son of God, Who loved me, and gave Himself for me" (Gal. 2:20)*. This is the exclusive place wherein we can truly worship God the Father as He desires – in spirit and truth.

CHAPTER 15

Faith Firmly Anchored

I CORINTHIANS 2:2

PREFACE

I t is amazing how much emphasis we can put on things in this world! As a young boy, I remember the toy section in this one particular grocery store my mom used to go to; as she shopped, she allowed me to spend the entire time in the toy aisle where inevitably I would choose the most important toy of my life. When she came to get me, I would plead my case on how badly I needed it, but most often I had to put it back.

As I grew up, so did my desire for age appropriate toys such as trucks, tools, motorcycles, high-tech gadgets, etc., and now making my own money, I purchased pretty much what I wanted. Each purchase was exciting, as was the time spent enjoying the item after I brought it home. Yet sometimes weeks or months prior to the purchase, I would ponder what I wanted as if it was the only thing that mattered. However, regardless of how important I felt the item was, after a time, the obsession faded, and the item either found its way into storage or was given away. Wow! The power of want! I saw, I wanted, and I made up my mind!

All this changed when I was introduced to my wife, Nancy. We became inseparable the moment we met and, in our love for each other, everything I once found important simply faded in the backdrop of life. We married three years later and my decisions were based on protecting and supporting Nancy's life and our daughters. The passion that drove my decisions was no longer based on my wants and desires, but on those of my family's needs and desires, and so I learned to become mindful because the consequences of my decisions impacted my family.

In our marriage, there were many decisions – some insignificant, others taking the time to make. I remember one decision that forever changed our lives. It was 1997. I had come to a place where I realized that neither Nancy nor any other person could help me with the war going on in my mind and the sin I was so desperately trying to overcome.

Nancy was my confidant, yet as much as she loved me, and as much as she tried to help, nothing was working. As I came to see this, it was clear I had but two choices: Man or God. Although this may seem like a rather easy choice, it was not. What I mean by seeking the answer through "Man" is the gamut of church sermons, bible studies, and Christian conferences, etc. What I mean by seeking God for the answer is an unwavering decision to look nowhere else but to God and His Word, without the influences of man. This decision took time because it was black and white for me. If I made the decision to seek God and His Word, it would be an exclusive decision with impenetrable borders, regardless of the cost.

With the support of Nancy in my decision, I chose to seek God without the influence of Man in any way. Looking back, I can now see it was the most important decision of my life. I believed if I earnestly devoted myself to this endeavor I would find the answer within a year, but it would be nine years before I came to see what I was in search of. When the answer came into view, it would not be because I studied, prayed, or even engaged a life of significant fasting – it was revealed because of God's love for me and my decision that turned into determination, yet even I did not uphold my determination. Looking back, I can easily see that God was my strength each time I made the ongoing decision because that is all that I had. All we truly have as Christians is the capacity to make decisions.

If the decision is made to seek God and Him alone for the answer, He will uphold this decision. When He unveils the answer, our ongoing decision to embrace it becomes the rampart of determination, and this is what the Apostle Paul is saying to us here in *I Corinthians 2:2*.

I Corinthians 2:2 – Subject Scripture undivided
For I determined not to know any thing among you, save Jesus Christ, and Him Crucified.

What an incredible statement we find unveiled in the Word of God – *"For I determined."* Assessing all things and regardless of the cost or circumstances, Paul made an unwavering decision. This decision was his to make; he could have digressed from the pursuit of triumph and holiness, but he did not. In Paul's perseverance, God taught him by the Revelation of Jesus Christ, wherein he came to understand God's Way for his triumph and holiness and made the unwavering decision not to know any other thing. While Paul was alive, his constant ponder was the magnificent work of the Cross, therein his Faith and will followed and he was not detoured *(Rom. 7:25; I Tim. 6:12; II Tim. 4:7)*.

By the Apostle Paul stating, *"For I determined not to know any thing among you,"* he is not saying that he determined not to know "anything" – he knew so much about the Law, its Ordinances, and everything within them. He is saying is that he understood the implications and magnitude of what even a little error would create. Therefore, he could not bend an iota and was determined not to know any other particular "thing" for his manner of living for God *"save Jesus Christ, and Him Crucified,"* thus, the way of Sanctification.

Today, we have so many other particular "things" referred to as teachings, telling us how to live for God. These other "things" are being brought forth from the most powerful positions in human history. From the pulpit, these other "things" are reaching millions unlike ever before, mostly by false preachers and teachers ultimately teaching doctrines of devils, whether realized or not *(II Cor. 11:3; Gal. 1:6-9).*

This is not to say that all those preaching errors are doing so with malicious intent. Rather, there are many in powerful positions today (as in Paul's day) who have made an assessed decision to preach their ideas even after they come to see their error. Though there are many facets of the intention for maintaining their position, it becomes hard to give up the income when one builds a kingdom *(Acts 8:18-23).*

Scripture warns us very clearly about such teachings and those that bring them, not because they might come, but because they have come – *"⁶I marvel that you are so soon removed from Him Who called you into the Grace of Christ unto another gospel: ⁷Which is not another; but there be some that trouble you, and would pervert the Gospel of Christ. ⁸But though we, or an Angel from Heaven, Preach any other gospel unto you than that which we have preached unto you, let him be accursed. ⁹As we said before, so say I now again, If any man Preach any other gospel unto you than that you have received, let him be accursed. ¹⁰For do I now persuade men, or God? Or do I seek to please men? For if I yet pleased men, I should not be the servant of Christ. ¹¹But I certify* you, Brethren, that the Gospel which was Preached of me is not after man. *¹²For I neither received it of man, neither was I taught it, but by the Revelation of Jesus Christ" (Gal. 1:6-12).*

Galatians 1:6-10 is the warning, and *verses 11 and 12* are the criteria. The Gospel that the Apostle Paul received was the Gospel of Jesus Christ, and Him Crucified for triumph and holiness (that is, Sanctification), and he was taught it by the Revelation of Jesus Christ. Therefore, this is the Gospel we are to adhere to as Paul did while he lived in his mortal body.

Every preacher with a sincere heart for God must ensure what they are preaching is biblically sound. In order to do this, they must ensure their applications are built on the one true foundation that has already been laid, which is Jesus Christ, and Him Crucified *(I Cor. 3:10-11)*. Unless it is built on this foundation, it errs from the Word of God.

The preacher may feel that people will become offended with such a Message, yet true Believers long for the Truth, and they need to be fed the Truth in order to live for God the way He desires. Love is not passive, and because Faith works by love *(Gal. 5:6)*, as the Gospel becomes preached in truth from a sincere and loving heart, the preacher trusting God can rest in the fact that He will build the church.

The Apostle Paul was given the great responsibility in delivering the Gospel Message of the Cross, and we should guard our heart and mind against any other gospel. The Apostle Paul was determined not to know any thing except that which would Save his soul and keep him free from the Law of Sin and Death; thus, we too should make the same determination. The bottom line is: Faith anchored in Jesus Christ, and Him Crucified, secured the Apostle Paul in the Will of the Father, and that says it all!

CHAPTER 16

The Faith

GALATIANS 2:20

PREFACE

Faith! In simple word structure, Faith is a noun and identifies a person, place, or thing. Yet unlike the word "believe," which is a consideration and acceptance of truth whereby invoking an objective (i.e., material action), Faith, although a consideration and an acceptance of truth, invokes a subjective action and stays within the immaterial realm of the mind.

We can associate "believe" with Salvation – *"9That if you shall confess with your mouth the Lord Jesus, and shall believe in your heart that God has raised Him from the dead, you shall be saved. 10For with the heart man believes unto Righteousness; and with the mouth confession is made unto Salvation" (Rom. 10:9-10).*

Yet after Salvation, this word "believe" seems to become shelved, so to speak; the word "Faith" becomes the choice word. Why is that? Before we come to Christ, we believe, and after we come to Christ, we have Faith *(Gal. 3:24-25)*. This does not antiquate the word "believe" because it is a vital component within our heart that does not go away after our Salvation. We believe in Jesus Christ, and we have Faith that what He has done through His death is enough, plus or minus nothing!

Before Salvation, the word "Faith" was distant; it seemed to be tied to religion, which is quite amazing because most unsaved people associate with it in the same way. Nevertheless, upon Salvation, something significant happens: all of a sudden we have Faith. This is because, upon our Salvation, the Faith of Jesus has been given to us *(Gal. 2:16)*.

The Apostle Paul writes, *"I live by the Faith of the Son of God..."* *(Gal. 2:20)*; we could say, "it is the Faith of the Son of God that I live by." Either way, it is as the Scripture bears out; the Apostle Paul lives by Jesus' Faith. Yet, why did Jesus need Faith? This is an important question, and by Paul writing, *"the Faith of the Son of God,"* he makes a marked distinction regarding Faith.

Many religions have made, and continue to make a cardinal mistake by believing that Jesus Christ was not God because they think that "the Son of God" means He was not co-existent with God. This is a remiss interpretation, and can be derived from *John 3:16* – *"For God so loved the world, that he Gave his Only Begotten Son, that whosoever believes in Him should not perish, but have Everlasting Life."*

The title *"Only Begotten"* within *John 3:16* means just that, He was the *"Only Begotten"* Son of God. This speaks of Jesus' humanity due to His virgin birth, not His Deity. The Man, Jesus, was one hundred percent Man, and He, in absolution, is one hundred percent God.

What must be understood is that the Man, Jesus, while in His humanity, did not cease to be God; God cannot cease from Himself. Therefore, in His humanity, He divested Himself as He walked in the likeness of men *(Phil. 2:5-8; Heb. 12:2)*. The profound implications of this go far beyond what any man or woman could write about in their lifetime *(John 21:25)*. Yet, the manifested purpose of Christ was to come in the likeness as a man (the last Adam *[I Cor. 15:45]*), to rectify the consequences of the first Adam. This had to be done by a man. No other way would have been in accordance with God's Divine Attributes of Truth, Justice, Judgment, and Whom He is – Love *(I John 4:8)*. In order to understand why Christ had to come into the world as the last Adam, we must understand how Lucifer brought the Fall of the first Adam, and thereby the Fall of Mankind.

In the Garden, Lucifer did not control or force Adam to eat from the Tree of the Knowledge of Good and Evil. Eve became deceived through Lucifer's twisted comments, which caused her to transgress and facilitate Adam in unbelief as a result. In his unbelief, Adam then used his physical body to partake of the Tree that he was commanded not to eat from. Not only did Lucifer's tactic bring the Fall of Adam and Eve, but his tactic also brought the Fall of Mankind through Adam's actions *(Gen. 3:6-9; Rom. 5:12)*, yet this was the extent of Lucifer's wisdom.

Therefore, the Fall of Lucifer had to be done through a man, and it had to be done without controlling or forcing Lucifer – this is the infinite wisdom of God *(Gen. 3:15)*. For this reason, the Epistle of *1 John 3:8* writes – *"He who commits sin is of the Devil; for the Devil sinneth from the beginning. For this purpose the Son of God was manifested, that He might destroy the works of the Devil."*

The Word God came in the likeness of men in order to *"destroy the works of the Devil."* Yet we must keep in mind that God, in the likeness of men, could not violate His Divine Attributes and Nature *(Titus 1:2)*. Meaning, because Lucifer did not control or force Adam in any way to bring about the Fall, likewise, God (in the likeness of men, the last Adam, the Man, Jesus) could not use His power as God to bring the Fall of Lucifer.

The last Adam (the Man, Jesus), never ceasing to be God, divested Himself and allowed Lucifer's pride to dictate the events that would forever seal Lucifer's eternal fate. For this reason, the Apostle Paul writes – *"Which none of the princes of this world knew: for had they known it, they would not have Crucified the Lord of Glory" (I Cor. 2:8).*

The word "divest" means that God did not allow Himself His Rights of Deity. The *"Only Begotten Son"* of God divested Himself of His rights, even though He ceased not to be God. Divesting Himself, He Authored Faith and was baptized by John, receiving the fullness of the Holy Spirit to be led in His manifested purpose (that is, the Cross), which was the Will of His Father Who is in Heaven *(John 3:16; Matt. 26:39).*

Though we see through a glass, darkly *(I Cor. 13:12)* for now, this is a look into the Revelation of the Mystery and Wisdom of God – the Cross. So, when the Apostle Paul wrote, *"I live by the Faith of the Son of God..." (Gal. 2:20),* he is literally saying that he lives by Jesus' Faith that was given to him upon his Salvation.

One might possibly understand that Jesus Authored Faith, but ask: "How is Jesus the Finisher of our Faith?" Let us look into *Hebrews 12:2 – "Looking unto Jesus the Author and Finisher of our Faith; Who for the joy that was set before Him endured the Cross, despising the shame, and is set down at the Right Hand of the Throne of God."*

We might have thought *Hebrews 12:2* meant that Jesus was finishing our Faith, but this is not what the Author of Hebrews is implying. Everything was finished at the Cross *(John 19:30).* If Jesus had to finish our Faith, it would be in conflict with His Word, His ways, and the tremendous Price He Paid for us. The Author is implying that Christ Jesus is now refining us as we learn obedience of Faith *(Rom. 16:26).*

In simple word structure, "Faith" is a noun identifying a person, place, or thing. Remarkably, this noun facilitates the full scope of defining a noun. The person is Jesus Christ, the place is Calvary, and the thing is the Cross, that is, the events surrounding Jesus Christ, and Him Crucified.

Therefore, Faith was Authored by the Man, Jesus, with the Cross as the very origin of its existence, and He finished Faith on the Cross. Jesus no longer needs Faith – we do – and He gave it to us upon our Salvation into Him.

Galatians 2:20 – Subject Scripture
I am Crucified with Christ: nevertheless I live; yet not I, but Christ lives in me: and the life which I now live in the flesh I live by the Faith of the Son of God, Who loved me, and gave Himself for me.

Galatians 2:20 – Portion I
"I am Crucified with Christ: nevertheless I live...;"

The Apostle Paul is giving us a most exciting and wonderful insight by stating, *"I am Crucified with Christ."* Paul could have written, "I am Crucified with Jesus." The Apostle did not because (as stated) the Man, Jesus, was one hundred percent Man, and He, in absolution, is one hundred percent God *(John 1:1, 14, 29; I Pet. 1:18-20)*. Meaning, the Man, Jesus, did not cease to be God; God cannot cease from Himself.

In His humanity, Jesus expressed His Deity as this – *"¹⁷Therefore does My Father love Me, because I lay down My life, that I might take it again. ¹⁸No man takes it from Me, but I lay it down of Myself. I have power to lay it down, and I have power to take it again. This Commandment have I received of My Father" (John 10:17-18).*

The significance of *John 10:17-18* is that no man can lay down his or her life and take it back up again – only God can do this. Upon the Cross, though His physical body was being Crucified, He never ceased to be God Eternal.

Because of the comprehensive nature of this, let us look into *Luke 23:46*. The Scripture has been divided with expositions to explain along the way – *"And when Jesus* (clearly signifying the Man *[Rom. 5:15; Heb. 10:12]*) *had cried with a loud voice, He said, Father, into Your hands I commend My Spirit* (the Spirit of God that came from the Father at His Baptism by John, went to the Father *[Matt. 3:16; Mark 1:10-13]*): *and having said thus, He gave up the ghost"* (to breathe His last with His physical body – to expire: NT: 1606; from NT: 1537 and NT: 4154).

As God, He had the power to lay down His bodily life and take it back up again – no one took it from Him. Upon the Cross, His Deity as God Alpha and Omega lives, never ceasing to be God during His Human Crucifixion, unto His Death. This was the inseparable work of the Cross *(John 10:17-18)*. The Apostle Paul is expressing the correlation and likeness by stating, *"I am Crucified with Christ."* Now living in this remarkable experience, though Crucified with Christ, he states, *"nevertheless I live."* The Apostle Paul is literally living in the likeness of Jesus' death and the likeness of His Resurrection *(II Cor. 4:10-11)*.

The Apostle Paul stated in *Romans 8:11* – *"But if the Spirit of Him Who raised up Jesus from the dead dwells in you, He that raised up Christ from the dead shall also quicken your mortal bodies by His Spirit that dwells in you."* The significance of *Romans 8:11* is that Jesus did not raise Himself; God the Father raised Jesus from the dead *(Acts 2:23-33)*. What is most remarkable about *Romans 8:11* is that, though Jesus was triumphant through His bodily death *(Col. 2:13-15)*, He (being fully God in open view for all principalities and powers to see) was still fully divested and dependent upon the Father for being raised from the dead. This is an amazing part of the correlation the Apostle Paul is experiencing as well. As Paul became fully dependent on the Father through Faith in Jesus Christ, and Him Crucified, he remained divested to his own efforts and carnal thinking.

As Christians, we must keep in the forefront of our belief and Faith that death must come first *(Rom. 6:7; 7:25)* in order to be raised from the dead in the likeness of Jesus' Resurrection *(Rom. 8:2, 11, 14)*. For this reason, as it was for Paul, the Cross must ever be the object of our Faith *(I Cor. 2:2; Gal. 6:14)*.

Galatians 2:20 – Subject Scripture
I am Crucified with Christ: nevertheless I live; **yet not I, but Christ lives in me: and the life which I now live in the flesh I live by the Faith of the Son of God,** Who loved me, and gave Himself for me.

Galatians 2:20 – Portion II
"…yet not I, but Christ lives in me: and the life which I now live in the flesh I live by the Faith of the Son of God…,"

Portion two of *Galatians 2:20* – *"yet not I, but Christ lives in me"* – speaks of the inseparableness of Jesus' Human death, and yet the life and power of His Deity as Christ Jesus, all taking place on the Cross. Paul, due to the Gift of Eternal Life he has in Christ, is seeing a correlation of this amazing event now taking place in him.

The Apostle Paul's proclamation – *"and the life which I now live in the flesh"* – is correlating the work of the Cross taking place in his flesh. The Apostle understands that his flesh, now Crucified in the likeness of Jesus' body, is simply a tangible physical tent that he lives within for the time being. This being the actual event and ongoing experience, he describes how it began – *"I live by the Faith of the Son of God."*

By the Apostle Paul making a marked distinction of the Faith he lives by, he unveils to all that the life he now lives in the flesh, he lives *"by the Faith of the Son of God."* Paul's statement – *"the Son of God"* – speaks of God's humanity, not His Deity, and the very reason He Authored Faith. Through His obedience unto the death *(Matt. 26:39; Heb. 10: 5-10)*, even the death of the Cross, He finished Faith *(John 19:30; Heb. 12:2)*. Through this precious work, God now gives this Faith to everyone who calls upon His Name, and as they walk with Him, He can finish their obedience to His Faith.

Galatians 2:20 – Subject Scripture

I am Crucified with Christ: nevertheless I live; yet not I, but Christ lives in me: and the life which I now live in the flesh I live by the Faith of the Son of God, **Who loved me, and gave Himself for me.**

Galatians 2:20 – Portion III
"...Who loved me, and Gave Himself for me."

Now in the balance of *verse 20*, this magnificent statement is the direct and personal reference to the Cross, and should cause all other ideas of looking anywhere else to fade away. This ending statement of *verse 20* is the very means and source of our life and living, and the resting place for our Faith.

The Revelation of the Cross, the magnitude of what took place, and the entire intention from Eternity past (being God's Love), was magnificently expressed like this. Though Man's understanding of God's Love has been significantly reduced due to the Fall, the impact and incomprehensible greatness of His Love remains unchanged, Eternal and comes with the promise of the Holy Spirit.

Though it is not possible to grasp the fullness of God's Love, what we can grasp as we wait for His Return is that our Creator came in the likeness of men for the sole purpose of Redeeming us and giving us the means through which we can now live for Him. The beauty of His greatness is so amazing! As we come to understand His Sacrifice was for both Salvation and Sanctification as Paul came to understand, our Faith will remain in Him and what He has done, and our profession will be – *"I am Crucified with Christ: nevertheless I live; yet not I, but Christ lives in me: and the life which I now live in the flesh I live by the Faith of the Son of God, Who loved me, and gave Himself for me."*

PART IV

The Offense of the Cross

CHAPTER 17

They Will Say Lord, Lord

MATTHEW 7:21-23

PREFACE

As we look around us, we can see the world racing by as if most know and understand what they are doing and where they are going. As we watch the news, it seems as if everybody and everything is coming apart, and we wonder why. Somehow, the problems of the world appear too big and people's pain too distant, but this is not so. It is all real, not only at the distance of news, but in those we may see around us, even if they are not showing it.

Depending upon the upbringing and propensities of any one person, his or her perspective view of the world may be too far different from another's to understand fully how he or she views life. The point I am driving toward is this: regardless of our view or whom we may think has it all together, regardless of what church we may go to or what pastor we may be listening to, each and every person falls short. Every book, writing and answer provided for mankind's problems will come woefully short unless they are grounded in the absolute Truth of God's Written Word. Yet even then, everything written and spoken about the Word of God comes short. The only absolute for us is the True Word of God itself.

We cannot depend on what we think is good or bad, or what he or she says. We all have the responsibility to know the biblical Truth, correct, in context, and then walk in the Truth. The biblical Truth is simple – believing it is the hardest part. Nonetheless, when it is known, believed, and understood, everything else that is not of the Truth will fade in comparison.

For every living human being, there is nothing more important than receiving the Gift of Eternal Life found only in Jesus Christ. Once Salvation is received, there is nothing more important than truly coming to know Jesus Christ, His Ways, and how He has made the way for us through His Life and death, and then walk in this Way as He desires.

It is His Way that is set apart, wherein we can find the only answer for the leading of the Holy Spirit unto the Will of the Father. If we are not led by the Holy Spirit, then we are about own will and, regardless of the effort, if it is not the Will of the Father, we will be qualified as not knowing Jesus Christ as God had intended.

As Christians, we have a deep desire to work out our Salvation *(Phil. 2:12)*, but it must be worked out through Jesus Christ in order to be in the Will of the Father *(I Cor. 2:2; I Pet. 1:7-9)*. To ensure this, the Apostle Paul instructs us to examine ourselves as Believers in order to see if we are in the Faith *(II Cor. 13:5)*. Therefore, it becomes paramount to know what *the Faith* truly means.

The Christian Faith was Authored, designed, walked out, and finished by the Man, Jesus. Now, Faith's object and resting place is Jesus Christ, and Him Crucified *(I Cor. 1:17-18; 2:2; Heb. 12:2)*. The reason we need to examine ourselves and be specific about this endeavor is to ensure that we are not deceiving ourselves in what we have come to believe as truth through those who have erred from the truth *(I Tim. 4:1)*. No one ever thinks it could be them, but that is the art of deception.

I have chosen three Scriptures disclosing a group of people who had done things we as Christians would think are good and right, but we will see that they had been done apart from the Will of the Father. This group of people could have avoided their catastrophic position had they humbly and truly examined themselves to see if they were in *the Faith*. Had they been in the Faith, the Holy Spirit would have led them unto the Will of the Father, and they would have truly known Jesus Christ.

Matthew 7:21 – Subject Scripture undivided
Not every one who says unto Me, Lord, Lord, shall enter into the kingdom of Heaven; but he who does the Will of My Father which is in Heaven.

"Not every one who says unto Me, Lord, Lord, shall enter into the Kingdom of Heaven" reveals that not all claiming the Name of Jesus (even as Lord) truly know Him. These words are followed up by drawing the line of specific criteria for knowing Him – *"but he who does the Will of My Father which is in Heaven."*

The criterion for entering into Heaven is direct and clear. However, we cannot know, nor can we do the Will of the Father apart from the Holy Spirit *(Rom. 7:18; 8:9-14)*. Each of us as a Christian man, woman, boy, or girl, can always do something, even great things, but without the leading of the Holy Spirit, it will not be the Will of the Father.

We are created in the image, after the likeness of God, so we have the power within ourselves to create, to rule, and the sovereignty to make our own decisions. All of this and everything associated with the power we have and the decisions we make has been given to us by God. Yet we are not nor can we ever be God. We have a beginning – God does not; we have love – God does not – He is Love *(I John 4:16).*

There is something deep within each of us that can cause us to believe we have the power to do what we want without consequences. Each one of us who call upon the Name of the Lord deals with this to one degree or the other. This is ultimately pride producing rebellion, regardless of how good it looks.

Nothing has changed since the beginning in regards to learning dependency on God. This is, for the time being, our journey. Aside from dependency on God the Father through Christ, we depend on ourselves; each of these dependent events is simply a form of godliness that has denied the power *(II Tim. 3:1-7).* A child of God is led by the Spirit of God *(Rom. 8:14).*

Matthew 7:22 – Subject Scripture
Many will say to Me in that day, Lord, Lord, have we not Prophesied in Your Name? and in Your Name have cast out devils? and in Your Name done many wonderful works?

Matthew 7:22 – Portion I
"Many will say to Me in that day…,"

"Many will say to Me" reveals these people, whomever they may be, will be directly accountable to Christ Jesus. Yet these people will make an effort in order to justify themselves, as we will come to see. Nevertheless, now before God, everything (including their intentions) will be revealed and will be irreversible. Christ' statement – *"in that day"* – reveals a Day to come.

Matthew 7:22 – Subject Scripture
Many will say to Me in that day, **Lord, Lord, have we not Prophesied in Your Name? and in Your Name have cast out devils? and in Your Name done many wonderful works?**

Matthew 7:22 – Portion II
**"Lord, Lord, have we not Prophesied in Your Name?
and in Your Name have cast out devils?
And in Your Name done many wonderful works?"**

The balance of *verse 22* is profound and staggering statements on many levels. Now before the Lord, the justifying efforts, based upon spiritual manifestations, begins. Nonetheless, their works may have been done in His Name, but they will come to realize too late what they had been doing was not within the Will of the Father.

The size of one's ministry, the eloquence of one's preaching or teaching, spiritual manifestations, miracles, wealth, or possessions, are not criteria in determining that an individual is in the Will of the Father *(II Pet., Chptr 2; Jude)*.

Matthew 7:23 – Subject Scripture
And then will I profess unto them, I never knew you: depart from Me, you who work iniquity.

Matthew 7:23 – Portion I
"And then will I profess unto them, I never knew you…"

"And then" reveals the Lord waited as they disclosed their ways by making their defense. Their defense is acknowledged and reply begins – *"I will Profess unto them, I never knew you"* – which will reveal all they had done while alive in their physical bodies, driven

by their intentions, had nothing to do with truly knowing Him. This incomprehensible statement – *"I never knew you"* – brings out the reality that using the Name of Jesus (even under the title "Christian") is not criteria for knowing Him. The Apostle Paul gives us a view into the central theme of Biblical Christianity, and what it means to know Christ Jesus as Lord in the following *Verses.*

"⁷But what things were gain to me, those I counted loss for Christ. ⁸Yea doubtless, and I count all things but loss for the excellency of the knowledge of Christ Jesus my Lord: for whom I have suffered the loss of all things, and do count them but dung, that I may win Christ, ⁹And be found in Him, not having my own righteousness, which is of the Law, but that which is through the Faith of Christ, the Righteousness which is of God by Faith: ¹⁰That I may know Him, and the power of His Resurrection, and the fellowship of His sufferings, being made conformable unto His death; ¹¹If by any means I might attain unto the Resurrection of the dead" (Phil. 3:7-11).

Philippians 3:7
"But what things were gain to me, those I counted loss for Christ."

This extraordinary *verse* takes on a variety of depths and seasons in our Christian walk. When we first receive Salvation, we are in the wonder of it all, yet as we begin to walk, we find it difficult to lay those things aside that so easily beset us *(Heb. 12:1)*. Along the path, we may stop for a while and set up camp where we are not meant to, but because we love the Lord, we learn to pack up and go on unto perfection, which is after Christ *(Phil. 3:12; Heb. 6:1)*. As we pack up, we realize we do not need the things we once did and we let them go until there is nothing left.

Philippians 3:8

"Yea doubtless, and I count all things but loss for the excellency of the knowledge of Christ Jesus my Lord: for whom I have suffered the loss of all things, and do count them but dung, that I may win Christ...,"

Paul begins *verse 8* with *"Yea doubtless,"* letting us know that, with a doubt, he has made the decision that everything pales in comparison to his pursuit, and writes, *"and I count all things but loss for the excellency of the knowledge of Christ Jesus my Lord."* Paul makes a marked distinction between a nominal walk, as opposed to a walk in what he describes as a walk in pursuit of *"the excellency of the knowledge of Christ Jesus my Lord."* By writing *"my Lord,"* he reveals his first love. There is knowledge of Christ Jesus, and then there is a decision to lay all things aside in order for one to lose "I" in this world and find themselves in Christ Jesus *(Mark 8:35)*. Here in the balance, Paul writes, *"for whom I have suffered the loss of all things, and do count them but dung, that I may win Christ."* When the decision is made to follow Christ and endeavor to truly follow Him, the things of the world will no longer cause us to stop.

Philippians 3:9

"...And be found in Him, not having my own righteousness, which is of the Law, but that which is through the Faith of Christ, the Righteousness which is of God by Faith...:"

Philippians verse 9 gives us great insight; within it, we see that to be found in Him is not possible by trying to live by the Law through any kind of self-effort, but quite the opposite – being found in Him can be done through *"the Faith of Christ."* This may be easily received by the Christian at first, but once again the Christian must understand that *"the Faith of Christ"* was Authored and finished with the Will of His Father as its very foundation. This foundation is the Cross, and this is the foundation upon which we build – there is no other. Yet we are to take heed how we are to build thereupon *(I Cor. 3:10)*. Jesus Christ was made manifest in these last times for us *(I Pet. 1:18-20)*. He did not need to satisfy the Law for Himself, nor did He need to die for Himself – these He did for us. The Mystery of this remarkable finished work was given to the Apostle Paul, and once he was taught it by the Revelation of Jesus Christ, he laid the foundation of his Gospel for us. Thus, we see his devoted intentions in *verse 10*.

*P*hilippians 3:10

*"...That I may know Him, and the power of His
Resurrection, and the fellowship of His sufferings,
being made conformable unto His death...;"*

There are four inseparable and phenomenal things going on within *verse 10*. First, *"That I may know Him"* comes as we begin to understand the purpose for which He came – this is the cornerstone of knowing Him.

Second, *"and the power of His Resurrection"* is the desired experience of all who believe; however, no one can experience the power of His Resurrection except through His death *(Gal. 2:20)*, and the knowledge of this death is found in the excellency of the knowledge of Christ Jesus. Within this knowledge is the Revelation of the Cross.

Third, *"and the fellowship of His sufferings"* embrace the Cross as the mainstay of Faith. There alone many sufferings will be experienced because this way, this walk, is not of this world *"and"* thus are the dynamics of *"the fellowship in His sufferings."* This is a good thing *(I Pet. 1:7)* and, regardless of the experience, the power of His Resurrection will bring us through because, as it was with the Lord Jesus, the Holy Spirit always leads us unto the Will of the Father when the Cross becomes the focal point of our life and living *(I Cor. 2:2; Gal. 6:14)*.

Fourth, *"being made conformable unto His death"* is the Mind of Christ, and we are to let this Mind be in us *(Phil. 2:5-8)*. The entire desire of Jesus our Lord was, is, and, ever shall be to do the Will of His Father. In His Love, He came in the likeness of men, divested Himself, and became conformable unto death, even the death of the Cross. God is Love – *Agape* Love – openly displayed on the Cross for us. Man has the limits of *Phileo* love and *Storge* love, and though these Greek descriptive titles are not found in the Bible, they nonetheless accurately describe human love. Yet these types of love need *Agape* Love or human love fades, remiss of True love *(John 21:15-17)*. Embracing the Cross is where *Agape* Love is found, and where we are made conformable unto Jesus' death. In this, the world, the flesh, and the Devil are overcome *(John 3:16; I Cor. 13:1-13; I John, Chptr 4)*.

Philippians 3:11
"...If by any means I might attain unto the Resurrection of the dead."

This amazing *verse* unveils the supernatural benefit that simply happens as a result of embracing *verses 7-10*, all of which are summed up in the Cross – Jesus Christ, and Him Crucified – God's established way of victory.

The Apostle Paul unveils within *Philippians 3:7-11* that the way for our victory in this present evil world is to be made conformable unto His death *(I Cor. 2:2; II Cor. 4:10-18; Phil. 2:5; 3:7-11)*, and that way is Faith resting in the Cross whereby giving the Spirit of Life the latitude in which He can quicken our mortal body unto the Will of the Father *(Rom. 7:25; 8:2, 11, 14)*.

This is what it means to function in the Law of the Spirit, and because this Law has been established in Christ Jesus through His death, we can rest in the fact that the Spirit of Life in Christ Jesus will raise us in the likeness of His Resurrection unto the Will of the Father while we are alive in this present evil world. This is *the Faith* wherein we can truly come to know Jesus as Lord, and this is the Faith of the Son of God wherein we live *(Gal. 2:19-20)*.

As we walk in this truth, we also experience freedom from lingering condemnation because the Righteousness of the Law remains fulfilled within us *(Rom. 8:1-4)*. This is an inexpressible place for us to be, and because we have entered into His rest apart from our own works and methods *(Heb. 4:3, 10)*, we will experience true joy *(I Pet. 1:8)*. Apart from this way of the Cross, we cannot come to know Christ Jesus as God the Father has intended *(Phil. 3:18-19)*, and Scripture bears out that we will not experience the leading of the Holy Spirit unto the Will of the Father as intended.

Whoever these people might be that were functioning outside the Will of the Father, and in that Day to come, the Lord will profess unto them, *"I never knew you."*

Matthew 7:23 – Subject Scripture
And then will I profess unto them, I never knew you: **depart from Me, you who work iniquity.**

Matthew 7:23 – Portion II
"...depart from Me, you who work iniquity."

These words that the Lord will profess – *"depart from me"* – are inconceivable to the human mind. The balance – *"you who work iniquity"* – qualifies the result of being outside the Will of the Father.

"Iniquity" is defined in biblical Greek within the word *anomia* (ἀ νομία, NT: 458, an-om-ee'-ah); from *anomos* (ἄνομος, NT: 459, an'-om-os); illegality, i.e., violation of law or (genitive case) wickedness, lawless. Within this Scripture context, *"iniquity"* has a double meaning. When one is functioning in Lawlessness, they will produce the fruits of death – *"iniquity."* Let us understand the reality of the Christian functioning in Lawlessness.

As Christians, we are delivered from the Law by the Body of Christ *(Rom. 7:4)*, but we are not Lawless *(Rom. 7:7, 25; I Cor. 9:21; Heb. 8:10-13; 10:16-17)*. The Apostle Paul writes, *"To them that are without Law, as without Law, (being not without Law to God, but under the Law to Christ,) that I might gain them that are without Law"* *(I Cor. 9:21)*. Within *I Corinthians 9:21*, we see *"being not without Law to God, but under the Law to Christ"* clearly revealing we are *"not without the Law to God,"* and furthermore, we are *"under the Law to Christ."*

The Apostle is not speaking of a set of rules in regards to *I Corinthians 9:21*; if this were the case, we would then be left trying to live by the Law in our own efforts. Instead, he is speaking of the spiritual Laws we are to function within so that we do not function in Lawlessness.

The most powerful Law wherein the Believer is insured of functioning within the Will of the Father is "the Law of the Spirit of Life in Christ Jesus" *(Rom. 8:2)*. When the Christian does not function within the parameters of the Law of the Spirit of Life, he or she will be functioning outside of the dynamics of that form of Doctrine *(Rom. 6:17-18)*. Meaning, ensconced within that form of Doctrine is the Law of Faith *(Rom. 3:27)*, the Law of God *(Rom. 7:25)*, the Law of the Spirit *(Rom. 8:2)*, the Law of Righteousness *(Rom. 9:31)*, the Law to Christ *(I Cor. 9:21)*, and the Law of Liberty *(Jam. 2:12)*.

Each one of these spiritual Laws has a dynamic in and of itself, and yet they are inseparable. For example, as I have previously stated, the Apostle Paul set the example for us to follow, whereby we are to serve the Law of God with our mind *(Rom. 7:25; Phil. 3:17)*. There is good reasoning behind this. The Law of God is not only the Mosaic Law fulfilled and Satisfied in Jesus Christ; all of the other spiritual Laws of Righteousness are also housed within it, which, at the very least, make up the foundation of that form of Doctrine *(Rom. 6:17-18)*.

By the Apostle setting the example of serving the Law of God with his mind, he is saying we are to look and think about where the Mosaic Law was fulfilled, Satisfied, and the Penalty Paid – the Cross (Jesus Christ, and Him Crucified). As we follow the Apostle Paul's example, we will have simply engaged all of the Laws of Righteousness, and because the Cross is the legal parameter the Spirit of Life works through, we experience his effectual power working within us *(I Cor. 1:17-18; Gal. 2:19-20; 6:14)*.

If we had to figure this out while we walked with Him, we really could not keep track of it, and so, in God's wonderful love, we have the simplicity that is in Christ *(II Cor. 11:3)*. The simplicity is that we can simply rest our Faith in the Cross *(I Cor. 2:2; Gal. 2:20)*. When this is done, we are simply within the guidelines of the Law of the Spirit and functioning within that form of Doctrine. Thus, we are not Lawless. Ultimately "Lawlessness" can be defined as anything done apart from the Will of the Father; we are either functioning in the Law of the Spirit of Life, or by default we will be functioning in Lawlessness.

As we peer once again into *Matthew 7:21* – *"Not every one who says unto Me, Lord, Lord, shall enter into the kingdom of Heaven; but he who does the Will of My Father which is in Heaven"* – we find that whoever these people may be, they did not do the Will of the Father Who is in Heaven. On this one fact alone, they had been qualified as not knowing the Lord, which is seen in *Matthew 7:23 – "And then will I profess unto them, I never knew you: depart from Me, you who work iniquity."*

Though these *verses* evade our full grasp, they will one day be a reality for some. The Tree in the Garden of Eden that was not to be eaten from was the Tree of the Knowledge of both good *and* evil, not just evil *(Gen. 2:9, 17)*. We must understand that it is the good whereby mankind is most often deceived, yet as Christians we are not excluded from this deception.

The unsaved sinner is constantly ruled by the sin nature; thereunder, he or she is in a perpetual cycle of trying to do good in order to overcome the knowledge of evil. However, because the strength of the sin nature is the Law, the sinner will never break out of this cycle unless Salvation is received.

Every sinner, regardless of how good or evil they may be, has set a standard that he or she lives by in order to avoid the moral standard set by God. When anyone cannot live up to or within their own standard, they argue and fight – this is where wars, murders, and every other type of sin originate.

For us who are Saved, we must learn that we cannot do good apart from God's established way of victory, and without embracing the way of victory (that is, the Cross), our senses will not be exercised to discern both good and evil *(Heb. 5:14)*. Without this discernment, it is not possible to discern the nature of sin wishing (willing) us to do good *(Rom. 7:21– NKJV)*. If we fall prey to the deception of good, the sin nature will revive, gain dominion, deceive and ultimately destroy our life. This is a reality which can be seen as we look around throughout today's mainstream Christianity, and those in this condition are ever more susceptible to ongoing deceptions.

The preacher has the potential to engage any one way of any method devised by an Angel, another, or him or herself. Once the deception is engaged, he or she will build a corrupt gospel on the wrong foundation and preach "another Jesus" with "another spirit" and bring "another gospel" *(II Cor. 11:4; Gal. 1:6-9; I Tim. 4:1)*. This will make the Message of the Cross of none effect not only in his or her own life, but also to those who embrace the heresy *(I Cor. 1:17; Phil. 3:18)*. Those that embrace the way of error will think their way is right, but this is the art of deception.

The catastrophic statement *"I never knew you: depart from Me, you who work iniquity"* was professed unto these people because they did not know Jesus. Had they truly desired to know Him, they would have known His Way and remained in the Will of the Father.

Our walk, and thus our relationship with God, is either by Faith or not. If Faith is the choice, we cannot choose to walk with Him our way *(Gal. 5:17)*, it must be the Way that God has established through Jesus Christ, and Him Crucified *(Rom. 7:25; I Cor. 2:2; Gal. 2:19-20; 6:14)*. Outside of this Way, it will be in the flesh by the Law *(Rom. 7:5)*.

We should never overlook the fact that the whole world is trying to either live by the Mosaic Law or some other law that they or others have devised, whether it is realized or not, and everything seems so right about it. Nonetheless, this cycle is due to the knowledge of good and evil from the Tree *(Gen. 3:6-9; Rom. 2:14-15; 5:12)*.

One of the Devil's great tactics and ploys is to make it seem as if there is something else, but there is not. It is either by God's established way of victory or it will be by self-imposed efforts of trying to live by the Law in one way or the other, and the penalty of the Law is bondage and death.

If we make the choice to walk by Faith, we must continue to remind ourselves that there is nothing within us (that is, in our flesh) to perform what good we might think or imagine we could do *(Rom. 7:18)*. Our will applied to our physical body becomes an illegal combination as it regards dealing with spiritual matters *(Rom. 7:18;*

8:10). Meaning, if we make this illegal combination in the effort to resist temptation, restrain sin or gain some idea of holiness instead of choosing the Cross it reveals, though we believe in Jesus, we have placed Faith within ourselves, which, once again, results in motions sins in the flesh by the Law.

Our will must come second place to the proper decision of Faith; this resonates determination, which is meant for maintaining Faith *(I Cor. 2:2; I Tim. 6:12).* Our will always defaults into our body, and when resonated becomes willpower. Thus, when the body is used, the evidence is our will is being done, and not the Will of the Father.

Our body is neutral, neither holy nor unholy. Our body is an instrument, a tent by which our spirit and our soul live in for now. Our body can be used for good unto the Will of the Father, but only when it is quickened by the Spirit of Life within us *(Rom. 8:2, 11-14).* Either way, we must all appear before the Judgment seat of Christ, where each one of us may receive the things done in our body according to what we have done, whether be it good or bad *(II Cor. 5:10).*

It is easy to think we can invoke God in our efforts, even in His Name, and when we see or feel manifestations, we can come to believe we are rightly using the Name of Jesus within the Will of the Father, when it is possible we are not. In no uncertain terms, unless our body is moved by the Spirit of God, it is of no profit unto the work of God *(John 6:63).*

Let us peer once again into *Matthew 7:22* in order to get a perspective on this – *"Many will say to Me in that day, Lord, Lord, have we not Prophesied in Your Name? and in Your Name have cast out devils? And in Your Name done many wonderful works?"*

Within *Matthew 7:22,* we see people doing what we, as Christians, would consider good things to do; yet these activities were accounted unto them as Lawlessness, as we came to see in *Matthew 7:23.* Once again, as Christians we are delivered from the Law by the Body of Christ *(Rom. 7:6)*, but we are not Lawless *(Rom. 7:25; 8:7; I Cor. 9:21)*. This means the dynamic of our life and living does not come by trying to live by the Law, or any other law or method coming from the mind of man or an Angel *(II Cor. 3:5; Col. 2:8, 20)*. As Christians, our life and living come from the power of God working within us.

This world and the god therein *(II Cor. 4:4)* have many spiritual counterfeits that have the appearance of spiritual truth, but will be revealed as erring from the Truth. For this reason, the Apostle Paul preached Jesus Christ, and Him Crucified *(I Cor. 1:17-18, 23)*. The Cross was the Will of the Father for Jesus as He walked in the likeness of men and framed Faith for us *(Matt. 26:39; Phil. 2:5-8; Heb. 12:2 – Author)*, and the Cross is ever and always to be the object of our Faith *(I Cor. 2:2; II Cor. 13:4-5; Gal. 2:19-20; 6:14)*. It is the Faith of Jesus Christ now given to us through His finished work at Calvary's Cross *(Heb. 12:2 – Finisher)*.

When the Trump of God sounds, we will be changed from this mortal body and put on immortality *(I Cor. 15:51-58; I Thess. 4:13-18)*, and the sin nature that is presently in our members *(Rom. 7:23)* will no longer be. Yes! Christ is risen, or our Faith is in vain and we are yet in our sins *(I Cor. 15:14-17)*, but while we wait for the Trump to sound, we are to be found in Him. This wonderful place in Him is found as we take up our cross daily *(Luke 9:23; Rom. 7:25; I Cor. 2:2)*. This means we must learn to remain dead to remain free from the deceit and power of sin *(Rom. 6:7)* moving and expressing itself through our mortal body *(Rom. 7:15, 20, 23)*. It is because our will and its power link up quite well with our body that it seems natural to try and accomplish resisting sin and attaining holiness by allowing this link-up to take place. Yet without realizing it, if we do this, we have come to rely on our own abilities and willpower through our carnal mind, and not the power of the Holy Spirit. Therein, the sin nature is given the legal right to revive *(Rom. 7:9)*.

"The sin nature" is what we must overcome because it is this nature of sin that can lead us into Lawlessness. The reason I am driving so hard toward the sin nature is because it is the core problem within Man *(Rom. 7:23)*, even though it is Satan who opposes us from the outside. The implications are profound, but it is really that basic. The problem comes when the sin nature revives within us and then we do not know how to gain victory over it, or we have made the decision that the only way of true victory through Faith anchored in the Cross is foolishness *(I Cor. 1:18; 2:14)*. If the sin nature revives and remains unrestrained, it will rule us and therein deceive us into embracing every other way of error. Meaning, we have a spirit and soul that live in a body, but within our members is the sin nature due to the Fall of Adam, and until we put on immortality, we have to die to self to remain free *(Rom. 6:7)*. The only way is the Cross.

Our Faith must remain in Whom He is, and What He has done for many vital and beneficial reasons. First, so the Righteousness of the Law remains fulfilled within us *(Rom. 8:4)*. Second, so we remain dead while we live *(Gal. 2:19-20)*. Third, so that the Spirit of Life in Christ Jesus can keep us free from the Law of Sin and Death *(Rom. 8:2)*. Fourth, so our walk after the Spirit will be free from condemnation *(Rom. 8:1)*. Fifth, so we remain in the Will of the Father *(Rom. 8:11-17)*. Sixth, so we do not function in Lawlessness *(Matt. 7:21-23)*. And lastly, so we can experience the presence and effectual energizing power of God in our life for Sanctification *(Gal. 6:14)*. The list can continue on, yet all the above and so much more take place as we determine not to know any other thing other than Jesus Christ, and Him Crucified, for our life and living *(I Cor. 2:2)*.

"I never knew you: depart from Me, you who work iniquity" reveals that these people, whoever they may be, were functioning

Daniel E. Armour

outside the Will of the Father. Now functioning in Lawlessness, they had been invoking miracles by some spirit and misusing the Name of Jesus. For this reason, many Christians today are overcome with so much demonic activity, and because they do not know the way of victory, they account this demonic activity as typical Christian warfare. Yet nothing could be further from the truth.

Yes, Satan is our evil opponent, but we have another opponent in our members, and because of the lack of knowledge in the way of victory, marriages and families are being ripped apart *(Hos. 4:6-8; I Cor. 1:17-18)*. As Christians, we are not under the Law, we are under Grace *(Rom. 6:14)*, yet we are not to live Lawless *(Rom. 7:25; I Cor. 9:21)*. Everything we are moved to do as Christians must come first through Faith and then, when we are fitly moved by the Spirit, all that will be done will be through the Spirit of God within us *(Rom. 8:11-14)*.

God does not require much of us, but He does require our Faith to find its resting place in the Cross so that the Spirit of Life can work effectually within our life. Here, we will be about the Will of our Father Who is in Heaven.

304

CHAPTER 18

Another gospel: Which is not another

GALATIANS 1:6-9

PREFACE

God has ordained the fivefold ministry of the Apostle, Prophet, Evangelist, Pastor and Teacher. This means that God has designed these positions to feed His people. Yet when any one of these ministries is delivering tainted food, it leaves His people unable to live right because they do not feel good.

Not knowing what is happening within them, they consume more tainted food. Eventually, the trace elements of the poison distort their mind, and their system builds an immunity that allows them to consume more and more until they die.

The consequences of eternal Hell pale in comparison to this. Meaning, what if in the end this was not dramatic enough to help change the direction of those on the wrong road?

Jesus said, "*²³And in hell he lift up his eyes, being in torments, and seeth Abraham afar off, and Lazarus in his bosom. ²⁴And he cried and said, Father Abraham, have mercy on me, and send Lazarus, that he may dip the tip of his finger in water, and cool my tongue; for I am tormented in this flame. ²⁵But Abraham said, Son, remember that you in your lifetime received your good things, and likewise Lazarus evil things: but now he is comforted, and thou art tormented*" (Luke 16:23-25). Though Jesus said this prior to His death on the Cross, He made these statements that we might understand that, in eternal Hell, all things will be remembered forever and ever.

The point is that error can cause us to lose hope in such a way that we can give up, and allow our Faith to fade away to such a degree, wherein we give up on God and denounce the very thing we once confessed *(I Tim. 1:19)*, all due to erroneous teaching (tainted food).

Galatians 1:6 – Subject Scripture
I marvel that you are so soon removed from Him Who called you into the Grace of Christ unto another gospel:

Galatians 1:6 – Portion I
"...I marvel that you are so soon removed from Him..."

This statement that the Apostle Paul makes reveals that the Believers in Galatia had moved their Faith from the Cross into another gospel. Although it is easy to read this kind of stern admonishment in the Word of God, these kinds of statements are rarely heard of today, for at least two reasons. First, the offense of the Cross has ceased within the lives of both the preachers and those believing in their teachings *(Gal. 5:11)*. Meaning, because the Cross has not, or is no longer the determined centerpiece for their life, and thus their Faith, the offense of the Cross has ceased. Second, this type of statement would more than likely get the preacher evicted from his or her church if he or she embraced the Cross.

Thank God that Paul understood the dire consequences and gave the stern admonishment. However, even though these types of admonishing statements are not heard of much today, this does not mean that we do not have the responsibility of working out our own Salvation with fear and trembling *(Phil. 2:12)*. Just because the Cross may not be preached, it does not remove the responsibility of seeking God for the answer to Sanctification.

As with Salvation, each person is given the freedom to respond to the drawing of the Father – Salvation is never forced *(John 3:16; 6:44)*. Likewise, after Salvation, each of us is given the freedom to respond to the Holy Spirit's desire to teach *(John 14:26; I John 2:27)* – Sanctification is not forced. When the Apostle presented to the Believers in Galatia that deception had overtaken them, they had the choice to receive the admonition and examine themselves as well. God does not violate the will of Man in regards to this matter.

Galatians 1:6 – Subject Scripture
I marvel that you are so soon removed from Him **Who called you into the Grace of Christ** unto another gospel:

Galatians 1:6 – Portion II
"…Who called you into the Grace of Christ…"

This reveals how our relationship with God began. We did not find God – He called us out of the darkness of our life through His Grace and drew us unto Himself for the purpose of fellowship with Him in His Light and Truth.

Galatians 1:6 – Subject Scripture
I marvel that you are so soon removed from Him Who called you into the Grace of Christ **unto another gospel:**

Galatians 1:6 – Portion III
"...unto another gospel...:"

We must keep in mind that Paul is speaking to Believers, and this portion of *verse 6* makes it very clear that there is *"another gospel."* What is *"another gospel"*?

Galatians 1:7 – Subject Scripture
Which is not another; but there be some that trouble you, and would pervert the Gospel of Christ.

Galatians 1:7 – Portion I
"Which is not another...;"

The Apostle Paul lays the groundwork in describing a "counterfeit" of his Gospel. In the ending portion of *Galatians 1:6*, the Apostle Paul wrote *"another gospel"* and though we may think of *"another gospel"* as one in stark contrast to Paul's Gospel, such as the false gospels of the Book of Mormon, and that of the Jehovah Witness's, yet this is not the case. Yes, any doctrines contrary to the foundation of Whom Jesus Christ Is, What He has done in His Life and on the Cross through His death and His Resurrection, are false gospels indeed. However, the Apostle Paul states *"another gospel"* coming from within the Christian Church.

This is a serious indictment, so let us see what this entails. If the Apostle Paul had only written – *"another gospel"* – and then stopping with that, we would restrict the guidelines of *"another gospel"* to those religions in obvious error. However, by the Apostle

Paul immediately describing *"another gospel"* with *"Which is not another,"* he has brought the guidelines of false gospels into the realm of Christian counterfeits. Meaning, a gospel that is created through the mind of a born again man or woman when he or she is under deception; creating *"⁶another gospel: ⁷Which is not another"* is a gospel created in such proximity effect simulation that it can be embraced as "the Gospel." Thus, *"another gospel"* coming in this way is not in such stark contrast as those in blatant blasphemy, and therefore can be received by undiscerning Christians.

Are those that create another gospel truly born again? If not, were they at one time born again? We do not know; what we do know is that Christians are susceptible to such gospels. What the Apostle Paul has written should not be taken lightly – it has been written to help all Christians understand that *"another gospel"* can have the Name of Jesus, but not be the same Jesus. In this, Christians will think that it is okay, regardless of what is being preached.

Let us qualify this by looking into *II Corinthians 11:4* – *"For if he who comes Preaching another Jesus, whom we have not Preached, or if you receive another spirit, which you have not received, or another gospel, which you have not accepted, you might well bear with him."*

Within *II Corinthians 11:4*, we can see that preachers will come; however, if these preachers are deceived, they will, in no uncertain terms, preach *"another Jesus"* and bring *"another spirit"* and *"another gospel."*

Any doctrines contrary to the foundation of Whom Jesus Christ Is, What He has done in His Life and on the Cross through His death and His Resurrection, are false gospels. More specifically, when Jesus Christ, and Him Crucified, are not the bedrock foundation for any teaching or preaching, what is being taught or preached is a counterfeit – it is that simple.

Does this mean that the Cross is to be preached within every sermon? No. However, when the Cross is understood for Sanctification, every message being preached will be easily discerned as to whether or not it is a counterfeit.

By the Apostle Paul writing *"⁶...another gospel: ⁷Which is not another...,"* he is giving us a clear guideline as to what a counterfeit gospel looks like. For example, all erroneous, so-called Christian gospels are proximity effect simulations of Paul's Gospel – all erroneous gospels will come in the Name of Jesus, yet they will bring another spirit that will produce proximity effect simulations such as healings, other tongues, being slain in the spirit, and many other signs and wonders. However, every one of them eventually results in confusion, chaos, and bondage.

Within erroneous gospels, the Salvation Message is most often brought forth as Paul's Gospel *(Rom. 10:9-10)*. In one way or the other, they lure the most seasoned Christians. Yet due to the fact that the Way of Sanctification is altogether altered, the essential Truth for Salvation unto Eternal Life is denied without the Christian realizing what he or she has done.

When "Him Crucified" is removed from the Way of Sanctification, the ways of deception will produce *"another Jesus"* with *"another spirit"* within a proximity effect simulation of *"⁶another gospel: ⁷Which is not another."*

My intention is to expound upon what the Apostle Paul has already revealed. In doing so, I understand that offense will be taken, regardless of how an explanation of erroneous gospels and settings is conveyed. Yet someone must take a stand for the hurting.

The bottom line is that all erroneous gospels are proximity effect simulations of Paul's Gospel, and therefore breed chaos and turmoil resulting in ongoing bondage. Chaos and turmoil can be very subtle for quite some time before giving birth to full-blown death. For this reason, the Apostle Paul writes – *"But I fear, lest by any means as the Serpent beguiled Eve through his subtilty, so your minds should be corrupted from the simplicity that is in Christ"* (II Cor. 11:3).

Within *II Corinthians 11:3, "the simplicity that is in Christ"* reveals the guideline for Paul's Gospel – simplicity. Erroneous gospels always end in human will working in combination with the physical body; therefore, there is no way around giving occasion for the sin nature to revive *(Rom. 7:5; I Cor. 15:56)*. The result is ambiguous complexity, which breeds chaos, confusion, and whirlwinds of darkness, stirring up more darkness *(Rom. 7:8-11, 15, 19 & 23)*.

Through Jesus Christ, God has made our walk a simple one, a walk in which simple Faith placed in His Son, and what His Son has done through His death, results in the ability to live for Him through His Spirit – it is really that simple. When this walk becomes the way of life and living, the context of all teaching will be revealed, whether it is Truth or whether it is *"⁶another gospel: ⁷Which is not another."*

Galatians 1:7 – Subject Scripture
Which is not another; **but there be some that trouble you, and would pervert the Gospel of Christ.**

Galatians 1:7 – Portion II
"...but there be some that trouble you,
and would pervert the Gospel of Christ."

As we begin portion two of *verse 7*, the Apostle's statement – *"but there be some that trouble you"* –indicates a description of the Believer leaving church with a sick and uneasy feeling because that which was preached was error. When the Believer discusses this with another, it brings up debates, and arguments, yet without the knowledge for true Sanctification, all of this is ongoing and troublesome.

Ending *verse 7,* there is much that can be said about Paul's statement – *"and would pervert the Gospel of Christ"* – but by Paul using the word *"pervert,"* he is stating that because the Gospel of Jesus Christ is finished, and therefore the Gospel cannot be changed *(John 19:30),* the only thing Satan, an Angel, a man, or women can now do is pervert it.

Galatians 1:8 – Subject Scripture undivided
But though we, or an Angel from Heaven, Preach any other gospel unto you than that which we have preached unto you, let him be accursed.

Galatians 1:8 is most profound. By Apostle Paul beginning this *verse* by stating, *"But though we, or an Angel from Heaven"* he, in no uncertain terms, is bringing the possibility into a reality that any preacher and/or one of his or her associates can become deceived and bring forth another gospel. Adding to this profundity is the actual reality of *"an Angel"* having the ability to use the faculty of a human in some way in order to bring forth another gospel. Moving on in *verse 8* – *"Preach any other gospel unto you than that which we have preached unto you"* reveals, if any preaching is not built on the foundation and bedrock of Jesus Christ, and Him Crucified, it is *"another gospel"* with *"another Jesus"* with *"another spirit" (II Cor. 11:4).* Thus, to the Preacher that is preaching such, the Apostle Paul states *"let him be accursed"* – doomed or eternally damned.

Galatians 1:9 – Subject Scripture undivided
As we said before, so say I now again, If any man Preach any other gospel unto you than that which you have received, let him be accursed.

Galatians 1:9 is a repeat of *verse 8,* letting all of us know (by this repetition) the importance of knowing the Truth, speaking the Truth, as well as the final result of preaching error and embracing error.

CHAPTER 19

The Offense of The Cross

GALATIANS 5:11

PREFACE

B ecause we love God so much and desire to serve him from a pure heart, judgment does not seem to fit in this type of setting. Satan knows this, and he will conspire and extort any way he can at every vantage point. It is so very important that we never lose sight of the tremendous Price that was Paid by our Lord and Saviour. Some have said that extremism is what causes church divisions, and for the most part they may be right. Yet when we come to understand and embrace God's established way for our victory, we will most often be set apart and viewed within a "not so popular" category, without a doubt. We are not called to please others to the point that we compromise from the Truth, and when we walk in the Truth, we will be persecuted by those in the Church that err from the Truth. We cannot say "I don't care" because we do, and to those to whom we say this, it sounds wrong and leaves the door open for more persecution.

However, we can say, "I cannot take on the care," because this allows grace upon those searching for the Truth and for us to look forward, leaving whatever is false behind in order to attain what God has called us to: His Truth.

Galatians 5:11 – Subject Scripture
And I, Brethren, if I yet Preach Circumcision, why do I yet suffer persecution? then is the offence of the Cross ceased.

Galatians 5:11 – Portion I
**"And I, Brethren, if I yet Preach Circumcision,
why do I yet suffer persecution?..."**

The Apostle Paul begins with quite a perplexing question to the Believers in the Roman province of Galatia. Paul had deep concern because the Believers in those communities had come under the influence of the Law embedded in religious activities and were no longer obeying the truth *(Gal. 5:7)*, which, as we know, is by Faith apart from works of the Law *(Gal. 2:16, 21; 5:4)*. They had also come to embrace many other false teachings that had come from men and Angels *(Gal. 1:6-9)*. Nonetheless, by the Apostle Paul proposing this rhetorical question – *"And I, Brethren, if I yet Preach Circumcision, why do I yet suffer persecution?"* – he is stating that if he preached Law, his preaching would be acceptable. However, because the Galatians already embraced these tainted and corrupt teachings, they had become deceived and had now taken offense when he presented the Truth.

Galatians 5:11 – Subject Scripture
And I, Brethren, if I yet Preach Circumcision, why do I yet suffer persecution? **then is the offence of the Cross ceased.**

Galatians 5:11 – Portion II
"…then is the offence of the Cross ceased."

By the Apostle Paul writing this portion of *verse 11* – *"then is the offence of the Cross ceased"* – he is revealing the same profound effect about the Cross, as he did in *I Corinthians 1:17* – *"lest the Cross of Christ should be made of none effect."* What is the profound effect of the Cross? Though Salvation is rejected on many levels by the unsaved, the idea that Sanctification takes place through the Cross goes against every one of the carnal ways of Saved Man. Thus, the Cross has a supernatural effect of offending! There is a reason Paul did not write, "then is the offense of the Resurrection ceased." For without the Cross, there would be no Resurrection, and this is the case for us who are Saved.

What is most staggering is that most of the unsaved world has no problem believing Jesus' Resurrection; the world celebrates His Resurrection with Easter and, with it, the Resurrection is most often never an offense. Yes, the Resurrection of Jesus Christ is violently rejected by religions that reject Jesus Christ altogether, yet today the Cross for Sanctification is most often rejected by those who are born again. This is the implication made in this portion of *Galatians 5:11*. Meaning, if the Apostle Paul compromised the Truth of the Cross by watering it down, those who embraced the unscriptural teaching would be happy with him. It does not take much – *"A little leaven leavens the whole lump" (Gal. 5:9)*. This was the case with the Galatians.

CHAPTER 20

Leaders That Preach Law

GALATIANS 6:12-14

PREFACE

It is most difficult to get a grip on the reality of our inability to satisfy the requirements of the Ten Commandments. Every day, each of us breaks these Laws. We may not think so, but we do. Assuring we do not deceive ourselves, Jesus takes the matter of the Law into the human heart. For example – *"But I say unto you, That whosoever looks on a woman to lust after her has committed adultery with her already in his heart" (Matt. 5:28).*

Yet we will continue going to great lengths in order to perfect ourselves, not realizing the consequences of what we are doing. This is our journey, and in it we learn – only God knows our heart. He knows, though we may stumble and fall, if our intentions in living for Him come from a pure and right heart. If they do, we will continue seeking Him for His ways, and He is faithful in revealing them.

It is only when we stop and decide that our ways or another's are better that we can get into significant trouble. This too is our journey, and in it we learn. However, this is a dangerous place which many have never left, and all too often, those never leaving are those preaching and teaching.

Chosen by God, the Apostle Paul was the first recipient of the Revelation of the Mystery – the way of Sanctification, the mystery of godliness. With this Revelation, we are able to go on unto perfection. Yet this magnificent Revelation also laid the foundation upon which all doctrine is built (thus, the litmus–test for all preaching and teaching).

Without this Revelation, due to our carnal mind, we reach the ceiling, never able to either discern or press through into the intimacy and presence of God for ongoing triumph and victory. Here we are left with the many resources of Man. Because the carnal mind intensely desires to live by the Law in one way or the other, we find ourselves overcome in chaos by the very thing we are trying to overcome. This is the plight without the Revelation, and we would never expect another to bring us into his or her vortex of darkness. Nevertheless, as we will come to see, this is the case.

Galatians 6:12 – Subject Scripture
As many as desire to make a fair show in the flesh, they constrain you to be Circumcised; only lest they should suffer persecution for the Cross of Christ.

Galatians 6:12 – Portion I
"As many as desire to make a fair show in the flesh...,"

This beginning portion of *Galatians 6:12* brings to light that nothing has changed since the days of Paul's preaching. The lust of the eyes, the lust of the flesh, and the pride of life *(Gen. 3:5-6)* can (and do) blind the preacher and laity alike who do not understand or have denied the power of God effectually working through Faith in the Cross *(I Cor. 1:17-18)*. If this truth we have in Christ is not understood or is denied, the only recourse is to live by the Law *(Rom. 7:5)*. The strength of sin is the Law *(I Cor. 15:56)*, so the only choice for those who live by it is to use more willpower applied to the physical body. This will work for a while, and for a while they will be proud of their efforts. Pride always puffs up, so they will disclose their temporal victory.

Galatians 6:12 – Subject Scripture
As many as desire to make a fair show in the flesh, **they constrain you to be Circumcised; only lest they should suffer persecution for the Cross of Christ.**

Galatians 6:12 – Portion II
**"…they constrain you to be Circumcised;
only lest they should suffer persecution for the Cross of Christ."**

As we begin portion two, the statement *"they constrain you to be Circumcised"* reveals that, during the temporal victory found in living by the Law, those living this way will boast of their carnal learning and efforts through false humility. Still, by doing so they bring you into bondage, not telling you of their failures, thinking that Sanctification will eventually be attained. In the balance of *Galatians 6:12*, the Apostle Paul is bringing to light that once we come to the knowledge of the Truth in Jesus Christ, and Him Crucified, we will either accept it or deny it. If it is denied, it will be based within one of two premises: we either believe it is foolishness, or we believe our own efforts are better *(I Cor. 1:23)*. Either way, if this Truth is denied, the only choice will be to live by the Law, which will result in failure time and time again *(I Cor. 15:56)*. The implications of the overall Scripture context are: those living by the law are blinded by pride and desire you to follow their way of error. Yet if they were to accept the Truth of the Cross, they would suffer persecution from the Believers who did not accept it as the truth. That is, *"they constrain you to be Circumcised; only lest they should suffer persecution for the Cross of Christ."*

Galatians 6:13 – Subject Scripture
For neither they themselves who are Circumcised keep the Law; but desire to have you Circumcised, that they may glory in your flesh.

Galatians 6:13 – Portion I
"For neither they themselves who are
Circumcised keep the Law…;"

This beginning portion of *verse 13* reveals the core truth of the matter – those who live by the Law do not keep the Law. We can see the same today; preachers and laity alike make their way of error clear unto those who know the Truth of the Cross, and they make their inadequate victory evident to all when they fall. This is due to their trying to live by the Law.

When we see them fall, it is a horrible thing to know and see because we were without the knowledge of the Cross for Sanctification at one time. So, as Believers, our hearts should be merciful toward them, but the Church can most often be the cruelest. When the world looks upon them, they rest their judgment in hypocrisy, yet the truth is the Christian does not want to sin.

There are those preaching today who clearly preach heresy and doctrines of demons, but there are those preaching today in both mega churches and smaller churches who love the Lord with all of their heart. Yet they who have not come to understand the Cross as it regards Sanctification continue to fail and fall, time and time again. If it is not Faith in the Cross, it is works by the Law, and because the strength of sin is the Law, they fall.

Galatians 6:13 – Subject Scripture
For neither they themselves who are Circumcised keep the Law; **but desire to have you Circumcised,** that they may glory in your flesh.

Galatians 6:13 – Portion II
"…but desire to have you Circumcised…,"

The Apostle Paul reveals another staggering fact in this second portion of *verse 13.* Those who try to live by the Law do not want you to have freedom, *"but desire to have you Circumcised."* Though it is difficult to believe that these would be the intentions of those trying to live by the Law, nonetheless, we must come to understand the dynamic going on because of their efforts. In other words, because the strength of the sin nature is the Law, those trying to live by the Law are therein ruled by the sin nature, and have fallen from Grace *(Gal. 5:4).* Therefore, there are those who do not understand what is going on *(I Cor. 1:10-18)*, and there are those who reject the power of the Cross *(Phil. 3:18).* Either way, the result produces a diabolical influence that enforces Law on everybody.

Those who have either denied or do not understand the Cross as it regards Sanctification are only able to desire that you use one or many of their laws and methods that are embedded in religious activities. This can be very subtle, but will result in failure, defeat, and bondage, simply because the strength of sin is the Law. Once again, it is difficult to believe that anybody would desire this of another Believer out of sheer malicious intent, but it is happening every day.

Galatians 6:13 – Subject Scripture
For neither they themselves who are Circumcised keep the Law; but desire to have you Circumcised, **that they may glory in your flesh.**

Galatians 6:13 – Portion III
"...that they may glory in your flesh."

The Apostle Paul reveals yet another staggering fact here in the balance of *Galatians 6:13*. Those who live by the Law desire that you live by the Law *"that they may glory in your flesh."* That is, they will teach and preach to those who listen through their temporal victories. Those who listen will gain their own victory for a while by embracing their methods, and those who have taught them will boast of how they have helped them. The context of these Scriptures is sternly spoken, yet the manifestation of this within today's churches can most often be subtle *(II Cor. 11:3)*.

Galatians 6:14 – Subject Scripture
But God forbid that I should glory, save in the Cross of our Lord Jesus Christ, by whom the world is Crucified unto me, and I unto the world.

Galatians 6:14 – Portion I
"...But God forbid that I should glory,
save in the Cross of our Lord Jesus Christ...,"

Before the work of the Cross, Man lived for God by Faith and by the Law in their own strength through their body. Though the main problem with this was the ongoing life of the sin nature to some degree, the more grievous problem was the accentuated pride that grew within those who gloried in their temporal victories.

After the finished work of the Cross, when we received Salvation, our body was made dead so that our body would not be used to live for God. The benefits are that the sin nature remains incapacitated and the Spirit of God would be our strength *(Rom. 8:10-11)*. This type of triumphant life for God is lived by Faith as well, and, instead of living by the Law, we now live through the Law *(Gal. 2:19)*. That is, we know the Ten Commandments, but because we cannot live by them by use of our body, Christ is now the end of the Law for Righteousness to everyone who believes *(Rom. 10:4)*. For this reason, as we place Faith whereupon the Law became Satisfied, the Righteousness of the Law remains fulfilled within us *(Rom. 8:3-4)*.

For the unsaved individual who is viewing some semblance of temporal victory, boasting will be about how his or her temporal victory was attained. Yet regardless of the method, their efforts are now part of the equation. Therein, the result is self-glorification, whether it is realized or not. Likewise, this same type of boasting takes place within the born again individual who is living by the Law. Regardless of the method, their efforts are now part of the equation, and the result is self-glorification, realized or not. However, when the Believer learns that the Law cannot be lived by, he or she will accept Christ as the end of the Law for Righteousness, and their Faith will rest in Jesus Christ, and Him Crucified, resulting in ongoing growth in Sanctification. Knowing that their ongoing Sanctification is through Faith apart from their own strength working through their body, he or she will give God all of the Glory. Therein, his or her thanksgiving will be – *"But God forbid that I should glory, save in the Cross of our Lord Jesus Christ."*

We must never separate Jesus Christ and His Atoning Sacrifice from His triumphant work because both the Redemption of mankind and the triumph over principalities and powers took place on Calvary's Cross. When ongoing Sanctification is evidenced as Faith is exercised in the Cross, then self becomes completely eliminated from the equation, and we come to realize it is all by Faith.

Galatians 6:14 – Subject Scripture
But God forbid that I should glory, save in the Cross of our Lord Jesus Christ, **by whom the world is Crucified unto me, and I unto the world.**

Galatians 6:14 – Portion II
**"...by whom the world is Crucified unto
me, and I unto the world."**

This statement made by the Apostle is the magnificent result determining not to know any other thing except Jesus Christ, and Him Crucified, for his intimate walk with God in the Sanctification process.

CHAPTER 21

Do You Realize
What Others Are Preaching?

II CORINTHIANS 11:4

PREFACE

C orrupt gospels are coming from many pulpits and technology
is able to disseminate these erred gospels to millions of people
throughout the world today. We are not called to judge those in the
world – that is the position of God in His time and on That Day.
Yet, as Christians, we have a responsibility to search the Scriptures
to see whether or not the message and doctrine of those preaching
and teaching lines up with Scripture. If error is found, much of
Christianity today refrains from judging, simply because we have
been taught not to judge. It seems right not to judge, but in many
cases it is wrong not to judge. Whether we realize it or not, we judge
every day, throughout the day. Every person has to make decisions
– some small, many big – but the most important decisions should

be those that guard our spirit, soul, and the Gift of Eternal Life. The Apostle Paul was faced with such decisions, yet he was not passive.

Real love does not allow error to continue because love sees that sin hurts. Furthermore, true love stands up in truth and does it on behalf of those in need. This chapter brings to light an erroneous gospel that preaches "another Jesus" *(II Cor. 11:4)*, and this gospel has led tens of thousands (if not millions) away from the Truth.

You will find in the Commentaries and Expositions that I have allowed the Scripture itself to bear the criteria for false preachers. Doing it like this allows you the liberty of the Holy Spirit revealing the truth, thereby exposing those that fit the criteria. There are many names that can be listed, yet the intention of this book is to bring understanding to the truth of God's established way of victory. In this, everything false will fade. It is not my intention or goal to scrutinize the preacher or teacher. However, it is the responsibility of every Christian to judge what is being preached and taught.

God has called us to bring this Message of Life to a dying and extremely hurting world, Christian and non-Christian alike. Our very intentions start and end in a sincere love for each Brother and Sister who desires an abundant life of triumph, joy, and peace in Christ. Yet love is not passive and cannot stand passive in the wake of this erroneous gospel – specifically "the spiritual death gospel," also known as "the spiritual death doctrine." The foundation for this erroneous teaching is based on the belief that the greatest defeat known to mankind is Jesus' death on the Cross. This false gospel proclaims that Jesus gave up his Deity as God on the Cross, took on the nature of Satan, and then went into the burning side of Hell. After three days and nights of Satan's torture, Jesus cried out to God, wherein He became born again and was delivered from hell as the first fruits of God.

These statements can be qualified via the internet – simply search "spiritual death gospel" or "spiritual death doctrine" or "another Jesus."

The Apostle Paul spoke of those who would bring "another Jesus" with "another gospel" with "another spirit" *(II Cor. 11:4)*; the "spiritual death doctrine" is a doctrine that brings the other pseudo saviour and gospel with another spirit, leading millions away from Saving Grace. It only takes one error within the non-negotiable of the Gospel of Jesus Christ in order to be blasphemy; we can clearly see six in the spiritual death gospel, which is no Gospel at all, but a doctrine of devils.

INVESTIGATING THE FOUNDATION OF BLASPHEMY

THE SPIRITUAL DEATH DOCTRINE
ANOTHER JESUS – II CORINTHIANS 11:4

Error One: This "other Jesus" gave up his deity.
Error Two: This "other Jesus" became sin.
Error Three: This "other Jesus" received the nature of Satan.
Error Four: This "other Jesus" went into the burning side of Hell.
Error Five: This "other Jesus" became born again.
Error Six: This "other Jesus" became the firstfruits by his born again experience.

PROPER BIBLICAL INTERPRETATION OF
JESUS CHRIST, AND HIS DEITY

Truth One: Our Biblical Jesus never gave up His Deity on the Cross. We are going to look into four Scriptures about this Truth: *Matthew 27:46, John 19:28, John 19:30,* and *Luke 23:46.* These Scriptures address the Deity of our Lord and Saviour Jesus Christ on the Cross before, during, and after His physical death.

Matthew 27:46 – Subject Scripture undivided
And about the ninth hour Jesus cried with a loud voice, saying, Eli, Eli, lama sabachthani? that is to say, My God, my God, why have You forsaken me?

In this profound *verse*, we see that this very question – *"My God, my God, why have You forsaken me?"* – reveals the Man, Jesus *(Rom. 5:15; I Tim. 2:5; Heb. 10:12)*, divested unto the very end in His seeking the Will of His Father Who is in Heaven *(Matt. 26:39)*. This was the purpose of His incarnation *(Rom. 8:3; Eph. 3:11; Phil. 2:5-8; Heb. 2:9; 10:5-10; 12:2; I John 3:8)*.

Never ceasing to be God, He divested Himself for the sake of the Cross in order to take upon Himself the Sin of the world, to take Sin away and condemn Sin in the flesh *(John 1:29; Rom. 8:3)*. Jesus, in His Sinless body, had become the once for all Atoning Sin Offering and Sacrifice upon the Cross through the Shedding of His Blood and the Offering of His body through death *(II Cor. 5:21; Heb. 9:12)*.

In this event, the Father looked not upon the iniquity *(Hab. 1:13)*. In these moments, and in no other place in Eternity, nor any other time in humanity, God the Word experienced the anguish of His Father's Love for Him and the anguish that He experienced for His Father. We cannot use the word "separated" in speaking of the moments when Jesus and His Father went through this because God cannot cease from Himself. Some have said that Heaven was silent for these moments.

John 19:28 – Subject Scripture undivided
After this, Jesus knowing that all things were now accomplished, that the scripture might be fulfilled, said, I thirst.

Beginning with *"After this, Jesus knowing that all things were now accomplished,"* speaks quite clearly that Jesus knew Who He Was, why He came, and that all He came to do was accomplished – the Redemption of mankind, the Mosaic Law Satisfied, the handwriting of Ordinances that were against us were Blotted out and taken out of the way, and principalities and powers were triumphed over through this event of the Cross *(Eph. 1:7; Col. 2:13-15)*. Though these things would be consummated through His death, *"all things were now accomplished."*

Moving on in *John 19:28*, the statement – *"that the Scripture might be fulfilled"* – refers to *Genesis 3:15* and *Psalm 69:21*, which speak of what He would come to do, and the purpose for His Incarnation, showing the Old Testament pointing to the New *(Heb. 10:7-9)*.

Here in the balance of *John 19:28*, Jesus said, *"I thirst,"* revealing to us that He did not grasp at His being equal with God. Jesus had the choice to use His Power as God, but did not *(Phil. 2:5-8)*. Moreover, as the Man, Jesus, His thirst was for Living Water, but they could not bring It *(John 7:38)*, nor did they know that He Is the Living Water *(John 4:10-11)*. Instead, they gave Him vinegar.

John 19:30 – Subject Scripture undivided
When Jesus therefore had received the vinegar, He said, It is finished: and He bowed His head, and gave up the ghost.

Within *John 19:30*, this remarkable statement *"It is finished"* says it all! What God the Father, God the Son, and God the Holy Spirit had foreordained before the foundation of the world, was now finished *(I Pet. 1:18-22)*. What God has finished is impossible to change, thus, because Satan and all those following him cannot change it, they pervert and corrupt it *(II Cor. 11:4; Gal. 1:6-9)*. The profound significance of *"He bowed His head, and gave up the ghost"* can be overlooked. Meaning, no human can voluntarily give up his or her ghost – only God could have done this *(John 10:17-18)*. Although stated earlier, I have placed it here because of the amazing statements of Scripture, but this explanation will also help you come to see the scope of events that had taken place on the Cross.

The Man, Jesus, was one hundred percent Man and He, in absolution, is one hundred percent God. What we must understand is that as the Man, Jesus, He did not cease to be God – God cannot cease from Himself. In His humanity, He divested Himself as He walked in the likeness of men. The profound implications of this go far beyond what could be written about in a lifetime. Nonetheless, the manifested purpose of Christ was to come in the likeness of men – the last Adam *(I Cor. 15:45)* – to rectify the consequences of the first Adam. This had to be done by a man. No other way would have been in accordance with God's Divine Attributes of Truth, Justice, Judgment, and Whom He Is – Love *(Psalms 89:14; John 14:6; I John 4:8)*. In order to understand why Christ had to come into the world in the likeness of sinful flesh as the last Adam, we must understand how Satan – Lucifer – brought the Fall of the first Adam.

In the Garden, Lucifer did not control or force Adam; through Lucifer's twisted comments, Eve became deceived, which caused her to transgress and facilitate Adam in unbelief. In his unbelief, Adam then used his physical body to partake of the Tree of the Knowledge of Good and Evil. Not only did Lucifer's tactic bring about the Fall of Adam and Eve – it brought the Fall of Mankind through Adam's actions *(I Tim. 2:14)*. Still, this was the extent of Lucifer's wisdom. Therefore, the Fall of Lucifer had to be done through a man, and it had to be done without controlling or forcing Lucifer – this is the infinite wisdom of God *(Gen. 3:15)*. For this reason, John writes – *"He who commits sin is of the Devil; for the Devil sinneth from the beginning. For this purpose the Son of God was manifested, that He might destroy the works of the Devil" (I John 3:8).*

The Word was made flesh – the last Adam – fully Man, and fully God. Yet we must keep in mind that God, in the likeness of men, could not violate His Divine Attributes and Nature *(Titus 1:2)*. Meaning, because Lucifer did not control or force Adam in any way, God in the likeness of men, could not use His power as God to bring the Fall of Lucifer. Therefore, the Man, Jesus, never ceasing to be God, divested Himself and allowed Lucifer's pride to dictate the events that would forever seal Lucifer's eternal fate. For this reason, the Apostle Paul writes – *"Which none of the princes of this world knew: for had they known it, they would not have Crucified the Lord of Glory" (I Cor. 2:8)*.

On the Cross, when Jesus knew that all things were now accomplished and said, *"It is finished...,"* He was saying all that needed to be done as a man was accomplished without violating the Divine Attributes and Nature of Who He Is – God. Once all things were accomplished according to the Will of His Father in Heaven, *"He bowed His head, and gave up the ghost."*

Luke 23:46 – Subject Scripture undivided

And when Jesus had cried with a loud voice, He said, Father, into Your hands I commend My Spirit: and having said thus, He gave up the ghost.

This beginning statement – *"And when Jesus"* – clearly signifies the Man, Jesus *(Rom. 5:15; Heb. 10:12)*. Jesus' statement – *"Father, into Your hands I commend My Spirit"* – qualifies that all things were now finished in accordance with the Will of His Father. As the Man, He now could express His Deity as God, which He did by commending His Spirit into the hands of His Father. However, because God cannot cease from Himself, He is speaking of the Spirit of God that descended upon Him at His being baptized by John.

"16And Jesus, when He was baptized, went up straightway out of the water: and, lo, the Heavens were opened unto Him, and He saw the Spirit of God descending like a dove, and lighting upon Him: 17And lo

331

a Voice from Heaven, saying, This is My Beloved Son, in Whom I am well pleased" (Matt. 3:16-17).

What must also be noted is that by Jesus saying *"I commend My Spirit,"* He was giving praise to His Father for the commendable work of the Holy Spirit, and the comfort He had in being led unto His Father's Will while He, as a Man, was divested

The balance of *Luke 23:46 – "He gave up the ghost"* – qualifies that the Spirit of God that He commended into His Father's hands was not the spirit of His humanity. Meaning, *Luke 23:46* begins with *"Father, into Your hands I commend My Spirit,"* and ends with *"He gave up the ghost,"* revealing to us both the *"Spirit"* and the *"ghost."*

The *"Spirit"* was for being led unto His Father's Will, and the *"ghost"* is what kept His human body alive *(e.g., Gen 25:8).* Therefore, the balance of *Luke 23:46 – "He gave up the ghost"* – is now addressing His humanity, and therefore is revealing that, as God, only He had the power to lay down His Life and take it back up again *(John 10:17-18).* This could be done because He had accomplished all things on the Cross as the Man, Jesus, in His Sinless Body *(John 19:28).* Therefore, *"He gave up the ghost"* – that is to say, to breathe His last with His Physical Body *(to breath His last – to expire: Strong's NT: 1606; from NT: 1537 and NT: 4154).* He, as God, gave up the ghost to His human body, and by doing so clearly signifies His Deity.

If anyone believes that Jesus became sin and took on the nature of Satan, it is a clear indication that they do not properly understand Who Jesus Is and what He Has done on the Cross through His death for us. Furthermore, to deny the Truth in the Word of God and teach "another Jesus" or "another gospel" is Satanic and is embedded within the doctrines of devils and fallen Angels, and has found its way into the mind of men who have now come as wolves in sheep clothing – those who have come and brought another gospel, which is not another *(Matt. 7:15; Acts 20:29; Gal. 1:6-9; I Cor. 10:20-21; II Cor. 11:4, 14; I Tim. 4:1).*

Truth Two: Our Biblical Jesus Is the once for all Sacrificial Offering.

Jesus never became sin. The proper interpretation is as the Bible reveals from *Genesis* to *Revelation*: our once for all "Sin Offering" by His Shed Blood and death on the Cross *(Rom. 8:3; Heb. 9:12-14).* Any other belief stands in the corridors of blasphemy. Everything that was needed to Satisfy the Law, deal with the handwriting of Ordinances, Redeem Man, and defeat the Devil was done through and by His body, Shed Blood, and physical death upon the Cross as the Man, Jesus *(Heb. 2:9-10).*

Jesus was not born through the seed of a fallen man *(Matt.1:20-21)*; therefore, He was without the nature of sin, the thought of sin, and the action of sin *(Heb. 4:15)*. Jesus never sinned, and He never became sin. He was, Is, and ever shall be God Alpha and Omega *(Rev. 1:8, 11; 21:6; 22:13)* – He alone became our Sin Offering *(Heb., Chptrs 9-10).*

Truth Three: Our biblical Jesus never relinquished His Deity.

As we know, the Man, Jesus, was one hundred percent Man and He, in absolution, is one hundred percent God *(John 1:1, 14, 29; Rom. 5:15; I Pet. 1:18-20).* He did not cease to be God – God cannot cease from Himself. He, in His humanity, divested Himself as He walked in the likeness of men to walk in Faith, to go to the Cross, to be Crucified, and to die. In all this, He was faithful to the Will of His Father *(Mark 26:39; John 19:30).*

Truth Four: Our biblical Jesus descended into Paradise, not Hell.

Many may believe that Jesus descended into Hell in order to pay the full ransom for the sin of mankind. However, Hades (Hebrew,

Sheol), Hades (Greek, Hell) was divided into the place of torment and Paradise. *Paradise is known as Abraham's bosom (Luke 16:19-31),* as we can clearly see in *Luke 23:43 – "Verily I say unto you, Today shall you be with Me in Paradise."* The Man, Jesus, Suffered death on the Cross, and the Bible unveils two events that took place in the lower parts of the earth.

Event One: Jesus, triumphant through His death on the Cross, descended into the lower parts of the earth into Paradise (Abraham's bosom). That is, He removed the Old Testament saints from Abraham's bosom and led them out of that region *(Eph. 4:8-10).*

Event Two: the Word God, Jesus Christ unchanged, as God, did not ascend to God the Father *(John 20:17)* before He Preached from Paradise unto the spirits in the burning side of Hell *(I Pet. 3:19),* as we can see the premise of in the literal account of Lazarus *(Luke 16:19-31).*

There was no need for Jesus Christ to suffer in Hell. Furthermore, we are not Saved by His sufferings – we are Saved by His Righteousness, Obedience, Vicarious Shed Blood, and death on the Cross.

Through proper interpretation, there is nothing from the Word of God indicating at all that Jesus went into the burning side of Hell for our Sins. He went to Calvary to be Crucified for our Sins and, as the Lamb of God upon the Cross, He became our Vicarious Atoning Sin Offering through the Shedding of His Own Blood and death.

Truth Five: Our Biblical Jesus did not need to become born again.

Jesus Christ is King Eternal, Immortal, Invisible, the only wise God *(Rom. 16:27; I Tim. 1:17),* Alpha and Omega *(Rev. 1:8, 11; 21:6; 22:13).* He never ceased to be God, nor did He change *(Heb. 2:16; Jam. 1:17).* His Proclamation *"It is finished"* is exactly what He meant – God's Word is never in conflict with itself, nor can He lie

(Titus 1:2). Furthermore, accomplishing all things *(John 19:28)*, it was through His death that He destroyed him who had the power of death, that is, the Devil *(Heb. 2:14-15)*. Therefore, by the death of His physical body upon the Cross, He Reigned triumphant *(Rom. 5:15-19; Col. 2:13-15; I John 3:18)* – He is Alpha and Omega, God Eternal and Unchanging.

Truth Six: Our biblical Jesus became the firstfruits for us.

Proper understanding shows that, upon Jesus' death on the Cross, He broke the hold of Death so we who are Saved would not be held by Death once we died a physical death, or alive at the Rapture. This is the meaning of firstfruits – the Lord Jesus Christ being risen from the dead *(I Cor. 15:20-23)* made the way for us and those who had died before the Lord went to the Cross, which is qualified by His Ascension *(Eph. 4:8-10)*. He never gave up His Deity or His position in the Godhead *(Col. 2:9)*, for He Is Eternal. This is not to be interpreted as Jesus being the first to become born again while in Hell, as the erroneous spiritual death doctrine teaches.

Everything that needed to be done was walked out, accomplished, and then finished on the Cross by the Man, Jesus, which we can clearly see in *I Corinthians 15:21* – *"For since by man came death* (Adam), *by Man* (the Man, Jesus) *came also the Resurrection of the dead."* Now, for those of us who are Saved, we can remain in continual victory because of His Atoning and triumphant work on the Cross, and we will not be held by Death once we die a physical death. Likewise, if we are alive when the Trump of God sounds, we will not be held by Death because Jesus Christ is the firstfruits being risen from the dead *(Acts 2:24; 10:40; 17:31; I Cor. 15:55; I Thess. 1:10; 4:13-18)*.

LET US TAKE A LOOK AT WHAT THE APOSTLE PAUL
WROTE ABOUT THE DEITY OF JESUS CHRIST

Philippians 2:5 – Subject Scripture undivided
Let this mind be in you, which was also in Christ Jesus:

Verse 5 is most remarkable in that to understand God the Word came from Eternity into time to be made in the likeness of men, yet never ceased to be God, is difficult to comprehend, but He did. He loves us so much that He made the choice in His foreknowledge and wisdom – way before the beginning of creation – to go to the Cross and die for us *(I Pet. 1:18-22)*. There must be something so incredibly special in His desire to spend Eternity with us; so extraordinary is His love for us that, in order to accomplish all that needed to be done as a man, He would not utilize His Power as God to get it done.

We are living in a miracle, a time that has been known by God in Eternity past and all who are Saved are soon to enter Eternity future. Though this is difficult to comprehend, it is true. All of creation depended on Jesus Christ not utilizing His Power as God; in describing this, I have chosen the word "divest." Though I have used this word a lot, it is the only word that properly defines one as depriving themselves of their rights. Christ Jesus has left all of us who call upon His Name with the greatest example as to what this truly means, and this is the mind that we are to have as well.

Philippians 2:6 – Subject Scripture undivided
Who, being in the form of God, thought it not robbery to be equal with God:

The Word God, no beginning or end, Was, Is, and ever shall be God Eternal *(John 1:1)*. The Apostle Paul's statement *"thought it not robbery to be equal with God"* speaks of Christ Jesus' position and participation in the Godhead *(Gen. 1:26; John 10:30)*.

Philippians 2:7 – Subject Scripture undivided
But made Himself of no reputation, and took upon Him the form of a servant, and was made in the likeness of men:

Beginning *verse 7* with the Apostle's statement – *"But made Himself of no reputation"* – refers to our Thrice Holy God making the choice in the foreordained plan that Mary would become the means through which God the Word would be made in fashion as a man *(Matt. 1:20; John 1:14)*. Yet He would be born in a manger and raised by a carpenter, as opposed to wealth, power, and recognition *(Luke 2:7-16)*. In the balance of *Philippians 2:7*, the Apostle Paul uses the word – *"likeness"* – that is, Jesus was not born through the seed of a man *(Matt. 1:20)*. Therefore, Jesus *"was made in the likeness of men."*

As stated, Lucifer – Satan – using the faculties of the Serpent, brought the Fall of Man by a man *(Rom. 5:12; Gen. 3:1-6)*; likewise, the fall of Satan had to be by a man *(Gen. 3:15; I Cor. 15:45)*. God could not violate Whom He Is *(Titus 1:2; I John 4:16)*. For this reason, He *"was made in the likeness of men"* to be Crucified as a man so that we would not be held in eternal death by the consequences of Adam's Sin.

Philippians 2:8 – Subject Scripture undivided
And being found in fashion as a man, He humbled Himself, and became obedient unto death, even the death of the Cross.

This statement that begins *verse 8* – *"And being found in fashion as a man"* – is a miracle and, if pondered properly, wades through the complexities of this world with its pains and disappointments and causes them to fade. As we move on in *verse 8* – *"He humbled Himself"* – refers to God divesting Himself of His Rights and reputation for the purpose of the Cross, never leaning on His Own Will or Power as God *(Matt. 26:39)*.

As we move on in *Philippians 2:8*, this first mention of death – *"and became obedient unto death"* – speaks of His Obedience to the Will of His Father in Heaven *(Mark 14:36)*. Meaning, Jesus Christ, in absolution being God, made the continual choice as a man to divest Himself for the sake of the Cross. This obedience unto death was a continuance in the Faith that He Authored as the Man, Jesus, as well. When He said, "It is finished," upon the Cross, this Faith would be given to all who would call upon His Name from then on. This is the Faith of the Son of God given to us, and this Faith always has the Cross before it *(Gal. 2:16-20; 6:14; Heb. 12:2)*. The balance of *Philippians 2:8* – *"even the death of the Cross"* – is the second mention of death, revering the focal epicenter of the Christian Faith.

The Word was made flesh in the likeness of sinful man as the last Adam *(I Cor. 15:45)*. Meaning, the first Adam was not formed by God with a sin nature – the nature of sin took eminent domain within mankind due to Adam's Sin. From then on, all mankind would be born into the original nature of sin that would reside within their members *(Psalms 51:5; Rom. 5:12; 7:23; I Cor. 15:22)*.

Since the first Adam did not have the nature of sin residing in his members when he sinned, God the Word was made in the likeness of men as the last Adam, free from the original nature of sin. In order for this to be done, He would have to bypass the seed of a fallen man; therefore, He (Christ – God the Word) would be made in the likeness of sinful flesh through Mary, a virgin *(Matt. 1:20)*. As the last Adam, Jesus Christ would be fully Man and fully God because He cannot cease to be God. Thus, He would divest Himself to accomplish and finish all things in His humanity.

We must understand that no human could have ever Atoned for Adam's Sin and destroyed the works of the Devil – it would have to be God Himself *(Col. 2:13-15; I John 3:8; 4:16)*. Therefore, the plan was foreordained that God the Word would come in the likeness of men so that He could be tempted like the first Adam *(Heb. 4:15)*, as a man. However, He would bear incomprehensively more due to Adam's Sin, and yet in His obedience unto death, even the death of the Cross, He Vicariously Atoned for the Penalty of Adam's Sin and triumphed over all principalities and powers on the Cross by His Sinless body through His Shed Blood and death. It was through His death that He destroyed the power of Death *(Heb. 2:14-15)*; the one Man, Jesus, did what Adam could not and, by His Own Blood, He entered once into the Holy Place, having obtained Eternal Redemption for us *(Heb. 9:12)*.

OUR RESPONSIBILITY TO FALSE DOCTRINE

There have always been and there will always be false prophets, teachers, and preachers – and more so today than ever before in human history *(Matt., Mark, Luke, Acts, Rom., I Cor., II Cor., Gal., II Tim., Titus, II Pet., I John, and Revelation)*. Within much of the New Testament, we are admonished and warned about them so we might not be deceived by them. We are deeply warned about corrupt gospels *(II Cor. 11:4; Gal. 1:6-9)*, not because they might come, but because they have come *(II Tim. 3:2-4)*.

Satan cannot change the Gospel because "It is finished" *(John 19:30)*. Nevertheless, in his efforts to circumvent it, he brings perverted and corrupt gospels through deceived men and fallen Angels. We should not marvel at this because Satan himself is transformed into an Angel of light *(II Cor. 11:14)*.

We as Christians are called to come out from their corrupt teachings *(II Tim. 2:18-21)*. Many Christians have told me that they see the error in their church, yet feel their presence can help change it. Though that might be, God is not the author of confusion – He is the Author of Peace *(I Cor. 14:33)* – so you can only do as the Holy

Spirit is leading you to do. Therefore, being led by the Holy Spirit is incredibly important.

It is possible we are at the very end of this dispensation, and the Resurrection (Rapture) of Christians is at hand. No man knows for sure, but ignorance toward false doctrine will not be justifiable before God. For this reason, no matter what, walk with God in His Truth because, if the Christian does not, it will be too late in the end *(Matt. 21-23; Phil. 3:18-19).*

PART V

Ending Commentaries

CHAPTER 22

The Lamb of God

†

COMMENTARY

T he Word God *(John 1:1)* was made flesh *(John 1:14)*, but not conceived through the seed of a man, for that which was conceived in Mary was of the Holy Ghost and His Name shall be called JESUS *(Matt. 1:20)*. Thus, Jesus was born in the likeness of sinful flesh without the sin nature *(Luke 2:5-16)*. He was made the last Adam *(I Cor. 15:45)* in order to Vicariously Pay the Penalty of the first Adam's Sin.

He was tempted in all points as we are, yet without sin *(Heb. 4:15)*. He was Crucified to take away the sin of the world *(Matt. 27:35; John 1:29)*, yet He did not sin in any way. He was the "Sin Offering" upon the Cross *(II Cor. 5:21)*, yet was not made Sin *(I John 3:5)*. Thereupon the Cross, He Blotted out the handwriting of Ordinances that was against us, which was contrary to us; took it out of the way, nailing it to His Cross. Having spoiled principalities and powers, He made a show of them openly, triumphing over them in it *(Col. 2:14-15)*.

Through His Cross, we now have peace being Reconciled to God *(Eph. 2:16)*. Through His Shed Blood, He Redeemed Man *(I Pet. 1:18-23)*, and fulfilled every seen and unseen facet of the Father's Will. He never ceased to be God, neither did He grasp at His being equal with God, but divested Himself for the sake of the Cross *(Matt. 26:39; John 19:28, 30; Luke 23:46)*.

After His death, He descended triumphant into the lower parts of the earth, into Paradise *(Abraham's bosom [Luke 16:19-31])*, and in that region He led all captive believing saints to freedom *(Eph. 4:8-10)*. He then ascended *(Matt. 28:6; Luke 24:34; I Cor. 15:20)*, yet without sin in any way, thought, or deed *(Isa. 53:10)*. When Jesus was raised, He first appeared to Mary Magdalene, out of whom he had cast seven devils *(Mark 16:9)*. After appearing to many more, He ascended into Heaven and ever shall be at the right Hand of the Majesty on High *(Rom. 8:34)*. This is the Jesus Christ of whom there is no other – in totality, all victory in every way was accomplished and finished on the Cross.

Though Satan is the god of this world, he, Death and Hell, his Angels, demons, and whosoever is not found written in the Book of Life will be cast into the Lake of Fire where they will remain forever *(Rev., Chptr 20)*.

CHAPTER 23

The Grace of God

✝

COMMENTARY

G race – what a remarkable word! Does Grace describe God's kindness? Is Grace like Faith? Or is Grace perhaps like love? Yes, Grace is the kind intention of God continually present toward all unmerited mankind. Yet Grace is like Faith, love, and Grace is also a plan – not a plan as we may think of perhaps in descriptive terms, but a living expression of God's kindness. An example would be a family plan to go on vacation. Though the family has a plan, once the plan is initiated, the family is living within the plan, and Grace is like this.

The plan of Grace was foreordained before the foundation of the world, and the Foundation of Grace was laid upon the Atoning and finished work of Jesus Christ on Calvary's Cross. Grace would be – and is today – the perpetual cohesion that allows Eternity and time to meet for the Divine Purpose of God's plan for mankind throughout the dispensation of time. God's Amazing Grace would become the exclusive means through which the kind intention of our Thrice Holy God could be expressed and present toward man, both Saved and unsaved. Grace always has abounded in the presence of sinful Man through and on the basis of Jesus Christ, and Him Crucified.

From cover to cover, the Word of God is about Jesus Christ, and Him Crucified. This word "Grace" – its substance, expression, and action – embodies the Cross, the Atoning and triumphant finished work of Jesus Christ, is the Foundation of God's Grace toward man.

One might reject the statement of God's ability to deal with Man on the basis of Jesus Christ and Him Crucified, yet for this very reason God's foreordained Plan of Jesus Christ and Him Crucified was established prior to the foundation of the world. Therein, this magnificent Plan would be melded in the Mind of God so that the kind intention of our Thrice Holy God could be continually expressed toward Man without destroying Man because of God's Absolute Holiness.

In the beginning, God knew the potential for Adam to Fall by the devices of Darkness, for Man is created – he is not God. Therefore, the Fall never came as a surprise to God – it was in this foreknowledge that He purposed to Give Himself as the Only Acceptable Sacrifice in order to Satisfy the demands of the Fall. In order for Him to accomplish this, He would become the Sin Offering for the entire consequences of the Fall. In order for God to become the Sin Offering, He would leave Eternity, enter into time to be made in the likeness of men for one purpose – to be Crucified at the hands of those who did not understand.

Through Vicariously Shedding His Blood and Giving His body on the Cross, He would Redeem Fallen Man and destroy the works of the Devil, toppling all principalities and powers. This foreordained Plan was and is Jesus Christ and Him Crucified, and it encompassed the expression of God's kind intentions – Grace.

Now, *"It is finished,"* yet Grace alone allows God to work even within the life of the Believer today who is Saved, but has fallen into sin, and it is Grace that allows God to be in the presence of unsaved, sinful Man in this present evil world right now and the days to come, until He Returns. Grace is God's kind intention expressed toward all mankind, and the foundation of Grace is Jesus Christ and Him Crucified.

CHAPTER 24

Until The Trump of God Sounds

†

COMMENTARY

Though the works of the Devil are destroyed *(I John 3:8)* and principalities and powers have been spoiled *(Col. 2:14-15)*, Satan is the god of this world *(II Cor. 4:4)* and sin rules and reigns in the unsaved *(Rom. 3:10; 5:12)*. Still, it can also revive and bring the Believer into captivity. Yet, because He was triumphant, we can be triumphant in Him, but only through His Spirit *(Rom. 7:25; 8:2, 11, 14)*. For now, Scripture reveals – *"Beloved, now are we the sons of God, and it does not yet appear what we shall be: but we know that, when He shall appear, we shall be like Him; for we shall see Him as He is" (I John 3:2)*.

While we wait, we have the two most powerful Laws ruling mankind right now, and every human is experiencing one of them in one way or another. They are the Law of the Spirit of Life in Christ Jesus, and the Law of Sin and Death *(Rom. 8:2)*. These two Laws are

349

more powerful than that of the human willpower *(Rom. 7:15, 20)*. Yet greater is the Spirit of Life in Christ Jesus in us who are Saved *(Rom. 8:2)* than Sin and Death that is in our members *(Rom. 7:23)*, which is in the world *(I John 4:4)*. Therefore, as we determine not to know any thing except Jesus Christ, and Him Crucified, we will remain free from the Law of Sin and Death to live in the likeness of His Resurrection and be led by the Spirit of Life unto the Will of the Father. This is God's established way of victory.

Afterword

B ecause of our love for Jesus Christ, we have a deep desire to overcome and grow in Him, yet most often (without realizing it) we can be doing this in our own efforts. When we walk in this manner, we can be held captive to the sin we are trying to overcome. The work of God for us is to believe in Him Who He sent – this is all that is required of us *(John 6:29)*. It seems as if we are to do more and, if we do not, we may condemn ourselves for not doing enough.

We were never to have the knowledge of good from the Tree – we were created, and made to know God. This racks the theology of the human race and can be one of the most difficult things to come to terms with. Yet when we realize the power and leading of the Spirit of Life is not effactually experienced in our life based upon our good efforts of doing, but based upon where we place our Faith, we come to terms with this.

The Apostle Paul came to understand this in his struggle to overcome. He came to understand that it was the good that he was deceived by *(Rom. 7:21-NKJV)*, as it is the good we most often can become deceived by. This is Satan's ploy today, as it has been since the Fall. Satan knows that if he can get Christians to do "good," they will build a kingdom, and though their kingdom will have an appearance of godliness, it will be built without God. Within this kingdom are visions of grandeur and freedom, yet oppression and bondage are all that is there.

When we received Salvation, it was the Sovereign act and work of God on His part – all that He required of us was to believe on Him Who He sent, repent, and confess. We then became His Child, He became our God, and our name was written in the *Lamb's Book of Life*. Our walk in Christ after Salvation is no different – this is why the Cross is the Power of God unto us who are Saved *(I Cor. 1:17-18)*.

We cannot do good, whatever "good" might appear as – we simply cannot do it without the help of the Holy Spirit. For this reason, thanks be unto God through Jesus Christ our Lord – He has made the Way! That Way is the Cross, and as your Faith finds rests in Jesus Christ, and Him Crucified, the hour will come that you will experience the Spirit of Life effectually working within your life, unlike what you may have ever known. It was for this reason that the Apostle Paul determined not to know any thing except Jesus Christ, and Him Crucified.

†

It is Finished!

TOPICAL INDEX

G

God cannot cease from Himself, 276, 279, 328, 330-331, 333

God cannot cease to be God Eternal, 249

God could have eliminated Satan at any time, 238

God did not design the Fall, 78

God does not operate based on what we do, 196

God has ordained the fivefold ministry of the Apostle, Prophet, Evangelist, Pastor and Teacher, 305

God Revealed a life-changing Truth not known by anyone before Paul, 33

God set Paul apart to receive the Gospel, 235

God's Law is the unchangeable moral code for mankind, 78

H

He, as God, gave up the ghost to His human body and, by doing so, this clearly signifies His Deity, 88

His triumphant Atoning Sacrifice on the Cross, 85

How is it possible for us to take the detour? 109

Human love remains unstable, 13

I

If death required a ceremonial baptism by water, then additional ceremonies would be required when one sinned, resulting in a life of ongoing ceremonies for cleansing, 251

If one does not think through the ways of the old man, the husband has nothing to enforce, 67

If the knowledge of good is not discerned properly, it is not possible to learn dependency on God the way He desires, 213

If we are without the knowledge of how to go on unto perfection, 258

If we do not take back up what has been taken out of the way through the Cross, but instead place our Faith in the Cross, the sin nature cannot revive, 102

If we do not think carnally in regards to Sanctification, we will not go after the Law unlawfully, 72

If we had to figure this out while we walked with Him, we really could not keep track of it, and so in His wonderful love, we have the simplicity that is in Christ, 298

If we make a decision whereby our Faith is improperly placed, 22

Illegal combination, 25, 52, 112, 121, 151, 194, 300-301

J

K

L

Lucifer plotted to the extent of his wisdom, 30, 213

M

Maintain properly placed Faith, 22
Man is a spirit with a soul, 9
Man was created a triune being, 9
Man's fallen condition, 77-78, 214
Many dangerous facets to the carnal mind, 152
Many will say to Me, 290
Materializing of the man, Adam, 17
Message of life through death, 33
Might be destroyed, 40, 42-44, 46
Might become exceeding sinful, 142-143, 145-146
Might destroy, 44, 277, 330
Misplaced Faith, 51, 82, 94, 256
Misplacing Faith is easy to do if the Cross is not clearly understood for maintaining death while alive; Faith needs the proper object, 51
Moral code for mankind, 77-78
Moral compass, 55, 65, 78-79, 98, 103, 105

N

Now born again, we can obey from our heart, 18
Now, with the clarity to see through a clean heart and a cleansed conscience, we no longer want to sin, 107

O

O wretched man that I am, 180
Objective performances, 23-24, 27
Old Testament Sacrifices, 79, 189, 256-257
Once the act of original human sin was complete, 231
One of the Devil's great tactics and ploys, 300
Ongoing death is experienced only through Faith placed exclusively in Jesus Christ, and Him Crucified, 27
Ongoing failure and condemnation, 30, 66
Ongoing growth in Sanctification, 323
Our baptism took place upon Salvation through Faith alone, 251
Our biblical Jesus became the firstfruits for us, 335
Our biblical Jesus descended into Paradise, not Hell, 333
Our biblical Jesus did not need to become born again, 334
Our biblical Jesus is the once for all Sacrificial Offering, 333
Our biblical Jesus never gave up His Deity on the Cross, 327
Our biblical Jesus never relinquished His Deity, 333
Our determination is more than sufficient to move our Faith into the Cross, 148
Our direct sovereignty, 45

P

Physical members as the facilitator, 123

Pondering view for our life and living, 49

Posture of understanding that there is another way other than a way of his own, or that of others, a posture that sees the human inability, yet sees the ability of God and His forgiveness, 163

Preached from Paradise unto the spirits in the burning side of Hell, 88, 334

Principle of apostasy, 64, 72

Principle of enforcement, 64, 68-70, 72, 165, 201

Principles of the husband, 64, 96

Propensities toward carnal thinking, 147

Properly placed Faith, 22, 26-27, 82, 95, 101, 196, 220, 225, 227-228

Properly walking with God cannot be avoided, 23

Proximity effect simulation, 309-310

Purpose of the Law, 41, 78, 140

Quickened by the Spirit of God, 16, 193

Reaching the required moral standard of the Mosaic Law is humanly impossible, 71

Referring to the intangibles of what Paul truly is; a spirit with a soul, and though both live in his physical body, he is not using his body to serve, 195

Refrain from believing a lie, 135

Remaining dead is the foundation to remaining free, 49

Resting our Faith in Jesus Christ, and Him Crucified, 83

Righteous requirements of the Law, 71, 79

Sanctification is through Faith, 323

Searching for the answer in all the wrong places, 94

Self-efforts, 42, 46, 82, 94, 111, 115, 134, 146, 153, 166, 207-208, 215, 227, 233

Set Faith in its designed resting place, 25

Seven principles to Biblical Christianity, 186

She is in adultery during this time of unlawful engagement, 74

She is required to live up to the whole of the Mosaic Law, 75

She saw herself for the first time, 65

Sinless Sacrifice, 85

T

U

V

W

We can become Crucified to this
world, 31
We can come to know the truths
and treasures of God within His
Word, 11
We can enter His rest, 83
We cannot depend on what we
think is good or bad, or what he
or she says, 288
We cannot do good, whatever
"good" might appear as, 352
We cannot use our physical body
to overcome, 81
We created other laws to avoid the
moral standard of the Law, 157
We do not have to die a physical
death to atone for our own sins,
nor could we ever, 250
We have been called to holiness,
and we have been called to
Sanctification, 80
We have three natures, 26
We learn to love in the likeness as
he Loves, 14
We might have thought Hebrews
12:2 meant that Jesus was
finishing our Faith, 278
We must be made conformable
unto Jesus' death, 83
We must never give up! 179
We must understand that it is the
"good" whereby mankind is
most often deceived, 299
We were in a fallen state, 13
We were never meant to have the
knowledge of good, 143
What is required of us who believe,
100

What was once unknown, and thus
unmanageable (the compelling
of the Commandment), is now
a known, manageable asset, an
essential principle compelling
him unto Righteousness, 142
When our Faith remains in Jesus
Christ, and Him Crucified,
because He kept the Law
perfectly, yet Vicariously Paid
the Penalty of our inability,
we receive the benefits of what
He has done for us. Therefore,
the Righteousness of the Law
remains fulfilled in us, and we
are not Lawless, 60, 79, 141
When subjective impulses are seen
in our mind, 23
When there is a battle, one
cannot simply avoid it without
consequences, 219
Who walk, 207
Will is then strengthened and
follows determination, 22
Will this happen instantly? 229
Willpower and physical body, 112,
121
Willpower is for the body, 25
Willpower naturally desires
to default into the objective
position, 25
Without knowing the way of
victory, 57
Without the discerning
capacity to manage the
compelling principle of the
Commandment, 138

Without the knowledge of the
    Cross for Sanctification after
    we become Saved, it is most
    difficult, if not impossible, to
    understand our relationship
    with the Law, 169

Yes! Christ is risen, 302

Word Index

accepted, 56, 65-66, 206, 261, 309

accepting, 77

accomplish, 25, 53, 143, 201, 249, 255, 302, 336, 338, 346

accomplished, 18, 45, 57, 87-88, 95, 101-102, 129, 154, 194, 200, 216, 233, 237, 239, 247, 328-329, 331-332, 335, 344

accomplishing, 335

accordance, 277, 330-331

according, 19, 40, 205, 209, 234-237, 239-242, 261, 301, 331

account, 3-9, 88, 304, 334

accountable, 290

accounted, 301

accounts, 3-5, 8

accurate, 243

accurately, 6, 73, 165, 295

accursed, 272, 312

accuse, 42, 66

accused, 89

accustomed, 143

achieve, 17

acknowledge, 97, 161, 201-202

acknowledged, 291

acknowledgement, 187

acknowledging, 187

acknowledgment, 244

acquiescence, 23, 25, 27

act, 30, 75, 123, 148, 193, 208, 210, 214, 231, 352

acted, 208

action, 10, 39-40, 80, 103, 109, 122, 133, 145, 150, 155, 212, 275, 333, 346

actions, 39, 80, 121, 154, 162, 187, 267, 277, 330

active, 22

activities, 5, 301, 314, 321

activity, 304

acts, 9, 12, 15, 87-88, 92, 215, 272, 280, 333, 335, 339

actual, 39, 49, 281, 312

actually, 75, 78, 116, 123, 127, 145, 150, 163, 167, 217, 230, 265

acute, 63, 111, 208, 210

acutely, 107

Adam, 3-10, 12, 17-19, 21, 26, 29-31, 38, 40, 64, 67, 77-78, 84, 96, 99, 118, 124, 133-135, 157-158, 164, 166-167, 200, 203, 206, 212-215, 229, 231, 264, 277-278, 303, 330-331, 335, 337-339, 343, 346

add, 100

adding, 78, 218, 312

addition, 10, 12, 18-19, 34, 61, 65, 69, 72, 95, 147, 170, 172, 188, 193

additional, 251

address, 327

addressed, 16, 218, 230

addresses, 97, 103, 156, 200

addressing, 104, 177, 332

adequately, 97

adhere, 273

admonished, 339

admonishing, 307

admonishment, 306-307

admonition, 307

adopting, 98

adoration, 263

adrenaline, 70

adulteress, 73-75

adultery, 63-64, 73-75, 317

adverse, 206

affect, 38, 265

affected, 10, 38, 137, 231, 265

affecting, 10

affection, 12

affects, 17, 265

afresh, 254, 257

afternoon, 132, 206, 212

afterword, 351

Against

   against (a giant), 188

   against (all odds), 122

   against (God), 19, 200, 202

   against (the Law of my mind), 40, 171-172, 176, 230

   against (the Law), 153

   against (the sin nature), 160

   against (the walk of Faith), 179

   against (us), 129, 214, 329, 343

Agape, 13-14, 295

age, 114, 205, 236, 269

aggression, 169

aggressively, 169

agitated, 124

agitates, 123

ago, 239

agree, 207, 209, 212, 235

agreed, 209

agreement, 23

agrees, 155

aid, 194, 211

aim, 223

air, 3

aisle, 269

alcohol, 126

alienated, 17

alike, 243, 319-320, 326

Alive

   alive (in the likeness of His Resurrection), 130

   alive (prior to Salvation), 17

alive (the ghost), 16

alive (the sin nature), 40, 63, 156, 164

alive (unable to utilize our mortal body in regards to spiritual matters), 53

allow, 85, 115, 127, 147, 149, 151-152, 245, 265, 278, 306, 326

allowed, 69, 117, 238, 269, 278, 326, 331

allowing, 57, 147, 249, 302

allows, 44, 224, 229, 305, 314, 326, 345, 347

Alone

   alone (feel), 30

   alone (His Word: governs our lives), 37

   alone (remarkable place), 32

   alone (the Answer, and Teacher), 163

   alone (through Faith), 51, 82, 154, 196-197, 215, 244, 251, 256

along, 280, 292

Alpha, 280, 333-335

already, 32, 50, 61, 68, 173, 178, 189, 206, 220, 273, 310, 314, 317

altered, 218, 310

altogether, 21, 52, 55, 78, 127, 133-134, 310, 315

ambiguous, 137, 311

Amen, 241-243

America, 205

amiss, 144, 173, 188

analogy, 16-17, 63-64, 68, 80

anchor, 130, 148

anchored, 24, 39, 46, 51, 53, 101, 193, 228, 269, 273, 303

anchoring, 198

arousing, 191

arrangements, 146

array, 13, 135, 240, 246

arrays, 243

art, 289, 300, 306

article, 6, 15, 38

ascend, 88, 334

ascended, 344

ascension, 196, 335

ascertain, 218

aside, 290, 292-293

ask, 10, 21, 225-226, 278

asked, 21, 227, 255

asking, 59, 100

aspect, 142, 157, 167

aspects, 69, 77

assent, 190

assess, 152

assessed, 26-27, 159, 272

assessing, 153, 271

assessment, 22, 153, 159, 168

asset, 141-142

associate, 44, 100, 275-276

associated, 15, 25, 30, 70-71, 84-85, 90-91, 125, 167, 192, 201, 210, 231, 249, 289

associates, 178, 230, 312

associating, 44

association, 5, 44

assorted, 201

assumption, 254

assurance, 122, 175

assured, 194

assuring, 317

astonished, 137

astonishing, 37, 100, 103, 111, 170

astounding, 96

ate, 30, 213

atmosphere, 7-8

atmospheric, 8

atomic, 70

atomically, 70-71

atoms, 70

Atone, 250, 256

Atoned, 176, 338-339

Atonement, 130, 231, 238-239, 257

Atoning, 72, 85, 107, 116, 120, 129, 170, 194, 206, 214, 226, 231, 255-256, 323, 328, 334-335, 345-346

attain, 32, 42, 47, 71, 82, 144, 158-159, 257, 264, 292, 295, 314

attained, 32, 83, 158, 193, 241, 251, 319, 323

attaining, 31, 71, 302

attempt, 42, 70-72, 161, 177

attempted, 29, 213, 215

attempts, 57, 73, 177, 207-208, 210-211

attending, 132

attitude, 186-188, 198

attraction, 12

attribute, 9-10, 137

attributes, 26, 31, 87, 102, 277, 330-331

Author, 18, 53, 86, 160, 235, 249, 256-258, 266, 278, 302, 339

Authored, 86, 171, 249, 278-279, 282, 288, 293, 338

Authoring, 249

authority, 26, 31, 70

authorizing, 108

avail, 192

available, 50, 86, 110, 241

availed, 7

avaricious, 42

average, 205

avoid, 42, 66, 90, 157, 168-169, 178, 219, 232, 299

avoided, 23, 108, 130, 192, 219, 289

avoiding, 57

awaiting, 155, 162

awakened, 13

aware, 65, 107, 122, 135, 194

awe, 10, 85

B

backdrop, 270

backed, 151, 166, 173

backing, 192

backs, 110

bad, 65, 70, 112, 115, 136, 173, 214, 288, 301

badly, 150, 266, 269

balance, 9, 23, 41, 46, 51, 53, 68, 74, 83, 94, 123, 130, 132, 139, 148, 152, 154, 161, 164, 177, 203, 266, 282, 291, 293, 296, 319, 322, 329, 332, 337-338

bang, 78

bankruptcy, 158

baptism, 224, 250-251, 280

baptisms, 254, 257

Baptist, 251

baptize, 250-252

baptized, 244, 251, 278, 331

base, 90, 212

based, 25, 38, 43, 72, 102, 118, 196, 210, 270, 291, 319, 326, 351

basic, 188, 303

basis, 154, 193, 215-216, 346

battle, 126, 219

beacon, 66

beam, 50

beams, 116

bear, 42, 85, 180, 309, 326, 339

bearing, 180

bears, 9, 38, 176, 276, 296

beauty, 283

bed, 6

bedrock, 309, 312

bedroom, 210

beforehand, 236

began, 4, 9, 66, 112, 114, 130, 132, 153, 163, 165, 169, 173, 179, 230, 234, 236-238, 242, 282, 307

begin, 3, 6, 14, 22, 43, 58, 68, 90, 97, 104, 108, 112, 116, 129, 140, 156, 169, 199, 224, 245, 253-254, 259, 292, 294, 311, 319

begotten, 276, 278

beguiled, 135, 311

begun, 254

behalf, 326

behavior, 48

behind, 22, 33, 37, 40, 43, 64, 130, 138, 155, 237, 248, 298, 314

behold, 40, 83, 129

being, 9-10, 15, 17, 27, 31-32, 43, 47-48, 52, 55, 65, 69, 72, 75, 82-84, 94-96, 110, 134, 150, 157-158, 164-166, 171, 173, 188, 195-196, 200, 209, 213-215, 217, 219, 225, 230-231, 248-251, 261, 265, 272, 280-282, 288, 290, 292-297, 301, 304, 306, 309-310, 326, 329, 331-332, 335-338, 340, 344

beings, 13, 30, 194

belief, 78, 82, 96, 110, 196, 199, 226, 255, 281, 326, 333

believe, 18, 24, 32, 39, 60-61, 71, 82, 85, 96, 98-101, 104, 109-111, 115, 118, 127, 130, 153-154, 158, 176, 179, 187, 192-193, 202, 216, 218, 229, 235, 237-240, 243, 251, 253, 258-259, 261, 264, 266, 275-276, 289-290, 294, 301, 319, 321, 333, 351-352

C

306-308, 310, 313-314, 325-326, 339, 343

calling, 33, 235

calls, 264, 282

calming, 175

Calvary, 279, 302, 324, 334, 345

camera, 211

cameramen, 210

camp, 292

capacity, 118, 128, 137-138, 151, 166, 214, 234, 271

captivated, 11

captivates, 148

captive, 115, 132, 177, 192, 200, 229, 263, 344, 351

captivity, 40, 115, 171, 176-177, 230, 349

cardinal, 276

care, 6, 74, 149, 313-314

careful, 45, 49, 57, 68, 85, 109, 146, 166, 194, 265

carnal, 19, 26, 42-43, 45, 47-49, 56, 63-65, 69-70, 75-76, 81, 89, 92, 98, 109, 118, 122, 124, 126, 130-131, 136, 139, 144, 146-150, 152, 155-156, 161-162, 165-168, 172-173, 177, 179, 185, 195, 198, 200-202, 209, 212, 217, 234, 253, 256-257, 260-261, 264, 281, 303, 315, 318-319

carnally, 72, 110

carpenter, 337

carried, 235

carry, 78, 108, 177, 179

case, 15, 24-25, 30, 43, 46, 67, 81, 112-113, 123, 131, 134, 152, 169, 206, 209, 212, 219, 229, 235, 251, 265, 269, 297, 308, 315, 318

cases, 67, 227, 325

cast, 230, 290-291, 301, 344

catalyst, 89, 113, 120

catastrophic, 30, 87, 159, 161, 212, 256, 260, 289, 300

catastrophically, 231

category, 313

cattle, 3

caught, 23, 210, 257

cause, 60, 71, 110, 124, 130, 136, 148, 150, 152, 177, 213, 247, 282, 290, 293, 306

caused, 6, 8, 30, 42, 96, 112, 124, 155, 167, 277, 330

causes, 39, 92, 148, 152, 205, 208, 218, 313, 337

causing, 89, 123, 163, 178

cave, 158

caverns, 30, 213

cease, 38, 218, 249, 276, 279, 328, 330-331, 333, 338

ceased, 278, 280, 306, 314-315, 334, 336, 344

ceasing, 88, 278, 280, 328, 331

ceiling, 318

celebrates, 315

celebrity, 210

center, 79, 210, 237

centerpiece, 306

central, 292

ceremonial, 102, 251-252, 255-256, 261

ceremonies, 102, 169, 251, 253, 255, 257

ceremony, 251, 256

certain, 261

certainly, 34, 79, 136, 153, 166, 218, 229

certainty, 4-5, 17, 40-41, 248

certify, 33, 235, 272

chance, 122

D

depended, 336

dependence, 31

dependency, 43, 81-82, 146, 157, 186, 198, 213, 290

dependent, 116, 133, 281, 290

depending, 75, 194, 198, 287

depicted, 131

deport, 207

depravity, 214

depress, 205

depression, 59, 205, 208-209, 214-215

deprimere, 205

depriving, 336

depth, 18, 34, 49, 214, 234, 238

depths, 198, 292

derivatives, 70, 228

derived, 253, 276

descended, 88, 255, 331, 333-334, 344

descending, 331

describe, 5, 137, 230, 246, 295, 345

described, 8, 243

describes, 5, 39, 92, 225, 282, 293

describing, 131, 175, 308-309, 336

description, 108, 152, 218, 243, 249-250, 311

descriptive, 40, 152, 186, 295, 345

desert, 50

deserving, 211

design, 3-4, 7, 37, 64, 78, 135

designed, 11, 25, 31, 70, 140, 203, 243, 263, 288, 305

desire, 4, 8, 18-19, 24, 30-33, 37, 42, 49, 52, 60, 63, 82, 97-100, 102, 109-110, 117, 121-122, 126, 129, 139-140, 144, 146, 149, 151, 155, 157, 159, 162-163, 165-166, 172, 176, 178-179, 188, 190-192, 196, 199, 213, 241, 243, 245, 250, 257, 261, 269, 288, 295, 307, 313, 318-322, 336, 351

desired, 8-9, 138, 143, 162, 170, 294, 300

desires, 25, 31, 42, 82, 105, 123, 131, 146, 148, 150, 172, 193-194, 196, 198, 200, 202, 207-209, 213-214, 241, 264, 267, 270, 273, 288, 318, 326

desiring, 49, 100

despair, 218, 242

desperate, 121, 127, 132, 170, 210, 244-245

desperately, 65, 138, 143, 155, 162, 264, 270

desperation, 111, 153, 179

despising, 86, 278

despite, 45, 110

destination, 215, 244

destined, 13

destroy, 44, 84, 130, 223, 240, 248, 277, 299, 330, 346

destroyed, 31, 40, 42-44, 46, 61, 176, 200, 231, 238, 335, 338-339, 349

destroying, 346

destruction, 158, 237-238

detail, 41, 108, 120, 171

details, 3, 9, 12, 111, 251

determination, 22, 25-27, 33, 91, 109-111, 113, 119, 122, 128, 137-138, 148, 151, 157, 166, 174-175, 190-192, 260, 271, 273, 301

determine, 6, 22, 90, 101, 111, 303, 350

determined, 5-6, 27, 33, 91, 154, 167, 174-175, 193-194, 220, 230, 271-273, 306, 352

determines, 194

determining, 95, 217, 291, 324

detour, 34, 101, 109-113, 137, 168, 229, 260

detoured, 108, 271

detours, 108, 168

detrimental, 148, 153

devices, 29, 213, 232, 346

Devil, 23, 31, 44-45, 61, 84, 107, 110, 130, 134-135, 155, 162, 176, 178, 200, 223, 226, 230-231, 235, 238-241, 247-248, 277, 295, 300, 330, 333, 335, 338, 346, 349

devils, 272, 290-291, 301, 327, 332, 344

devise, 232

devised, 42, 92, 161, 178, 220, 253, 260, 264, 299-300

devote, 207, 209

devoted, 209, 271, 294

devotion, 207-208

diabolical, 143, 168, 173, 321

dichotomy, 142

dictate, 278, 331

dictates, 22

diction, 178

did, 160

die, 49, 51, 53, 59, 70-71, 80, 89, 115, 132-133, 227, 250, 252, 255, 264, 294, 303, 305, 333, 335-336

died, 15, 24, 51-52, 68-69, 84-85, 107, 111, 115, 124, 126-128, 132, 139, 170, 226-227, 335

dies, 17, 67, 74

dieting, 210

difference, 108, 110, 112, 115, 167, 190, 198, 208, 225

different, 8, 21, 52, 55, 58, 84, 94, 101, 127, 133-134, 147, 159, 171, 174, 178, 206, 212, 230, 287, 352

differently, 34, 75

difficult, 21, 84, 96-97, 99, 108, 110, 130, 138, 146, 153, 155, 160-162,

164, 169, 194, 212, 292, 317, 321, 336, 351

difficulty, 77-78

digressed, 271

dilemma, 31, 113, 119, 121, 125, 218

dimly, 65, 172

dimming, 65

dip, 306

dire, 71, 84, 125, 191, 215-216, 307

direct, 17, 19, 26, 40, 44-45, 99, 121, 149, 172, 192, 282, 289

directed, 121-122, 258

directing, 108, 121, 135, 190-191

direction, 22, 134, 220, 305

directly, 15, 17, 30, 39, 43, 55, 145, 148, 156, 169, 200, 265, 290

directs, 109, 120-121, 133, 141

disability, 205

disallows, 208

disappointments, 337

disassociated, 15

discern, 13, 19, 114, 136, 147, 150, 155, 157, 162-163, 167, 171, 173, 214, 246, 299, 318

discerned, 108, 139, 164, 185, 213, 310

discerning, 133, 138, 172

discernment, 108, 136, 149, 154, 159, 163, 166, 173, 185, 197, 212, 299

discerns, 163

disclose, 111, 169, 266, 319

disclosed, 40-41, 52, 114, 122, 164, 170, 185, 241-242, 291

discloses, 117

disclosing, 123, 150, 154, 289

disclosure, 32, 41, 114-115, 122, 150, 154, 164

disclosures, 130

discover, 38, 188, 199, 243

discovered, 57, 117, 162, 164, 197

discovering, 166

discovery, 154

discuss, 21

discusses, 311

discussion, 4

disillusionment, 44

dismantles, 259

disobedience, 84

disorders, 210

dispensation, 77-79, 133, 340, 345

dispensational, 77

display, 78, 247

displayed, 74, 137, 295

disseminate, 325

dissolve, 44

distance, 287

distant, 276, 287

distantly, 154

distinction, 276, 282, 293

distort, 263, 305

distorted, 21

distracted, 264

distraction, 178

distraught, 170

ditch, 144

Divest, 250, 278, 336, 338

Divested, 88, 249, 276, 278, 281, 295, 328, 330-333, 344

Divesting, 234, 240, 249-250, 278, 337

divide, 186, 218

divided, 246, 280, 334

divides, 190

Divine, 4-5, 26, 31, 87, 102, 241, 277, 330-331, 345

division, 14

divisions, 155, 162, 252, 313

divorce, 67, 210

do, 160

Doctrine

Doctrine (Biblical), 144, 193, 198, 215, 217-218, 237, 243, 254-258, 297-298, 318, 325

doctrine (False), 272, 308-309, 320, 325-327, 332, 335, 340

document, 67

doer, 196

does, 161

doing, 47, 50, 60, 66, 71, 82, 88, 98, 100, 115, 118, 137, 146, 149, 152, 154-155, 158, 161, 165, 169-170, 219, 232, 238, 248, 272, 287, 291, 301, 310, 317, 319, 326, 332, 351

domain, 64, 168, 338

dominate, 267

dominated, 65, 190

dominates, 190

dominating, 126

dominion, 3, 39-40, 45, 56-61, 69, 149, 154, 165, 168, 178, 229, 248, 299

done, 158

doom, 59, 155, 162, 238, 247

doomed, 312

door, 50, 152, 313

doorway, 41

double, 297

doubt, 30, 119, 129, 134, 213, 293, 313

doubtless, 32, 292-293

dove, 331

down, 44, 46, 49, 85-87, 188, 194, 205, 217, 219, 239, 259, 278-280, 315, 332

dozen, 211

draft, 40, 120

drafted, 34

drafting, 120

dramatic, 132, 165, 214, 305

F

fruit, 80, 86-89, 91-93, 125, 131

fruits, 297, 326

frustration, 188

fulfill, 59, 102

fulfilled, 59-60, 71, 79, 81, 83, 85, 94-95, 141, 176, 202, 207-208, 215-217, 260, 296, 298, 303, 323, 328-329, 344

fulfilling, 153

fulfillment, 94

full, 6, 21, 39-41, 77-78, 81, 95, 101, 114, 118, 142, 146, 186, 198, 203, 206, 208, 215, 227, 236, 239, 257, 261, 279, 299, 310, 333

fullness, 218, 234, 238-239, 241-242, 278, 283

fully, 9, 30, 41, 72, 78, 83, 114, 120, 195, 200, 231, 236, 258, 280-281, 287, 330, 338

function, 10, 13, 19, 38, 50, 57-58, 98, 104-105, 112, 124, 140-141, 163, 169, 177, 212, 296-297, 303

functioning, 19, 58, 91-92, 98, 101, 131, 149, 155, 162, 170, 193, 220, 227, 296-298, 303-304

functions, 90, 144, 178, 193, 199, 212, 224

fundamental, 41, 49, 151, 155, 178, 198-199, 256-257

further, 16, 32, 40-41, 75, 97, 108, 113, 116, 120, 144, 152, 161, 180, 193, 304

furthermore, 40, 43, 46, 48, 50, 58, 60, 84, 101, 119, 139, 176, 193, 200, 202, 227, 256, 266, 297, 326, 332, 334-335

future, 10, 39, 80-82, 180, 336

G

gadgets, 269

gain, 32, 41, 50, 64, 81, 114, 163, 234, 244-245, 254, 292, 297, 299, 301, 303, 322

gained, 30, 213-214

gaining, 254, 256

Galatia, 306-307, 314

gamut, 270

gap, 13, 77, 116-118, 121-122, 128, 145

garden, 29, 133, 143, 213, 277, 299, 330

gate, 168-169

general, 12, 30, 190, 214, 219, 246

genitive, 297

gentiles, 235

gentle, 9

gentleness, 9

gently, 75

getting, 102, 144

ghost, 9-10, 15-17, 19, 83-84, 87-88, 129, 239, 280, 329, 331-332, 343

giant, 188

Gift, 13, 241, 254, 257, 281, 288, 326

girl, 84, 142, 197, 201, 211, 289

glance, 15, 98, 180, 186

glass, 14, 19, 99, 203, 278

glean, 242

glimpse, 9, 21, 248

gloried, 323

glorification, 323

glorious, 44, 168, 248

glory, 27, 53, 101, 111, 129, 189, 233-236, 238, 241-243, 247, 251, 278, 320-324, 331

go, 13, 22, 50-51, 58, 71-72, 75, 103, 108, 111, 124-125, 137, 170-171, 174, 179, 188-189, 200-202, 213, 217, 219,

heavenly, 254, 257

heavens, 331

heavily, 41, 173, 263

heavy, 82, 180

heed, 294

heinous, 132, 145, 211, 238

held, 69, 94-96, 200, 229, 259, 335, 337, 351

helicopter, 210-211

Hell, 45, 87-88, 206, 215, 244, 305-306, 326-327, 333-335, 344

help, 21, 40, 44, 48, 89, 91, 97, 109, 121, 131, 134-135, 167, 172, 186, 188, 194, 201-202, 211, 224, 229, 257, 270, 305, 309, 330, 339, 352

helped, 102, 322

helpful, 33

helping, 100, 103, 216, 229-230

helps, 242

hence, 64, 67, 177, 190, 225, 227, 264

henceforth, 40, 42-43, 46

hereby, 208

herein, 86, 91, 109, 122, 236, 255

heresy, 178, 260, 300, 320

herself, 65-66, 211, 299

hidden, 209, 233, 236

hide, 14

high, 33, 55-56, 98, 105, 146, 269, 344

highly, 8, 44, 70, 129

highway, 50

history, 119, 272, 339

hold, 38, 49, 113, 143, 186, 229, 235, 335

holding, 19, 108-109, 141

holds, 52, 108, 141, 187, 226, 242-243, 245

holiness, 34, 42, 47-48, 57, 80-81, 87, 105, 119, 135, 141, 144-145, 149, 155, 158, 162, 175, 189, 192, 198, 225, 234, 241-243, 271, 273, 301-302, 346

Holy, 4, 31, 39, 41, 47-48, 55-56, 58, 64, 82-84, 87, 90, 97, 105, 109-110, 112, 134, 140-141, 144, 147, 150, 157-158, 164-166, 173, 186-187, 190, 198, 209, 212, 214-216, 223-224, 229-230, 235, 237, 241, 243-245, 248-249, 254, 257, 262, 265, 267, 278, 282, 288-289, 295-296, 301, 303, 307, 326, 329, 332, 337, 339-340, 343, 346, 352

home, 99, 269

hope, 32-34, 59, 130, 152, 175, 203, 212, 218, 306

hoped, 11, 128, 175, 211

hopeless, 218

hopelessness, 127

horrendous, 211

horrible, 127, 153, 320

horrific, 132, 154

horrors, 154

hostile, 19

hostility, 202

hour, 193, 264, 328, 352

house, 258

housed, 171, 215, 298

howbeit, 233

human, 5, 9-10, 12-15, 17, 21-27, 30, 38-39, 50, 55, 70-71, 84-85, 88-89, 91-92, 96, 113, 119, 126, 131, 144, 146, 148, 154, 158, 163-164, 168, 179, 194, 200, 212-215, 223, 225, 229, 231, 234, 254, 261, 272, 280-281, 288, 295-296, 311-312, 317, 329, 332, 338-339, 349-351

humane, 12

humanity, 38, 88, 147, 173, 231, 249-250, 276, 279, 282, 328, 330, 332-333, 338

humanly, 30, 71, 84

399

I

inadequate, 95, 320

incapable, 99, 212

incapacitated, 13, 16, 39, 44-46, 48, 68, 72, 80, 103, 107, 124, 148, 157, 165, 170, 200, 247, 263-264, 323

incarnation, 328-329

included, 8

including, 56, 84, 104, 140, 290

income, 272

incomprehensible, 9, 29, 123, 213, 238, 263, 282, 292

incomprehensively, 339

inconceivable, 296

incorporeal, 10

incorrect, 124

incorruptible, 267

increase, 78, 153

increased, 210

incredible, 271

incredibly, 169, 178, 199, 263, 336, 340

indeed, 100, 129, 150, 159, 180, 190, 199-200, 227, 235, 239, 251, 308

independent, 116

indescribable, 132

indicate, 50

indicates, 311

indicating, 334

indication, 17, 332

indictment, 24, 75, 308

individual, 18, 31, 45, 89, 126, 132, 179, 210, 251, 291, 323

indwelling, 158

ineffective, 26, 93, 124, 248

inevitable, 212

inevitably, 151, 269

inexpressible, 30, 43, 217, 230, 296

infective, 130

infinite, 29, 213, 277, 330

influence, 12, 17, 44-45, 149, 263, 270, 314, 321

influenced, 39

influences, 230, 265, 270

inherent, 99

iniquity, 64, 291, 296-297, 299-300, 303, 328

initial, 138

initiated, 78, 120, 133, 345

initiation, 116-117

innate, 102, 118, 252

innately, 174

inseparable, 63, 67, 73, 96, 116, 202, 270, 280, 294, 298

inseparableness, 281

insight, 7, 41, 50, 64, 83, 114, 156, 163, 174, 225, 227, 234, 254-255, 279, 293

insightful, 7

insights, 6, 52, 234, 242

insignificant, 65, 210, 224, 270

inspiration, 235, 241

inspire, 11

inspires, 12

instant, 26, 116, 229

instantaneously, 114

instantly, 229

instead, 26, 50, 57, 59, 81, 91, 93, 98, 102, 135, 157, 164, 188, 197, 202, 224, 238, 260, 297, 301, 323, 329

institute, 205

instruct, 140

instructing, 147, 171, 197

instructs, 56, 72, 79, 98, 103, 105, 113, 139-140, 201, 288

instrument, 118, 140, 200, 242, 266, 301

instruments, 117

J

lifetime, 37, 230, 277, 306, 330

lift, 306

light, 33, 55-57, 65-66, 72, 75, 79, 98, 103, 107-110, 112-113, 115, 125, 139-141, 147, 154, 161-162, 164, 170-171, 197, 209, 238, 259, 266, 307, 318-319, 326, 339

lighting, 331

lightly, 159, 309

lights, 105

liken, 163

likened, 16, 38

likeness, 3-4, 6-8, 11, 13-14, 26-27, 29, 31-33, 47, 49, 52, 59, 61, 78, 81-85, 94, 98-99, 130, 171, 189, 202, 220-221, 227, 229, 231, 237-238, 240, 244, 248-251, 253, 264, 276-277, 280-281, 283, 289, 295-296, 302, 330-331, 333, 336-338, 343, 346, 350

limit, 19

limited, 45, 135

limits, 44, 295

line, 95, 206, 219, 231, 273, 289, 310

lineage, 64, 74

lines, 325

lingering, 296

link, 99, 302

list, 303

listed, 326

listen, 265, 322

listening, 287

listens, 74

lit, 108

literal, 3-4, 6-7, 38-40, 43, 69, 88, 103, 114, 128, 136, 143, 146, 148, 156, 161, 218-219, 334

literally, 15, 17, 43-45, 47, 73, 97, 117-118, 123, 137, 144, 146, 148, 157, 177, 194, 201, 208, 266, 278, 280

litmus, 318

little, 34, 149, 193, 218, 272, 315

liveth (uniqueness of Romans 7:2-3), 66-68, 73-74

location, 172, 199

locking, 152

long, 16, 39, 46, 48, 58-59, 66-68, 80, 86, 96, 104, 122, 228, 264, 273

longer, 42, 56, 61, 69, 74, 79, 92, 94, 103-104, 107, 125, 155, 157, 167, 190, 197, 199-200, 208, 219, 227, 230, 244-245, 251, 258, 270, 279, 293, 302, 306, 314

longing, 193

looked, 76, 118, 163, 165, 189, 211, 236, 328

looking, 3-4, 9, 29, 47, 83, 86, 97, 108, 130, 153-154, 156, 202, 210, 270-271, 278, 282, 309

looks, 125, 169, 290, 310, 317, 320

looming, 59, 126, 173, 208, 214, 217

loose, 44

loosed, 66, 68-69

loosen, 44

loosing, 230

Lord, 3, 6-9, 11, 18, 24, 27, 32, 44, 53, 83, 86, 101, 117, 125, 133-135, 150, 159, 161, 163, 168, 178-180, 185-189, 194-195, 198-199, 202-203, 209, 219, 229, 234, 238, 241, 244, 247, 253, 256, 275, 278, 287, 289-293, 295-296, 298-299, 301, 313, 321-324, 327, 331, 335, 352

lose, 152, 210, 257, 293, 306, 313

losing, 210

loss, 32, 210, 292-293

lost, 90, 207, 210, 218

lot, 9, 102, 132, 192, 223, 265, 336

loud, 280, 328, 331

M

manifested, 13, 22-23, 44, 110, 124, 165, 193, 240, 277-278, 330

manifesting, 92, 114, 125, 267

manifests, 265

manifold, 101, 200

mankind, 12, 29-30, 37-38, 40, 55, 61, 77-78, 83, 87, 120, 134, 141, 158, 168, 201, 206, 212-214, 237, 241-243, 262, 266, 277, 287, 299, 323, 326, 329-330, 333, 338, 345, 347, 349

manmade, 70, 109

manner, 16, 24, 72, 111, 114, 117, 119, 123, 154, 177, 180, 187, 191, 207, 224, 246, 249-250, 260, 272, 351

many, 12, 14, 31, 37, 45, 55, 60, 77, 82, 89, 91-92, 94, 98, 102, 113, 118, 126-127, 132, 137, 152, 155, 160-161, 169-170, 176-179, 185-186, 196, 201, 210, 213, 216, 218-219, 229, 243, 251-253, 257, 259-260, 264-265, 270, 272, 276, 290-291, 294, 301-304, 310, 314-315, 318-319, 321, 325-326, 333, 339, 344

mark, 4, 15, 18, 33, 39, 80, 109, 112, 280, 293, 333, 338-339, 344

marked, 276, 282, 293

marriage, 64, 67-69, 75, 86, 96, 270

marriages, 304

married, 67, 73-75, 79, 86-88, 125, 270

marry, 65

Martin, 188

marvel, 41, 272, 306-308, 339

marveling, 245

marvelous, 218

Mary, 39, 83-84, 337-338, 343-344

match, 160

material, 7-8, 10, 13, 23, 275

materializing, 17

materials, 5, 99

matter, 34, 39, 41, 46, 50, 82, 97, 137, 162, 193, 206, 307, 317, 320, 340

mattered, 269

matters, 16, 25-26, 42, 47, 52-53, 64, 69, 92, 118, 121, 128, 131, 136, 139, 149, 151, 153, 156, 158, 177, 191, 194-196, 231, 300

mature, 155, 162, 188, 234, 237

meant, 21-22, 25-26, 33-34, 89, 113, 132, 137, 143, 166, 174, 200, 212-214, 278, 292, 301, 334

measure, 77, 117, 214, 264

meat, 100, 114

mediating, 10

medications, 212

meekness, 87

meet, 77, 345

meeting, 78

mega, 321

melded, 26, 346

melt, 44

member, 12

members, 39-41, 45, 64, 80, 89, 91-93, 123, 131, 145, 148, 154-155, 162, 164, 168, 171-172, 176-178, 224, 230, 263, 266, 302-304, 338, 350

men, 15, 59, 126, 132, 161, 248-249, 261, 272, 276-278, 283, 295, 302, 314, 330-333, 336-339, 346

mental, 190, 196, 205, 210

mention, 338

mentioned, 210, 220

merciful, 320

mercy, 136, 211-212, 306

mere, 90, 124

merges, 265

message, 33, 101, 119-120, 122, 133, 160, 181, 234-235, 241, 259, 265, 273, 300, 310, 325-326

N

O

odds, 122, 265

off, 44, 61, 97, 147, 152, 210, 229, 306

offence, 314-315

offend, 39

offended, 273

offending, 315

offense, 285, 306, 310, 313-315

offer, 122

offered, 66

offering, 130, 187, 189, 255, 328, 333-334, 343, 346

officer, 211

officers, 211

often, 12, 76, 98, 111, 125-126, 146, 153, 168-169, 179, 210-211, 232, 269, 299, 310, 313, 315, 318, 320, 322, 351

okay, 22, 309

old, 4, 15-16, 37-38, 40, 42-43, 45-49, 56-57, 63-69, 75, 79, 81, 88, 96, 98, 107, 120, 124, 126, 130, 144-145, 147, 156-157, 164-166, 168, 170, 177, 189, 195, 205, 236, 241, 251, 255-257, 264, 267, 329, 334

older, 65

oldest, 243

oldness, 94-96, 98, 100-102, 177

Omega, 280, 333-335

omission, 218

oneself, 207-209, 223

ongoing, 22-23, 27, 30, 33, 43, 53, 66, 72, 82, 91-92, 119-120, 125, 130, 137, 174, 176, 188-189, 191, 193, 198, 248, 251, 256, 271, 282, 299, 310-311, 318, 322-324

only (Answer), 25, 27, 30-31, 39, 51, 53, 60, 82-84, 87, 90, 95, 97, 116, 119, 126, 130, 138, 147, 154-155, 174, 176, 186-187, 189, 202-203, 215, 218, 220, 223, 232-233, 252, 264, 267, 288, 303

onto, 21, 38, 168

open, 51, 65, 109, 149, 219, 223, 254, 257, 259, 280, 313

opened, 30, 88, 214, 331

opening, 1, 111

openly, 45, 87, 120, 129, 141, 211, 295, 344

opens, 180

operate, 196

operates, 196, 225, 227

operating, 23

operation, 225-227

opinion, 219

opponent, 304

opportunity, 7, 13, 19, 31, 42, 56, 96, 99, 113-114, 123, 125, 130, 175, 189, 193, 203

opposed, 14, 175, 208, 293, 337

opposes, 303

opposite, 50, 91, 253, 293

oppression, 152, 173, 215, 352

option, 22, 127, 213

ordained, 57, 108-109, 111-112, 115, 118, 121, 133-136, 139, 141-142, 145, 169, 233, 305

ordinances, 129, 176, 214, 260, 272, 329, 333, 343

ordination, 133

organization, 205

origin, 29, 119, 279

original, 38, 40, 96, 133, 135, 206, 231, 338

originally, 11, 65, 203, 264

originate, 299

originated, 17, 121, 139-141, 147, 166

originates, 146, 208

originating, 134, 139

particular, 34, 112, 269, 272

parts, 88, 174, 334, 344

pass, 50, 70-71, 186, 188, 202, 208

passage, 5-6, 12, 40, 50, 254

passages, 5, 169-170, 207

passed, 38, 50, 168, 189

passing, 71

passion, 270

passive, 23-25, 27, 273, 326

passively, 23

past, 4, 29, 80-81, 91-92, 129, 131, 180, 213, 228, 239, 261-262, 282, 336

pastor, 206, 287, 305

pastors, 209

pat, 207

path, 75, 147, 292

patterns, 192

Paul, 16, 24, 27, 32-33, 38, 40-43, 47-48, 50-53, 55, 58-60, 63-64, 66-67, 71, 75, 80, 82-83, 91-92, 96-97, 101, 103-104, 108, 111-128, 130-140, 142-145, 147-156, 158-167, 169-173, 175, 177-181, 185-191, 194-201, 203, 206-208, 215-218, 220-221, 224, 228, 230, 233-238, 241-246, 248-253, 258-261, 265, 267, 271-273, 276, 278-283, 288, 292-295, 297-298, 302, 306-312, 314-315, 318-319, 321-322, 326-327, 331, 336-337, 351-352

Pauline, 49

pausing, 8

pay, 13, 79, 333, 343

paying, 77, 202

peace, 154, 176, 193, 230, 244, 326, 339, 344

peculiar, 30

peer, 154, 186, 298, 301

peering, 9, 162

peers, 211

penalty, 52, 59-60, 71, 77, 79, 81, 85, 153, 176, 201-203, 206, 214-216, 220, 244, 298, 300, 339, 343

penned, 80-81, 199

people, 83-84, 154, 205, 212, 260, 273, 276, 287, 289-290, 296, 298, 300-301, 303, 305, 325

perceived, 43, 82, 237

perceives, 190, 212

percent, 276, 279, 330, 333

perception, 179, 212

perfect, 32, 85, 199, 201, 220, 227, 233-234, 317

perfected, 46

perfection, 71, 80, 254, 256-258, 292, 318

perfectly, 16, 60, 84, 187, 212

perform, 23-25, 47, 97, 115, 117-118, 137, 144, 156, 158-160, 165-167, 174-175, 194, 257, 266, 300

performance, 38, 97, 115, 135

performances, 23-24, 27, 135, 256, 261, 267

performed, 4

performing, 7, 97

perhaps, 6, 154, 158, 169-170, 345

period, 31

perish, 253, 258, 276

perishes, 100

permissible, 117, 177

permit, 254, 257

perpetual, 299, 345

perplexing, 314

perplexity, 16, 245

persecuted, 313

persecution, 259, 313-314, 318-320

perseverance, 271

person, 30, 39, 67, 84, 206, 211, 270, 275, 279, 287, 307, 325

positions, 173, 272, 305

possessed, 229

possession, 154

possessions, 291

possibility, 159, 312

possible, 8, 30, 83, 91, 109, 112, 130, 160, 167, 178, 191, 194, 207, 213, 218, 234, 283, 293, 299, 301, 340

possibly, 65, 226, 278

post, 156

posture, 163, 186

potential, 29, 73, 78, 149, 213, 299, 346

potter, 6

pounds, 210

Power

    power (Evil), 17, 38, 44-45, 69, 81, 85, 87, 102, 104, 111-113, 117, 128, 176, 247, 302, 339

    power (example: nuclear), 69-71, 75, 81

    power (God), 9, 22, 31-32, 43, 47, 60, 82-83, 85, 87, 89, 98, 101, 116, 119, 128, 131, 144, 176, 188-189, 193, 196, 216, 230, 234-240, 242, 246, 252-253, 258-259, 261-264, 279-281, 292, 294, 298, 302-303, 324, 329, 331-332, 339, 352

    power (human), 23-25, 45, 93, 98, 137, 139, 146, 151, 158, 161, 187, 270, 289-290, 302, 351

powerful, 38, 47, 93, 111, 263, 272, 297, 349-350

powers, 44-45, 85, 129, 237-240, 242, 254, 257, 281, 324, 329, 339, 344, 346, 349

practice, 151

praise, 209, 259, 265, 332

praising, 265

pray, 174

prayed, 271

prayer, 33

preach, 101, 247, 250, 252, 259-261, 272, 300, 309, 312, 314, 317, 320, 322

preached, 33, 88, 119, 235, 252, 259-260, 272-273, 302, 307, 309-312, 314, 326, 334

preacher, 259, 273, 299, 307, 312, 319, 326

preachers, 272, 306, 309, 320, 326, 339

preaches, 326

preaching, 34, 234, 236-237, 242, 252-253, 258-260, 272-273, 291, 309, 312, 314, 318, 320, 325

precede, 25, 150

preceding, 64

precious, 256, 282

precise, 117

prefacing, 58

premise, 43, 254, 267, 334

premises, 319

preposition, 224

prescription, 126

presence, 60, 116, 134, 150, 191, 217, 224, 229-230, 248, 254, 264, 303, 318, 339, 346-347

presentation, 213

presented, 75, 86, 110, 206, 210-211, 258, 307, 314

presenting, 142-143, 252

presently, 59, 266, 302

presents, 167

preserve, 15

press, 33, 150, 188, 193, 205, 318

pressing, 6, 188

pretty, 269

prevalent, 59, 215

previous, 149

previously, 98, 107, 115, 130, 195, 197, 215, 264, 298

prey, 56, 105, 140, 299

price, 242, 278, 313

pride, 23, 238, 261, 278, 290, 319-320, 323, 331

primary, 44, 73, 89, 238

princes, 233-234, 247, 278, 331

principalities, 44-45, 129, 237-239, 242, 280, 324, 329, 339, 344, 346, 349

principle, 56-59, 64, 67-70, 72-73, 105, 108, 113, 115, 118-119, 121, 124, 127, 134, 136-138, 142, 147, 165, 169, 186-189, 195, 198-199, 201, 203

principles, 33-34, 37-38, 40-41, 56-57, 63-64, 66-67, 75-76, 96, 112, 116-117, 119-120, 122, 130, 140, 147, 150, 155, 157, 162, 165, 167, 169-170, 185-186, 190, 195, 198-199, 201, 243-244, 254-257

prior, 7-8, 17-19, 40, 47, 79, 84, 86, 103-104, 131, 134, 142, 156, 160, 188, 199, 202, 214, 244, 269, 306, 346

priority, 248

prison, 152, 208, 218

private, 162

prize, 33, 39

probationary, 9, 31

problem, 25, 43, 45, 47, 50, 63, 69, 71, 111, 124, 132, 161, 165, 169, 195, 210, 229-230, 256, 260, 264, 303, 315, 322-323

problems, 153, 287-288

process, 25, 50, 80, 119, 156, 159, 165, 232, 258, 324

proclaim, 267

proclaimed, 37

proclaiming, 239

proclaims, 87, 239, 326

proclamation, 281, 334

produce, 7, 16-17, 92, 127, 197, 297, 310

produced, 8, 89, 154, 175, 212

produces, 93, 178, 256, 321

producing, 92, 290

product, 70-72, 174

products, 70

profess, 291, 296, 299

professed, 113, 300

profession, 113, 283

profit, 301

profound, 48, 56, 105, 116, 140, 155, 188, 235, 277, 291, 303, 312, 315, 328-330

profundity, 312

progressive, 258

promise, 282

promises, 178, 242

pronouns, 4

propensities, 118, 147, 149, 287

propensity, 147-149

proper, 22, 24-27, 51-53, 70, 97, 99, 112-113, 119, 126, 128, 131, 138, 151, 157, 166, 168, 174-175, 191, 194, 202, 219, 242, 254, 267, 301, 327, 333-335

properly, 5, 13, 16, 19, 22-23, 26-27, 39, 52, 61, 75, 82, 86, 91, 95, 97, 99, 101-103, 109-110, 113, 117, 121-122, 137, 142, 147, 150, 163, 167, 174, 190, 193, 196-197, 199, 213, 218, 220, 225, 227-228, 230, 252, 267, 332, 336-337

prophesied, 290-291, 301

prophet, 83, 251, 305

prophets, 236, 239-241, 339

proposed, 100-101, 211

proposing, 314

416

regarding, 27, 45, 49, 112, 150, 154, 165, 196, 276

region, 88, 255, 334, 344

regulate, 55

reign, 17, 40-42, 92-93, 157

reigned, 335

reigns, 349

reinforce, 196, 200

reject, 257-258, 315, 321, 346

rejected, 211, 253, 257, 261, 315

rejection, 65

rejoice, 259

rejoices, 239

related, 17

relating, 10

relationship, 6, 8, 29, 31, 38, 41, 58, 60, 77, 79, 82, 169, 186, 203, 219, 243, 300, 307

relationships, 212

released, 45, 229

reliance, 125, 148

reliant, 30, 214

relies, 177

relieve, 147

religion, 215, 276

religions, 102, 169, 276, 308, 315

religious, 90, 178, 260, 265, 314, 321

relinquished, 333

rely, 19, 89, 109, 150, 261, 302

remain, 25, 39, 43, 45-53, 57, 59, 61, 71-72, 80-83, 92, 103, 110, 119, 123, 125, 130, 144, 165-166, 189, 196, 203, 207, 215-217, 227-228, 237, 240, 248, 261, 263-264, 266-267, 283, 302-303, 335, 344, 350

remained, 42, 82, 157, 188, 190, 226-227, 281, 300

remaining, 27, 45, 49, 60, 81-82, 95, 98, 207-208, 216, 264, 266

remains, 13, 25, 39, 45, 48-49, 60-61, 71, 79, 85-86, 92, 125, 137, 141, 166, 174, 187, 192, 202, 217, 228, 239, 264, 282, 296, 303, 323

remarked, 211

remarks, 211

remember, 99, 110, 113, 126, 149, 165, 168, 194, 206, 232, 252, 269-270, 306

remembered, 144, 306

remind, 108, 253, 300

remiss, 13, 168, 253, 276, 295

remission, 79, 255-256

remove, 168, 307

removed, 18, 124, 218, 226-227, 272, 306-308, 310, 334

removing, 219, 226-227

render, 43

rendered, 16-17, 26, 47, 93, 118, 156-157, 232

renew, 254, 257

renewed, 48-49, 76, 130, 145, 187

repeat, 312

repeated, 256

repeatedly, 256

repent, 91, 154, 158, 251, 258, 352

repentance, 254, 256-258

repentant, 255

repented, 158

repenting, 256

repetition, 312

repetitious, 200

repetitively, 137

replace, 78, 178

replaced, 78, 218

reply, 291

reporter, 209

reproofs, 56, 72, 98, 103, 139-140

S

seeing, 66, 175, 254, 257, 281

seek, 18, 46, 114, 161, 179-180, 190, 192, 198, 239, 270-272

seeker, 259

seeketh, 264, 266

seeking, 18, 144, 163, 179-180, 233, 270, 307, 317, 328

seeks, 163

seem, 16, 118, 123, 126, 130, 132, 135, 137, 149, 186, 206, 210, 224, 270, 300, 313

seemed, 48, 128, 153, 276

seemingly, 57, 118, 135, 197, 213

seems, 47, 110-111, 118, 168, 199, 216, 275, 287, 300, 302, 325, 351

seen, 4-5, 11, 23, 30, 50, 64-65, 67-69, 73-75, 77-78, 85, 88, 99, 108, 114-116, 150, 155, 161-162, 166, 175, 179, 185, 192, 198, 214, 217, 219, 223, 230, 246, 299, 344

sees, 14, 31, 99, 129, 139, 151, 163, 170, 258, 326

seeth, 306

self, 15, 30, 42, 46, 49, 57, 72, 82, 94, 111, 115, 118, 134, 146, 149, 153, 159, 166, 174, 177, 207-208, 210, 212, 214-215, 227, 233, 252, 293, 300, 303, 323-324

self-efforts, 42, 46, 63, 82, 94, 111, 115, 134, 146, 153, 166, 207-208, 215, 227, 233

selfishness, 13

semblance, 30, 42, 158, 219, 323

send, 206, 306

sending, 85, 94

sense, 5, 26, 30-31, 47, 65, 100, 135, 191, 208, 212, 227

senses, 114, 299

sensitive, 259

sent, 100-101, 211, 250, 252, 255, 351-352

sentence, 206, 224

separate, 323

separated, 10-11, 30, 129, 214, 228, 235, 242, 328

separating, 8, 220

separation, 8, 30, 206

sequence, 25, 243

series, 211

serious, 75, 308

sermon, 310

sermons, 270

Serpent, 134-135, 311, 337

servant, 235, 242, 248, 272, 337

serve, 31, 40, 42-43, 46, 57, 60, 94-99, 101-102, 185-190, 194-195, 197-203, 216, 298, 313

served, 57, 79

serves, 190-191

service, 97

serving, 40, 97-101, 177, 190, 195, 197-200, 202, 209, 215-216, 224, 298

set, 8, 19, 25, 38, 69, 81, 86, 91, 98, 100, 104, 111, 137, 139, 149, 181, 193, 215, 235, 248, 278, 288, 292, 297-299, 313

sets, 60, 198-199, 254

setting, 5-6, 12, 76, 185, 213, 298, 313

settings, 310

seven, 186-187, 203, 235, 344

seventeen, 38

seventh, 8, 41

several, 206, 226

severely, 218

sexual, 12, 126

shadow, 257

shadows, 79, 189, 255-258, 261

shame, 86, 254, 257, 278

shape, 6, 188

shaped, 187

shapen, 64

shapes, 116

share, 39, 74

sharing, 206

sheath, 14

Shed, 61, 71, 75, 79, 86, 107, 175, 187, 194, 200, 202, 206, 238, 251, 255, 257, 333-334, 339, 344

Shedding, 31, 61, 74, 79, 130, 239, 255, 328, 334, 346

sheep, 109, 332

sheer, 322

shelved, 275

Sheol, 334

shine, 65

shined, 115, 170

shines, 55, 108-109

shining, 109

shipwreck, 130, 229

shocking, 87

shopped, 269

shore, 210-211

short, 48, 243, 287-288

show, 180, 214, 318-319, 344

showed, 211

showing, 74, 146, 287, 329

shown, 86-87, 215

shows, 57, 74, 131, 141, 146, 216, 335

shy, 211

sick, 311

side, 12, 50, 88, 189, 212, 217, 326-327, 334

sides, 212

sight, 313

significance, 4, 7-8, 175, 280, 329

significantly, 7, 10, 48, 93, 282

signifies, 88, 331-332

signifying, 280

signs, 310

silent, 328

similar, 75, 166

simple, 119, 197, 275, 279, 288, 309, 311

simpler, 119

simplest, 89

simplicity, 119, 133, 135, 178, 216, 223, 234, 240, 259, 264, 298, 311

simply, 8, 14, 16, 23-24, 26, 34, 61, 67, 82-83, 90, 94-95, 97, 100, 108, 112, 118-119, 131-132, 135, 137, 143, 149, 155, 157-159, 161-162, 166, 168-170, 173-175, 178, 190-191, 193, 198, 201, 203, 209, 212, 216-217, 219-220, 224, 229, 232, 235, 255, 259, 270, 281, 290, 295, 298, 321, 325-326, 352

simulation, 309-310

simulations, 310

simultaneous, 5

simultaneously, 202

sin, 10-11, 13, 16-17, 24, 26-27, 38-49, 51-53, 56-58, 63, 67-69, 72, 75, 78, 80-81, 84-85, 90-96, 102-105, 107-118, 120-151, 154-162, 164-180, 185-192, 195-198, 200, 203, 206-208, 211, 214-215, 218-219, 223-224, 228-232, 238, 240, 243, 245, 247-248, 254-256, 263, 265-266, 270, 273, 277, 299, 301-303, 311, 319-323, 326-328, 330, 332-334, 337-339, 343-344, 346-347, 349-351

since, 5, 52, 194, 201, 215, 230, 234, 236-238, 242, 290, 318, 335, 338, 351

sincere, 34, 135, 237, 245, 257, 273, 326

U

V

vacation, 345
vaguely, 150
vain, 126, 302
valid, 227
validated, 241
validity, 241
value, 194
valued, 30
vantage, 313
variant, 235
variety, 13, 178, 292
vast, 21, 137, 235, 259
vastly, 101, 147, 174, 206
veil, 19, 240
veiled, 245
verb, 4-5, 44, 73
verbiage, 190, 252
verbs, 4
verdict, 206
versa, 202
version, 17, 163-164, 218
versus, 172, 174
vessel, 108
viable, 157
Vicarious, 31, 86, 116, 130, 170, 187, 200, 255, 334
Vicariously, 60, 71, 77, 85, 141, 175, 194, 201-202, 339, 343, 346
vice, 202
victories, 322-323
victorious, 47, 83, 88, 209
victoriously, 33, 93, 236, 255
victory, 33, 40-41, 46-47, 57, 91, 101, 116, 120, 125-127, 129-130, 142, 150, 152, 154-155, 161, 163, 167, 178, 183, 186-187, 192-194, 196, 198-200, 218-219, 226, 239, 245-246, 248, 253, 295, 299-300, 303-304, 313, 318-320, 322-323, 326, 335, 344, 350
view, 3, 5-6, 9, 40, 43, 49, 51, 53, 64-65, 81, 84-85, 90, 94, 98-99, 108-109, 114, 117, 149, 151-152, 156, 161, 171, 191, 197, 202, 210, 212, 238, 271, 280, 287, 292
viewed, 23, 57, 73, 81, 104, 109, 202, 231, 313
viewing, 108, 149, 151, 226, 323
views, 16, 77, 98, 190, 211, 287
vile, 132, 168, 265
vinegar, 129, 329
violate, 18, 43, 46, 75, 78, 190, 277, 307, 331, 337
violates, 228
violating, 331
violation, 297
violently, 315
virgin, 75, 83, 276, 338
virgins, 86
visions, 352
vital, 144, 157, 167, 174, 276, 303
vitality, 13
vivid, 206
voice, 30, 213, 238, 280, 328, 331-332
void, 29-30
voids, 30-31
volition, 18
voluntarily, 329
vortex, 318
votary, 207
votus, 207

W

wades, 337
waged, 93

wages, 93, 132

wait, 12, 44, 48, 173, 283, 302, 349

waited, 9, 291

waiting, 131, 239

waits, 74

wake, 326

Walk

    walk (a simple walk) , 311

    walk (after the Spirit), 16, 85,
        90-91, 94-95, 209, 215, 217-218,
        221, 303

    walk (away) , 67

    walk (in holiness) , 241

    walk (in integrity) , 219

    walk (in newness of life) , 251

    walk (in search) , 49-50

    walk (in triumph), 198

    walk (in Truth) , 83, 288, 296,
        313, 340

    walk (intimately) , 18, 31, 33, 60

    walk (joyful) , 22, 43, 60

    walk (of Faith), 110, 122, 179-180,
        300

    walk (upon the Main Road) , 112

    walk (with God) , 21, 29, 32-33,
        39, 49, 100, 119, 193, 196, 209

walked, 24, 29, 75, 109, 149, 156, 196,
    211-213, 220, 238, 246, 276, 288,
    298, 302, 330, 333, 335

walking, 16, 23, 85, 90-91, 95, 99, 119,
    154, 157, 169, 176, 187, 189, 192,
    203, 205-206, 208-209, 215-216,
    219, 249, 260

want, 8, 21, 23, 47, 63, 82, 99-100, 107,
    115, 117, 119, 137, 144, 149, 152, 155,
    160-163, 170, 173-174, 193-194, 231,
    266, 270, 290, 320-321

wanted, 65, 118, 136, 138, 150, 195,
    269-270

wants, 39, 44, 47, 151, 160, 167, 190,
    195, 270

war, 27, 93, 107, 172-173, 175-176, 270

warfare, 47, 118, 121, 304

warned, 339

warning, 273

warns, 126, 272

warring, 40, 171-172, 176, 230

wars, 155, 162, 299

wash, 255

washed, 107, 124, 170, 206, 226

watch, 210, 287

watching, 210

water, 251, 306, 329, 331

watered, 7-8, 259

watering, 219, 315

wavering, 261

Ways

    ways (of evil) , 163-168

    ways (of God), 31, 33, 38, 41-42,
        47, 186-203

    ways (of our old man), 37-53

weak, 85, 94

weaknesses, 14

wealth, 242, 291, 337

weeks, 34, 269

weeping, 179

weight, 210

weights, 180

went, 7-8, 41, 103, 111, 150, 171, 244,
    250, 280, 326-328, 331, 334-335

western, 259

whirlwind, 175, 191

whirlwinds, 91, 311

white, 270

whoever, 296, 298, 303

whole, 7-9, 15, 57, 59, 72, 75, 300, 315

whomever, 290

434

whose, 5

whosoever, 179, 241, 257, 276, 317, 344

wicked, 18, 264

wickedness, 18, 297

wide, 15, 65

widely, 90

widespread, 215

wife, 12, 270

Will

will (our will), 18-19, 21-27, 30, 50, 52, 60, 70-72, 78, 91, 97-98, 109-113, 119, 121-122, 126-128, 131-132, 137-140, 145, 149-151, 156, 158-160, 163-167, 172-178, 185, 187, 190-194, 196, 199-200, 265, 271, 288, 300-301, 307, 311

Will (the Father's Will), 24, 26, 48, 50, 60, 83, 88, 90, 100, 102, 113, 126-127, 176, 190, 193, 216, 218, 248-250, 259, 278, 288-289, 291, 294-298, 300-304, 331-333, 338, 344, 350

willing, 164, 172, 299

willpower, 22-26, 32, 50, 52-53, 81, 89, 92, 97, 109-110, 112-113, 117, 121, 124, 126, 128, 131, 137-138, 148, 155-157, 159, 165-166, 173, 175-176, 191-192, 194, 301-302, 319, 350

wills, 163-164, 177

win, 32, 292-293

window, 210

wisdom, 30, 78, 87, 101, 163, 212-213, 233-237, 241-243, 247-248, 250, 252, 259, 261-262, 277-278, 330, 336

wise, 241-243, 334

wish, 150

wishing, 299

withholding, 30, 213

Without

without (a body), 10

without (being born again) , 17, 215

without (breaching into the Law of Sin), 173

without (coercion) , 56, 105, 113, 117, 140, 146

without (God) , 13, 144, 159, 174, 193

without (hands) , 69, 125, 170, 199, 251

without (Love) , 13

without (realizing) , 98, 110, 158, 169, 243, 245, 302, 310

without (stopping) , 50

without (the knowledge) , 24, 57, 94, 136, 138, 160, 165, 167, 169-170, 172, 176, 185, 209, 218, 230, 234, 248, 258, 299, 311, 318, 320, 351

without (the moral compass) , 78

without (the sin nature) , 80

without (the use of the physical body) , 172

withstand, 70

witness, 42, 65, 89, 124, 169, 176, 308

witnesses, 113

woefully, 81, 93, 117, 121, 148, 191-192, 261, 288

wolves, 332

woman, 63-64, 66-68, 73, 75, 80, 84, 86, 102, 142, 197, 201, 277, 289, 309, 317

womb, 64

women, 132, 312

wonder, 29, 31-32, 245, 287, 292

wonderful, 9, 21, 27, 32-33, 186, 193, 220, 237, 261, 263, 279, 290-291, 298, 301-302

wonderfully, 26, 55, 68, 158

Y

Z

Printed in the United States
By Bookmasters